Speaking of Race and Class

Speaking of Race and Class

*The Student Experience
at an Elite College*

Elizabeth Aries
with Richard Berman

TEMPLE UNIVERSITY PRESS
PHILADELPHIA

TEMPLE UNIVERSITY PRESS
Philadelphia, Pennsylvania 19122
www.temple.edu/tempress

Library of Congress Cataloging-in-Publication Data

Aries, Elizabeth.
  Speaking of race and class : the student experience at an elite college /
Elizabeth Aries, Richard Berman.
    p. cm.
  Includes bibliographical references and index.
  ISBN 978-1-4399-0966-9 (hardback : alk. paper) —
ISBN 978-1-4399-0967-6 (paper : alk. paper) —
ISBN 978-1-4399-0968-3 (e-book) 1. Amherst College—Freshman—
Social conditions—Case studies. 2. Private universities and colleges—
Social aspects—Massachusetts—Amherst—Case studies. 3. Minority
college students—Massachusetts—Amherst—Social conditions—Case
studies. 4. College students—Massachusetts—Amherst—Social
conditions—Case studies. 5. Universities and colleges—Social aspects—
United States. 6. Elite (Social sciences)—United States. I. Berman,
Richard, 1948– II. Title.
  LD156.A76 2012
  378.744'23—dc23
                                                      2012015448

∞ The paper used in this publication meets the requirements of the
American National Standard for Information Sciences—Permanence
of Paper for Printed Library Materials, ANSI Z39.48-1992

Printed in the United States of America

2 4 6 8 9 7 5 3 1

To Rose Olver

Contents

Preface

This book is a continuation of a study I began in 2005. Its aim is to help us better understand how race and class shape students' experiences and learning on campus. In *Race and Class Matters at an Elite College* (2008), I described the challenges based on their race and class that fifty-eight students from four distinct groups (affluent black, affluent white, lower-income black, and lower-income white) faced and what they learned from living in a diverse community during their first year at Amherst College. The current book, written in collaboration with my husband, Richard Berman, presents the views of fifty-five of the original fifty-eight study participants as they looked back on what they experienced and learned over their four years at the college. In their final interviews in the spring of 2009, most of the students in the study agreed to give up confidentiality. They remain identified by their original pseudonyms, but their permission to use more identifying information has made it possible to bring individuals more sharply to life and to profile some students and their experiences more fully.

This book centers on students' voices. Because students answered questions in their interviews about topics that often they had not previously considered or spoken about, their speech was spontaneous and conversational. To improve readability, I have removed false starts and repetitions, including the repeated use of "like," "you know," "kind of," and "sort of." In this book, the voices of many students are heard, but students who were particularly representative of their group's concerns or who were particularly articulate are profiled in greater detail.

When I recruited the participants for my study in 2005, I explained that my goal was to gain information that could be used to make Amherst College a better place for its students. Since that time, this goal has expanded. I hope that the voices of these students will help all those in U.S. academia who are concerned with ensuring the success of every student, improving campus climates, and promoting diversity programming that will support students and help them learn from their differences.

Elizabeth Aries
January 2012

Acknowledgments

My deepest gratitude goes to the students who participated in this study. Their experiences over four years at Amherst College are the focus of this book. Their willingness to speak openly in their interviews about the challenges they faced and what they learned during their college careers has taught me an enormous amount about the lived experience of race and class on campus.

Very special thanks go to my summer research assistant, Southey Saul. She originally worked with me on the analysis of the freshman-year data, and I was extremely fortunate to have her return to assist with the analysis of the senior-year data. Southey's interest in and dedication to this project, her meticulous coding of the interview data, her skillful data analysis using SPSS statistical software, and her hard work and enthusiasm in the face of the many more tedious tasks were inspiring. I could not have asked for a better assistant. I was also very fortunate that Rebecca (Becky) Lieberman volunteered her time during her summer break from college to gain research experience by assisting with the data analysis. I greatly valued Becky's energy, commitment, and skills as a coder.

In order to write the final chapter to this book, which steps back from Amherst to look at the broader literature on diversity programming, I hired three wonderful students as research assistants: Tyler Chapman, Aleksandra (Sasha) Margolina, and Spencer Russell. They identified, read critically, and summarized articles from scores of publications, working with consistent competence and enthusiasm. Their careful research, review, and summarization were invaluable to me.

I thank Nancy Aries, Rhonda Cobham-Sander, and Jessica Salvatore, who read chapters and offered references and feedback. My sincere appreciation goes to Micah Kleit at Temple University Press for his belief in my research and his support of this project, to Maryanne Alos for the wonderful job she did indexing the book, and to everyone at Temple University Press who has seen the book through to production.

This study could not have been carried out without funding. The research was supported in part by a grant from the Amherst College Faculty Research Award Program, as funded by the H. Axel Schupf '57 Fund for Intellectual Life.

My heartfelt thanks go to Richard Berman, my husband and cowriter, for his extraordinary commitment to this book and for his perseverance over the two-year writing process. I asked him to join me as coauthor because I knew that as a writer, he had the skills to bring the interview material to life in a way that I could not. Richard has an eye for narrative and a gift with words. A singer-songwriter by profession, Richard put his songwriting aside to help transform my academic writing into a much more engaging style. Involved in this project from the start, Richard conducted interviews with eight of the students at the beginning and the end of freshman year and with eighteen of the students in the final round of interviews. The students' incredible openness in the interviews that Richard conducted speaks to his remarkable ability to draw people out. He wrote the narratives about the students in this book and played a major editorial role in rewriting chapters to sharpen the focus, strengthen the organization, and present the issues in a clearer and more captivating style. His contribution to this book was a labor of love, for which I am forever deeply thankful. His faith in the importance of this work has never wavered.

Elizabeth Aries
January 2012

I join Elizabeth in thanking the students whose voices are the focus of this book and whose generous openness shed so much light on the experience of race and class at Amherst. I thank you, Elizabeth, for giving me the opportunity to be a part of this important study. It has been an education for me. My awareness of and concern about issues of race and class have grown enormously. And I thank you for your steady belief that my writing was of value to your work.

Richard Berman
May 2012

1

Race and Class on Campus

Four Students' Stories

"**I** kind of feel like I've been dropped on Mars. . . . I mean, it's *so* different." These few words reflected Emily's experience of her first weeks at Amherst College in the fall of 2005. Had you passed Emily walking across the campus of her elite New England liberal arts school, she would not have stood out from other young white women in casual clothes on their way to class. Given the school's past reputation, you might have assumed she came from relative wealth and privilege. But a closer look would have revealed she was not in designer jeans and did not sport the markers of wealth that some students chose. In fact, Emily came from a small farming community of six hundred in South Dakota. Her father, a farmer and truck driver, had quit school after eighth grade; her mother had never made it through college and was now at home, unable to work at her hospital job since becoming ill. Emily was one of nineteen students in her high school graduating class in a K–12 school of three hundred students, and in four years of high school, she had written one research paper. Her school had no library—Emily did her research online, and her main source was Wikipedia. Her community was white, and most referred to black people as "niggers," but there were few black people in town to take offense. The use of the term was "prominent" and went unchallenged.

The Bigger Picture

Lower-income white students like Emily, whose parents were not college educated, would have been difficult to find at Amherst or other elite colleges and universities forty years ago. The Amherst College that Emily entered in the fall of 2005 bore little resemblance to the college back then. Over the succeeding four decades, Amherst had undergone a sea change, from an all-male, largely affluent, prep-schooled, legacy-rich student body to one that was half women and more than a third nonwhite, with more than half its students receiving financial aid. Today, elite colleges and universities like Amherst recruit both underrepresented minority students and white students with high need for financial assistance and/or limited family education. This recruitment is both purposeful and expensive. A quarter of the college's operating budget each year goes to financial aid.

What has prompted this move to diversity at Amherst and schools like it? Changes in admission policy began with the emergence of the civil rights movement and growing civil unrest in the 1960s. The idea of "affirmative action" arose to help remedy past discrimination, creating more opportunities for African Americans in many areas, including college admissions. The changes in admissions policy were both a response to black discontent and a reflection of a new concern on the part of universities and colleges like Amherst to open up the educational opportunities they offer to a wider range of students in an effort to promote equity and social mobility. Over time, however, as affirmative action came under attack, arguments shifted away from compensating for past discrimination to the need for "diversity" for reasons other than social justice.[1] Leading educators made the case that potential educational benefits existed in having students of different races and classes interacting with one another. To be prepared to become citizens in this fast-evolving, increasingly diverse society, to thrive in it, and to compete in a rapidly expanding global economy, students need to understand and be able to work with those different from themselves. They need to have previous assumptions and prejudices challenged, and ideally, they should acquire the motivation to work for equality. According to Census Bureau projections, by 2042 non-Hispanic white people will no longer be in the majority in the United States.[2] As Neil Rudenstine, former Harvard University president argues:

> In our world today, it is not enough for us and our students to acknowledge, in an abstract sense, that other kinds of people, with other modes of thought and feeling and action, exist somewhere— unseen, unheard, unvisited, and unknown. We must interact directly with a substantial portion of that larger universe. There must be opportunities to hear different views directly—face to face—from people who embody them. No formal academic study can replace continued association with others who are different from ourselves, and who challenge our preconceptions, prejudices, and assumptions, even as we challenge theirs.[3]

While Amherst College, along with many other colleges and universities, has done much to create a diverse student community, two important questions need to be answered: To what extent does learning from diversity actually take place? And what distinct challenges arise for students— affluent, lower-income, black, white—living in this diverse community? The answers to these two questions are the focus of this book.

In Search of Answers

To help us attain those answers, 58 students out of the 431 entering students in the class of 2009 at Amherst College agreed to participate in a longitudinal study of race and class at the college. The fifty-eight students came from four distinct groups: (1) affluent white, (2) affluent black, (3) lower-income white, and (4) lower-income black. Through online questionnaires and face-to-face interviews at the beginning and the end of their freshman year and again at the end of four years, the fifty-eight students (roughly fifteen from each group and balanced by gender) laid out their thoughts about how race and class had shaped their college experience.[4]

How were the groups defined? The students in the two "affluent" groups had no need for financial assistance from the college. In contrast, the "lower-income" students had significant need for financial assistance. The average financial aid award for lower-income students in the study was $34,203 to cover the $43,360 fee for full tuition and room and board. Half of these students were first generation—their parents had not attended college.[5]

In this study, race was limited to students who, on their admission applications, self-identified as either "white or Caucasian" or "African American, black." Race is obviously more complicated than "black" and "white," and a number of other races were represented on the Amherst campus. Optimally, other racial minorities would have been included in the study—in particular, Hispanics, who are one of the two racial groups that have faced the greatest challenges in attaining college degrees (African Americans are the other racial group).[6] While forty-one students in the class of 2009 self-identified as "African American, black," only twenty-seven students self-identified as "Hispanic." The number of Hispanics was too small to produce a meaningful sample for this study. Forty-five entering students self-identified as "Asian/Asian American," but these students made up an extremely diverse group in terms of families' national origins and cultural heritage. A much larger sample of students would be needed to meaningfully study this group.

Race and Class Matters at an Elite College, an earlier book by the first author, describes the challenges students faced and the lessons they learned about race and class during their first year at the college.[7] That book contains details on the participants' backgrounds and the research methods. This book expands on the earlier work in two ways. It presents students' views on what they experienced and learned at Amherst over *four* years at the college, rather than a single year. Those reflections are enriched because, of the fifty-five students who took part in the final wave of data collection, all but six agreed to give up confidentiality and allowed identifying information to be used.[8] This book thus gives greater depth to individual students, the issues they encountered, and what they learned.

To give a sense of what students in each of the four groups experienced and learned at Amherst, we present the stories of Emily, Matthew, Andrea, and Marc. Each of these students comes from a different group in the study. Each of them speaks to some of the common issues that other students of his or her race and class experienced, and each one's story illustrates the potential for learning from diversity. But these four students are not fully representative of their groups, as considerable variability in students' experiences and learning existed within each of the groups. Their profiles are portraits of individuals.

Emily

Early one afternoon in her first weeks on campus as a freshman, Emily took a seat for lunch at a table in Valentine, Amherst's college-wide dining room, and was soon joined by three black male students. These students were friendly and affable, but Emily sat in silence. "I didn't know what to say, how to begin a conversation." She was worried about what words might come out of her mouth, possibly something "politically incorrect." Having grown up with TV as her only exposure to black people, Emily had developed powerful stereotypes. "I have those in my head," she noted at the time, "and yet I don't really want them." She continued, "To combat that is really difficult."

For Emily, the wealth of some of Amherst's students was an eye-opener but not a cause for envy. On seeing students in coordinated outfits with well-chosen accessories or visiting another girl's room, she observed, "The piles of shoes and clothes—and everything I own in a trash bag—it's funny to me, because when I see someone who is all decked out, I think, 'Why would you want to appear that way? Why would you want to show off the fact that you're rich?'"

Yet Emily had chosen to come to Amherst, aware that she was taking herself out of her community and into a wider world, however stressful the transition might be. As she put it that first week, "I want to be very open. I want to meet people who are of different races. I mean, that's why I'm here. I want to see diversity in action. I want to be a part of that. I want to go out of my way to make friends who are different than me." She achieved that goal. By the end of her freshman year, Emily was part of a close circle of seven female friends, and she was the only white person in the group. The others were Chinese, Indonesian, black, and biracial. The racial diversity that Emily experienced in her first year remained an integral part of her Amherst world all the way through her senior year.

Whereas the races of the friends she chose to live with were diverse, none of the students in her group of close friends came from wealthy backgrounds. When asked at the end of her senior year about the importance of having friends of the same social class, Emily responded that when she had first arrived, she had not thought it would be important. "But looking back, it has been extremely important for me to have that. I think just having that day-to-day help, and not to feel alone, just to navigate it with someone. I mean, there's a lot going on here and just to have someone to go through it with you."

That said, Emily did form close friendships with two wealthy white students over her four years. It was not as though she was trying to. As she explained, "I've made friends with people, not social classes." But Emily felt that it had taken more work to form those friendships. She mused, "Maybe not on their part—on mine—letting go of the stereotype that they're not going to understand." There were things they could not understand, like why Emily worked so many hours a week off campus. "But they appreciate it," she said. Talking about the wide gap she felt between herself and wealthy students at the college, Emily noted, "People still ask me, 'How many hours a week do you work? Why do you work so much?' . . . If I saw somebody working a lot, I would think, 'Oh, they need the money.' I don't get any deep joy out of doing dishes at Val [Valentine dining hall]." Emily worked over twenty hours a week and sent money home to help support her teenage sister, who has two children. In response to questions from affluent students about her working, Emily reflected, "We've had two totally different lives. And in the same way that I'm looking at them through a cage of 'How did you get this way?' they're also looking at me." The disparity in social position between Emily and Josh, one of her two wealthy friends, was highlighted when he told her he did not know how to cash a check. She thought about how long she had been working and how getting her paycheck every week made her feel "so excited." She remarked, "I would never have thought that someone twenty-two years old would not know that."

In discussing her relationship with Josh, Emily noted, "I think the reason we are close is that he's very comfortable talking about his class." Josh did not shy away from acknowledging his wealth. Emily also noted that, unlike Josh, many students tended to "close off about themselves" when they discovered she had limited resources. She was not sure if "it's because 'I don't want to be friends with you' or if it's because 'I don't want to make you uncomfortable.'" She tended to give them the benefit of the doubt and assumed that students were trying to avoid creating discomfort for everyone.

For Emily, what she could tell friends from her class differed from what she could tell her wealthy friends about the day-to-day issues that involve class. With friends of the same class Emily could discuss "not having the money to do this or that" or what she referred to as "the implications of class," confident that the concerns she voiced would fall on sympathetic ears. In contrast, with Josh, she said, "I would feel more like I was whining. . . . He really doesn't know, and I don't expect him to know, what I mean."

One incident that occurred in her freshman year stuck with her painfully. Emily was at a party with her other wealthy white friend, Abby, and at some point, Abby's boyfriend called Emily "white trash." The comment not only made her think poorly of him but also raised concerns about how *other* people viewed her. "If I say, 'Oh, I'm low income,' do they automatically assume something else?" Although Emily held on to the idea that this was not "the general attitude," she said, "I definitely think there are people here who just do look down on people who [are low income]."

Emily's journey to Amherst put more than physical distance between her and the family and community she had left back home. She arrived on campus "proud of the people at home, just the way that they got by and could make things work and didn't have a lot of outside help." Over the course of her freshman year, she began to see people at home as being more closed-minded, judgmental, and "very behind the times." Yet she did not assign blame to her home community. "I can sympathize and say, 'You grew up in a totally different way; you grew up in an older generation. You have no experiences outside of that bubble to make you different.'" But she faced a seemingly insurmountable disconnect between home and college. "I can move in between, but there's no bringing them together."

By the end of her last year at Amherst, she oscillated between positive and negative views of her community. When asked then about whether her feelings had changed, she responded, "That's something that's changed a lot over the four years." She still saw a benefit in the way she grew up, but now she also looked at her home community as "so isolated and so not what I want." She explained, "I would love it if the whole world were like Amherst in that it had a whole mix of people interacting." That was not the case, and Emily said with certainty, "I would never want to bring my gay friend home or my black friend." She would not want her friends to experience her community's closed-minded reaction. There *was* no bringing her two worlds together.

Matthew

Had Matthew, an affluent white prep-school grad, passed Emily on a walk across the Amherst campus that freshman year and sized up her position on the social-class ladder, he might well have turned his gaze away. "College is so much about making connections," he asserted in his fall interview, "and your relationships with people. I mean, it is about learning, but the most important thing is *networking* at college. Period. The networking will help you get jobs or know people, or whatever. And the people who are more likely to help you get the jobs you're looking for are of a certain class. That's not to say that kids of another class won't extend this, but the probability that a relationship is going to help you later down the line is going to be much higher if it's a person from a higher class than another."

Matthew had attended Deerfield Academy. His father raised money for Historic Deerfield Village, and his mother was a career counselor at Smith College. They were wealthy enough to send Matthew to Amherst with no financial aid, and he was not the first in his family to go to Amherst. He followed in the wake of his father, his uncle, his sister, and a cousin. "We have pictures of my sister and me wrapped in Amherst blankets when we were two." Upon arrival, Matthew envisioned himself gravitating toward students from the upper class, from the Upper East Side of New York or Greenwich, Connecticut—students like those he had been surrounded by in boarding school—a far cry from a young woman from rural South Dakota.

If Emily had noticed Matthew as she walked across campus at some point in their freshman year, she might well have assumed he was one of the wealthy preppies at the college. He was always in neatly creased khakis and polo shirts, ever ready with a polite smile and a hello to all he passed, a legacy of his years of socialization at Deerfield. According to his description, "The way I dressed was very preppy. But also the way I acted was just sort of, not 'snobby' but sort of as if I had the ability, money-wise, to do anything I wanted, which could not be further from the truth."

Matthew's desire to become friends with very wealthy students lessened over the course of his freshman year. Many of the students he got to know during that year were unlike those he had anticipated meeting and befriending. "I remember my cousin's Amherst, and my dad's Amherst, and my uncle's Amherst, and my sister's Amherst, and being the fifth in my family to go here, I had all those stories floating around of what Amherst is like. It just could not have been more different than what I thought."

In freshman year, the college assigned Matthew to a double room with Ruben, a lower-income Mexican American. Matthew learned that Ruben had moved out of his home as a junior in high school, had gotten his own lodging, and had supported himself by working two jobs while getting through his last two years of high school. Matthew got close to Ruben that year, but Ruben was not the only person from a dissimilar background who became an integral part of Matthew's friendship group. That group consisted of a number of people whom he might well never have imagined would be important to him when he first arrived. By the end of that year, when he spoke of social relationships, he stated, "Your close friends you're friends with because you like them as people and not because you think they will be successful."

In his senior year Matthew lived off campus with Ruben and two other male students. Matthew described one of them, a black student, as being "in the lowest 1 percent" financially at Amherst, like Ruben—not exactly an obvious choice if you are looking for relationships that are "going to help you later down the line." That friend had been in and out of college because he had no father at home, and "he needed to be the man of the house, [to] work and support the family, and he couldn't be off getting an education." After helping the family with its financial and social problems,

Matthew's roommate returned to the college. When asked about how they had become roommates, Matthew responded, "I chose to live with him because I would have never gotten to know him unless I was sort of thrust against him and made to know him. And he's an awesome guy." Asked how this roommate factored into what he learned about race and class at Amherst, Matthew acknowledged his importance, adding, "It's not just him; it's many different situations."

What explains the long journey that Matthew made at Amherst from newly arrived network-focused freshman bent on finding people in positions to advance his career plans to departing senior with a social world of friends, many of whom were from much less affluent circumstances than his own? Part of the answer, it would seem, is serendipity, the pairing that brought Matthew together with his freshman roommate and gave him a window into a world he had never been exposed to. Part of the answer lies in Matthew himself. Once introduced to students whose lives had been so different from his, he did not turn away. He embraced the exposure, the learning, and the people he met and liked, all the while increasing his awareness of his relative privilege. And part of the explanation lies in those fellow classmates. Matthew admired and learned from these friends and the rougher roads they had traveled.

Interestingly enough, given the relationships and experiences Matthew had with black students over his four years at Amherst, he acknowledged, "[On some deep level,] I think I still have pretty significant stereotypes about blacks that need to be broken down, despite the fact that I'm very close friends with a lot of black people. . . . When I get to know somebody who is black I stop thinking of them as that race. I sort of take them out of the pool of black people—and there's still all the other black people." And an awkwardness persisted for him in certain social situations, a self-consciousness about his being a white person and not knowing how to act around black people. Perhaps the following anecdote captures literally and metaphorically the discomfort Matthew struggled with. He vividly remembered a time when all his black friends were hanging out and "putting on really heavy rap music, getting up and dancing." He continued, "I was like, 'What am I doing? I have no idea what's going on,' but they were very accepting; they were like, 'Come on in'—making fun of me because I didn't know how to dance like they did, [but] they were good-natured about it. It wasn't like they were mean about it, but I felt so awkward." For Matthew, experiences like those, of being a distinct minority in a social situation, gave him "an appreciation for how [black students] must feel all the time."

Matthew graduated with a degree in economics and a career in investment banking awaiting him in New York. He was thinking he might room with one of his close Amherst friends who would be working for a nonprofit. They would not split the rent evenly. But Matthew's social world was not exclusively composed of those less well-off than he. His friends stood on many different rungs of the social ladder. In his senior interview

Matthew echoed his spring, freshman-year sentiments when he noted, "When I look for friends, I don't really look or care about their social class at all." But he reiterated his even longer-standing belief that "connections are absolutely the most important thing." "And," he added, reflecting on the connections he had made and the resulting investment banking position he had awaiting him on Wall Street, "I think I did a good job, too."

Andrea

Like Matthew, Andrea needed no financial assistance from Amherst. But Andrea is black, and her race and class and the intersection of the two presented issues that were not a part of Matthew's experience. Andrea's mother was a creative director at an ad agency. Her father, whom she described as "an out-of-practice pediatrician," served as "Mr. Mom" to the children when they were young and later as the caretaker for his aging parents. Andrea had a brother who had graduated from Dartmouth and another who had graduated from Haverford College. She began her own college journey with uncertainties and concerns about race and class—where she fit in, how she saw herself, how others saw her, and how she wished to be seen by others in regard to those two important social identities. She would leave with increased understanding, self-acceptance, and confidence.

"I'm going home for the weekend." A simple statement of fact, yet in pronouncing it, Andrea, whose home was New York City, recognized a new perspective she had gained over her four years at Amherst: an awareness of her relative wealth. She had acquired that perspective, in part, from her close friendship with a classmate, Brenda, who could not afford to travel home for a weekend. As Andrea reflected in her senior year, "I have more appreciation for where I've come from and how easy things are for me in relation to her." But Amherst afforded another, seemingly paradoxical, change in Andrea's perspective. The wide economic variability at the college enabled Andrea to see herself as not all that wealthy. As she put it in the fall of her freshman year, "A lot of people here have more money than me." She was aware of students who went out to eat almost every night and students who had BMWs sitting in the student parking lot—things that caused her to feel "some jealousy." She was struck by remarks of classmates such as "Money, that doesn't matter. . . . I lost this; I'll replace it." Or "Oh, I crashed my car. My parents are just going to buy me another one."

Andrea found much to admire in Brenda, her lower-income friend. Andrea noted that if Brenda "goes out and buys something, she'll appreciate it more." Andrea watched as Brenda went through the whole financial aid process, impressed at how she "rolls with the punches better in terms of money. . . . She's like, '[If] I'm not getting this money, I'll find a way to make up for it.'" Brenda was trying to pay off her loans early by working in the college dining hall. Andrea realized, "She's more aware of future problems or issues than I am. I don't think about that right now. I don't know if I ever will have to. . . . She's shown me that coming from a different social class makes you think differently about how to deal with these things now and in the future." Andrea's experience with Brenda and others at the college caused her to conclude that students who are "middle [class] or anything below upper are more grounded in reality."

Andrea's feelings about class ranged from "tension" and a bit of "jealousy" toward more affluent students to discomfort about her own relative wealth when she was around lower-income students. That discomfort led her to wish to hide her class background in certain situations during her freshman year. In her spring interview back then, Andrea explained, "I'm not on financial aid. I don't say that generally around most of my friends because they're on financial aid." But if asked directly if she is on financial aid, Andrea said she answers, "Not now." She continued, "I'll try to say it in a way that's not like 'No. I don't need financial aid.' . . . I definitely play down the fact that I'm not on financial aid."

Andrea was also reluctant to tell classmates where she lived, as assumptions were made about her on the basis of that information—assumptions she felt uncomfortable with and took steps to avoid.

> My neighborhood is Jamaica Estates [Queens]. It's the nice part of Jamaica, and every time I say it, everyone's like, "Ooh, ooh," like "Big shot." So I find myself just saying I live in Jamaica more than I do the specific neighborhood. And I have a country house out in Southampton, on Long Island, and as soon as the word "Southampton" comes out of my mouth, it's "Oh, she has a pool and a mansion, and she lives next to some movie stars," which is definitely not true. People have definitely made assumptions just by normal facts about me. I live in a nice neighborhood [and before] you know—boom! [I'm] automatically superwealthy. It kind of bothered me a little bit last semester whenever I said it, so I avoided saying it pretty much. But now I've kind of grown into it, [and I] shrug it off.

In addition to assumptions around class, Andrea dealt with assumptions, as well as expectations and pressures, based on her race. Many of these assumptions ran counter to those based on class. At times students assumed she was "superwealthy" and living in a "mansion," but she also faced stereotypic beliefs that black people are poor, that she did not "come from a fancy neighborhood" and that she lived in "an apartment building, someplace run-down." In her freshman year, she said, other black students "actually assumed that I was from a lower class [and that I] was on financial aid."

Over Andrea's years at Amherst, classmates voiced expectations about how she "should speak": "I should not be speaking proper English; it should be Ebonics. I shouldn't be able to pronounce things correctly or a certain way." Some classmates assumed she listened to rap music. She noted, "I don't listen to rap that much; I'm more alternative and rock and stuff like that. People walk by my room, and they'll hear the music that I'm listening to, and they do a double take. I can definitely see that someone's like, 'What are you listening to?' [As if] I should be listening to rap and R&B." She recalled talking about Amherst's step dance club and being told, "You should be in it." Andrea continued, "And I was like, 'I don't do step.' 'But you're *black*.'" And being black brought expectations from some classmates that she should dress "like a hipster," in "skinny jeans" with "alternative T-shirts" sporting "black clothing name brands." She fit none of these stereotypes. If Andrea mentioned where she shopped, "other students [were] like, 'Oh, you shop there? That's a really *white* store.'" And Andrea's response was "What the hell does that mean?"

According to Andrea, among classmates, "if I said I was dating someone, they would assume that I was dating a black person if they didn't know me . . . or know who he was." Andrea's serious relationships with white men at Amherst violated more than the *assumptions* of some black students—they violated their *expectations*. "I'm supposed to be dating black men mostly. But I generally only date white men. I've never heard anyone say anything to my face, but I get vibes from black male friends of mine that they don't approve of me dating outside of my race. And no one would ever say it because, you know, it's 2009. What are you going to tell someone, 'You can't date outside of your race'? But I definitely feel the tension there." Talking about the reaction she got to a specific white boyfriend who was "upper class, really wealthy," Andrea noted, "I definitely felt negativity from black men."

When asked at the end of her freshman year what difference, if any, her race had had on her experience at Amherst socially, Andrea reflected, "A lot of people assume that black people are always just going to hang out with black people" and that they date others of their race and party with them. "And that's not [me]. I don't cut myself off to any other people just because they're not black." Andrea sensed a general feeling among some black classmates: "You should want to be with people of your race." She got invited to be in groups with other black students—invitations that came with the message "We're the black students in '09, and we have to stick together" or "We all have to band together and stay strong." But, as Andrea observed, that was not her. "I have black friends, and I have white friends. I have Asian friends." She felt open to everyone while acknowledging that race "definitely affects you socially—how you think about who you're friends with, how people see you because of who you're hanging out with or who you're dating and stuff like that. So it definitely affects the social atmosphere."

Andrea experienced an element of surprise and disappointment that "people group together," that "they don't want to branch out," that they do not want to "see what else is out there, see what it's like to be friends with someone from a different culture," that they do not "embrace it." In high school she was aware that some students desired to hang out in same-race groups, but she had expected students to reach across race lines in college "because you're living with these people, you're with them 24-7, you party with them, you work with them . . . you share personal space with them." It made her realize some students "really like being in this bubble."

Andrea was not one of them. In her senior year Andrea lived in a suite with four white students. She noted, "I find it easier to make friends with people that are not my own race. . . . I think it's because I grew up in a very white neighborhood. I went to a high school where I [could] count the black people on my hand." As a senior looking back, Andrea spoke of having had "a lot of racial issues" when she was younger about "not being black enough and being called 'white' all the time" because of what she liked. She continued, "And then I just started working with those issues, and [now I] don't care about that anymore. . . . Race has taken a back burner in how I socialize with other people." When asked how she explained this profound change, she said simply, "I think I've become more confident in myself."

Over her years at Amherst, race may have been relegated to the back burner for Andrea, but even in her suite at times she came up against the assumption that she represented "black people" and thus could shed light on the behavior of other black students that was puzzling to her suitemates. One of them might note a particular behavior she had observed and wonder why "black people act like that." All eyes would turn to Andrea. "And I'm like, 'Well, I don't know. I don't [know] what to tell [you].'" And there were times when Andrea would turn to her suitemates to gain an understanding of their perceptions of members of her race. If they were watching a movie with "a very stereotypical" portrayal of black people, she would ask them, "Does it have an effect on you as a white person? If I start acting like this, are you going to think, 'She's just being black . . . as opposed to just being who she is'?" She added, "We've had several conversations about it."

For Andrea, representing her race to white students was not confined to her suite. She found herself in that position in classes, too. She recalled times in black studies courses when a student would pose a question and the professor would turn to Andrea and suggest, "Well, Andrea, why don't you talk about it?" In her "Introduction to Black Studies" course, she reported, "There were about five to seven black people in a class of twenty, and we're constantly asked to speak for [black people]. 'Why are black people so hostile and angry about race? Why do they always bring up slavery?' And it's like, 'I don't know. I don't bring up slavery in my daily conversations.' A lot of times we're expected to know everything about our race and talk about that." Reflecting on her experience in her "African Education" class, she noted, "I'm African *American*. I don't have any family ties in Africa, but because I was black, people kind of just assumed that

I knew more than they did when it came to Africa." When asked if she felt these unwarranted expectations from her classmates were an opportunity to inform, she responded, "I felt it was more of a burden."

Marc

As a black student at Amherst, Marc had experiences in the classroom that closely paralleled Andrea's regarding expectations that he could speak for his race. "There have been times, especially in literature classes where we're reading slave narratives; we'll read Frederick Douglass . . . and I'm supposed to be the authority. Teachers will literally say, 'Well, Marc, how did this book make you feel?'"

But while Marc felt many of the same pressures and expectations concerning race as Andrea, there were differences—large class differences. He was a lower-income black student from inner-city Hartford whose parents had emigrated from Jamaica in the early 1980s. Marc's dad, who had not attended college, made helicopter blades. Marc's mother, who had started college in Jamaica but had never finished, worked as an insurance agent. She had always had hopes that her children would have a better life than she and her husband had been able to achieve and provide for their family. When Marc finished sixth grade and his parochial school abruptly discontinued its seventh and eighth grades, thus threatening to thwart her educational goals for Marc, his mother mobilized. One day that summer, with Marc in hand, she arrived on the campus of Kingswood-Oxford, a prep school she passed as she commuted to and from work each day. One thing led to another, and in the fall Marc entered the school on scholarship. A decade later, as Marc began his senior year at Amherst, his younger sister started her freshman year at Trinity College.

Given his family's circumstances, unlike Andrea, Marc never had to worry about hiding his wealth. In fact, he arrived on campus with a strong interest in making wealth. Money and earning a living out in the world loomed much larger in his thinking than in Andrea's. But there were other pulls within Marc. In the fall of freshman year he had mused, "I wonder what it's like to experience life through someone else's eyes or someone else's skin and understand what experiences they go through, or what's different for them just because of their skin color." At an earlier point in that interview, he stated his view that for him, "a lot of college is exposure to different people and new ideas." Over the next four years, Marc allowed himself that exposure, and a tension developed within him between doing well and doing good, fueled largely by the diverse friendship group he chose to become a part of. In so choosing, he embarked on a remarkable journey across class and race lines that eventually changed him and his life goals.

When he arrived on campus as a freshman, Marc joined a varsity team, having been lightly recruited after his high school career. The team provided a ready-made friendship group with similar interests to eat dinner with every night. Marc summed up the way he saw it as an entering student: "I want friends. I need a group of friends at Amherst, and this is the most accessible group, so it's really going to be easy to make friends with them and stay in this comfort zone." In the spring of his freshman year, some friends not on the team invited Marc into a room draw group for sophomore housing, and Marc's decision to join that group led to a new friendship group that stayed intact for the rest of college. "I've distanced myself from the team as I've gotten more comfortable with a different group," he explained. Marc realized that he was socializing with teammates out of necessity and not necessarily because he really wanted to. And it was the new group of friends that had such a strong impact on him and set in motion many of the changes he went through. "Our group's really diverse. There's three white friends, two black friends, [and] two Latinos, and they're all male—and of varying social classes." Other friends were not part of the core group of eight and lived in different locations on campus, he said, "but we still keep in touch and go to meals and things."

When asked how he learned about the social class of his various friends, Marc reported, "Conversations over time, especially because Amherst does a really good job of making these sorts of conversations happen a lot." Marc spoke of attending talks at the college with his friends where "really tough questions about social class and interactions between varying social classes" at Amherst and beyond were raised. "I think that what my group of friends does really well is take those conversations back to the dorm rooms. . . . There have been countless nights when we'll stay up and actually talk about what it means to have this really diverse group."

The entire group of friends Marc lived with sophomore year joined the Hispanic affinity group La Causa, and that experience had an enormous impact on his awareness of class and of race. He talked about the influence of La Causa and other cultural groups on campus: "I think those groups do an amazing job of making social class and race a conversation piece. A lot of what they'll do in those groups, as far as throwing events on campus, is to base them around social class and different aspects of race. I think that having been in that group and having the majority of my friends in [La Causa] has definitely led us to be more social-class conscious."

One of Marc's close friends, a wealthy white student he lived with, became the chair of La Causa and, as such, "got to decide what topics will be discussed. . . . Often a lot of the meetings that he led were about social class." Marc had never thought "the wealthy cared about lower social classes." His friend's strong interest in understanding the experiences and concerns of those from less-affluent circumstances opened Marc's eyes on that score. On a more personal level, he shared, "This person showed me that I can have a completely normal, completely healthy, and great relationship with someone who's incredibly . . . out of my social class."

When he arrived at Amherst, Marc planned to become a lawyer. He had gained direct exposure to the law at a Hartford law firm for which he worked over summers and winter breaks through college, initially doing office chores and then paralegal work. He explained, "I remember having conversations with my mom, and a lot of her impetus for my doing law was just make money and 'do better than we did . . . and be able to raise a family comfortably.'" Those ideas were a part of Marc's thinking, too. But something happened. As he described it, "A lot of people who I originally thought were going to take lucrative jobs, like even myself . . . went through a change." His desire to pursue law was overtaken by a desire "to touch the lives of the next generation to come." And he knew how he would go about it: "I really want to teach at any cost, whatever it takes." Marc emerged from his four years pointed in a new direction, propelled by changes in perspective and values.

To attribute Marc's changes in attitude and direction solely to Amherst would be unfair to Marc. He placed himself in positions that gave him exposure to new people and ideas and, like Matthew in *his* way, allowed those experiences to have great effect. And not all of Marc's Amherst experiences were so welcomed.

When, at the end of his senior year, Marc was asked how salient his race was on a day-to-day basis at Amherst, he responded, "On a daily basis maybe once per day something will remind me." When might that occur? Maybe at lunch in Valentine, "thinking about who is sitting with who and noticing a group of black students will more often than not sit together." Marc reflected, "It's not necessarily that the black students want to sit by themselves but just that they're sitting with their friends and their friends happen to be black, not the other way around." For Marc, over his four years at the college, the vast majority of his reminders were observations without emotional charge. A few, however, stood out and were remembered for the self-consciousness or pain they caused. One example might have been the remark by his coach when pairing Marc up with a black recruit visiting Amherst: "You guys should understand each other." Or a teammate's biting put-down: "If you were a white with your [level of athletic skill], you wouldn't have gotten in here." Perhaps an example was a question, not typical but memorable, in a literature class about a work by Frederick Douglass: "Well, Marc, how did this book make you feel?" Or maybe another example was a racist remark on the Amherst Confessional, a website that allowed students to post anonymous comments about one another. One comment Marc remembers was "how minorities are easing their way through Amherst and don't deserve to be here because affirmative action got them here." It went on to say, "They're bringing down the level of prestige at Amherst." Thinking back on some of the things he had seen written in the Confessional about people of his race, Marc offered these reflections:

> To be honest, it's disillusioning . . . because you've got to think you're going to school with some of the most intelligent people in

the nation, and for these ugly things to be said about other people, you just wonder where it comes from. You walk around, and it could be any of the people that you're walking around with, having lunch with, having dinner with in the cafeteria. And everyone seems perfectly well-adjusted, and no one says anything like that when it's face-to-face conversation. You introduce this form of anonymity, being able to say whatever you want, and all of a sudden people are incredibly nasty to each other. . . . It always makes me sad to think there are people who I very well could be friends with or acquaintances with who are harboring these thoughts.

Looking ahead to his life after graduation, Marc contemplated going back to Hartford to teach. Yet going back would not be a seamless transition. He had changed over his four years at Amherst. He no longer went to church, he had experienced interracial dating, and he was comfortable with gay people marrying. He had brought family members around to tolerating some of his positions, even if they disagreed. Some chasms were too wide to bridge. He explained, "They're very negative toward gay marriage rights and things like that. I have a friend who is very 'out' and very outspoken about the gay community. He's the head of Pride Alliance right now, and through his eyes I've seen what the gay struggle is and what some of their main issues are. I think I've become more sensitive to that, and my family just doesn't get it at all."

Marc had issues with his black friends in Hartford who voiced concerns about "staying true to your race."

They see me off gallivanting with whites in Massachusetts, and that's offensive to them. The way I talk, they feel it's very affected. I use all these big words, so now I [must] feel like I'm better than them. . . . The majority of us are going through the college experience. But I think that being at Amherst is very different from being at one of the community colleges. . . . Whenever I try to relate the experiences that I'm having, it's kind of a disconnect between me and my friends just because they don't have the same [experiences]. . . . What I'm thinking about in particular are some of the lectures on race and class issues that are not only part of the Amherst community but extend past that globally. I don't think they are getting that same exposure. So they're like, "Yeah, that's cool, but why does that matter?" or "Whatever." It becomes tough to explain constantly [why] we should be conscious of what's happening outside of our own bubble.

As his life at Amherst was drawing to a close, Marc was poised to re-enter that Hartford "bubble." He commented, "I feel like I've done a good job of taking the Hartford stuff and bringing it to Amherst." But the hard part for Marc, as for Emily with her community, he said, would be "bringing Amherst back to Hartford because it's a place that doesn't change and isn't as accepting. The only way I feel the gap would ever be bridged is to just keep rubbing those two worlds up against each other until something gives, and once you find that thing, maybe you can start to bring in more. . . . Since I've been away from Hartford, I miss being home a lot. I actually want to go back and make changes."

Why This Study Matters

We can view the world of the undergraduates at Amherst College as a microcosm. In their everyday interactions, students face a great challenge that also confronts the larger society today—how to address differences and inequalities in order to build a community. Like numerous Americans, many of the students in the study had little close contact with people of another race or class before leaving home for college.[9] Like numerous Americans, they had internalized stereotypes and prejudices based on race and class that are widespread in our society. The study participants give us an unusual and valuable perspective by revealing their personal perceptions of their experiences and their learning. Through their eyes we see, for example, difficulties they faced and how some moved beyond stereotypic views of race and class toward greater understanding and appreciation of those whose lives have been so unlike their own. We observe the learning about self and others that can come from students' efforts to build relationships with those different from themselves and students' discovery of more commonalities than they had believed existed. We learn too about the emotional costs of moving on and moving beyond families and communities students have left behind.

The outcomes of students' experiences with diverse classmates on campus are important. These students will carry what they have learned about diversity into their interactions in the world beyond Amherst and will be better able to help bridge differences in that larger world as a result. As Emily explained, "The opportunities or the experiences that I've had outside of the classroom with friends is going to make me better in the outside world. It's going to make me more willing to interact with people of different races, different backgrounds. And that's something that, if I hadn't had this step, if I had just gone from South Dakota to out in the real world, . . . would have been a lot more difficult. And Amherst has definitely provided a stronger bridge than I could have done on my own."

What follows in this book are the study participants' perceptions of and responses to the challenges of class and race on campus and to the learning opportunities that diversity presented. Most of what we know regarding students' living and learning among diverse peers comes from large-scale survey studies, which are reviewed in Chapter 9. Yet what we learn from the fifty-eight students at Amherst contributes something important. Psychologist Jim Sidanius and his colleagues conclude their longitudinal survey study of the challenges of diversity at UCLA with the comment "We were not able to connect the mountains of very useful quantitative data with the students' own subjective understandings of their lives and the challenges facing them over the college years."[10] Throughout this book the reader hears the voices of students in the study, who provide their individual perspectives on and responses to the issues raised by having to navigate their way in unfamiliar, challenging waters. In Chapter 9, we step back from Amherst and look at other institutions of higher education across the country—how they are addressing the challenges of diversity and which programming and practices have proved successful.

2

Moving In and the Challenges of Class

"I don't really think there's anything the college really could've done to prepare students for as big a change as it was." So mused Robert, a lower-income white student raised in an almost exclusively white town with a little over four thousand residents, three thousand miles from the college. He was thinking back to his transition to Amherst, including his first night in his bare room in a near-empty residence hall; his black roommate was off at a football team meeting, and Robert was left feeling "kinda empty and a little scared."

Although he was alone with his thoughts that night, Robert was not alone in experiencing a great deal of newness and challenge in settling into the college. Living in a socially and racially diverse community 24-7 was a big change for many students. And the challenges students faced regarding race and class were not limited to their initial entry into the community; some challenges extended over the four years the students were on campus, and new ones emerged over time. This chapter begins with a look at what the transition was like for students in the study during their first days and weeks at the college. The discussion then moves on to explore the class challenges students confronted over the next four years and how they dealt with these challenges.

Moving In

Perhaps not surprisingly, the transition to the world at Amherst was easier for the affluent students in the study than for their lower-income classmates. They were in the majority. Some of them had boarded at prep school, and for those students, coming to Amherst was a continuation of life as they had known it their previous four years. They were in a familiar world, in which ample resources were a given, the grounds were manicured, the facilities were impressive, and many of their fellow students had, like them, led privileged lives. Most of the other students from wealthy backgrounds had gone to either private day schools or to well-funded public high schools. What might have been more difficult to anticipate was the fact that among the lower-income students, black students had an easier entry than their lower-income white classmates like Robert. Why was that? The experiences of the two lower-income students, one black and one white, that follow shed light on the answers.

Trina, a lower-income black student from Brooklyn, arrived at Amherst in the fall of 2005 with financial aid. At age ten she had been accepted into New York's Prep for Prep, one of a number of private organizations around the country that identify and then prepare talented black youth for placement into elite independent day and boarding schools. The program provides follow-up support for those students throughout high school. During the years before college, Prep for Prep students attending different independent schools have numerous chances to get together, share experiences, and build friendships. Trina was not the only Prep for Prep student in her entering class at Amherst. When she walked onto campus she was not confronting a world of total strangers. She explained, "Most of my freshman friends I'd known from elementary school because we were all in Prep for Prep." Even before she arrived at Amherst, Trina took steps to reduce her concerns about her minority status: "I was on Facebook every day to see how many brown people joined . . . not because I'm not open to meeting people who aren't brown, but I think that sometimes you want to meet people that you have a cultural affinity with. . . . Yeah, I was really afraid that there weren't going to be any black people. I was afraid that being at Amherst was just going to be like white Anglo-Saxon New Englanders."

Trina and her entering black cohort had no trouble identifying one another and were the recipients of warm welcomes from some of the black students already at the school. In her fall interview in her freshman year, she reported that black classmates on campus were "very excited that there's a lot of new black kids at Amherst." She continued, "A lot of the kids on my floor don't know upperclassmen, but I know upperclassmen 'cause they Facebook me and they talk to me in the hallways and stuff like that because they're like, 'Oh! She's black and she's at Amherst!'" Her entering class had forty-one students who identified as African American or black, over 50 percent more than in the class that had entered the previous year. "They're very excited that there are more brown people. . . . When you're black at Amherst, you're already a member of a minority group, and other minority [students] are more inclined to say hi to you. I've had random black students at Amherst just come up and say, 'Hi, my name is so-and-so. I've never seen you before.' . . . I think that was very welcoming when I first got here."

Having gone to Trinity School in New York, Trina was already familiar with the world of white wealth. There she had met people "whose last name is Rockefeller" and people who "have Learjets," and she felt "already sort of acclimated to it." But unlike at her high school, Trina was not an outlier at Amherst in not being well-off, and she drew comfort when, as she recalled, the director of admissions at Amherst told the entering class, "Fifty percent of all Amherst students in [Trina's] class are on financial aid." In her high school, few students were on financial aid, and those on aid were mostly black classmates. "It made you stand out, especially because socioeconomics was coupled with racial distinctions." Asked how she felt when she learned of her new situation at Amherst, she responded, "I felt kind of like part of the group!" Far from making her feel like an outsider, Trina found that her lack of wealth had a certain status and that having great means could cause social discomfort. "People make fun of the kids whose parents came back to buy all their books with credit cards. . . . It's sort of weird that they're making fun of the rich people, 'cause at my high school there were people making fun of the poor people." For Trina, paying for her own books made her feel "included in complaining about how much [they] cost." Given her prior experiences at Trinity and the social supports in place for her at the college, entering the Amherst community turned out to be "no great transition." And to varying degrees, that was true for other newly arriving lower-income black students, two-thirds of whom had attended private high schools with the help of financial aid.

In contrast to Trina, but like many other lower-income white students, Robert had had no direct exposure to the kind of affluence and privilege that awaited him at the college. Where he was raised there are "a few people who own businesses around town, but the majority of people either work for the railway or work in the tourism industry, and everyone seem[s] on the same level." He noted, "The kind of looks that I see here now, some of these kids, boggles my mind." Robert spoke of a girl whose great-grandfather was someone he had "heard of before":

> He owns this bank, her family has a billion dollars, [and] they just got back from the Hamptons. These are things you see on TV. Or like an Audi Quattro—in the small town where I'm from, if a car drives through like that, it's like, "Oh my God! Wow! You see that car he had?" And here, there's like four kids who just got their licenses whippin' around in them. It boggles my mind. . . . I see people here with more money than I've ever imagined.

Perhaps even more unsettling, yet not unwelcome, was Robert's exposure to his black classmates. His roommate was black, "a really nice guy," and several other black students were living on his floor. He explained, "All that I really knew about black culture before I came here was what I'd seen on TV." What Robert had seen were black people depicted as "rappers" or by "their different dialects, how they talk differently, stuff like that." He went on, "And then I come here and actually meet people who are like that. . . . I hope I'm not sounding racist or anything like that, because it's great for me." Robert described a particular evening: "All four of them were in my room, and they were all very comfortable, laughing, joking around. And I didn't really know, especially as a white man, how I fit into this, and if their stereotypes of me would affect how they judge me. . . . They were all dancing [and there's the] stereotype—white men can't dance. But it was true. I couldn't do any of the things those guys were doing." According to Robert, those four students "didn't act like anything was different. And even though I didn't feel as comfortable with them, I don't think they excluded me just because of my race. They still went about their business and didn't change anything and didn't act any different for me, which was good."

Back then, in the fall of his freshman year, Robert wondered whether there might be other white students "more comfortable with the little mannerisms like that, [who] slide right in there." He said, "But for me, to be honest, it's different, and I just don't want to offend anyone." Long term, Robert was optimistic: "I'm sure we'll become good friends and get to know a lot more about each others' backgrounds and culture and stuff like that." Entering the Amherst community, though, Robert, unlike Trina, was definitely out of his comfort zone.

Specific factors went into making Amherst an easier, more welcoming place for many lower-income black students to transition into than it was for some lower-income white students. Black students, both lower income and affluent, had a number of social advantages when they arrived on campus that were not present for lower-income white students, which helped them meet the challenges of being in a minority. To begin with, they merely had to look around to find one another. And many of their black classmates already at Amherst were ready to invite them into a strong black community. Comments such as these were common from black students in the study: "There's always camaraderie amongst black people, so from there you meet black people just because you're black"; "There's a community of black students on the campus, and if you want to be involved in that community, it's very easy, and I think that's a good thing. It's very inclusive." Regardless of how involved they chose to be in it, most black students appreciated the presence and benefits of the strong black community, for the ease of "finding friends of your race" and the advantages of networking within the black community—"We help each other out."

No comparable, readily identifiable community of lower-income students, black or white, existed on campus to welcome them or help them connect to others like themselves. However, it is not the case that such connections were not valued. Lower-income students spoke of their desire to have friends with common backgrounds, who had "similar experiences" and "a lot of similarities and common things that are going in [their] lives." Once found and formed, those connections were helpful to them in dealing with class-related problems on campus. What Emily, the South Dakotan, said of the special value she attached to having close friends from the same social class bears repeating: She stressed the importance of "just having that day-to-day help [in order] to not feel alone and just to [be able to] navigate [the world of Amherst] with someone." After four years, many lower-income students reported that they had formed a core group of close friends "from the same working-class background" or of "a similar social class." But it generally took much longer for lower-income white students to find each other than it did for their black counterparts.

Many of the black students who were so welcoming belonged to the Black Student Union (BSU), an organization whose mission was to support black students and to foster programming around race. BSU members were instrumental in acclimating incoming black students to Amherst. Regardless of whether students wished to join the BSU, most black students at Amherst appreciated its presence and spoke positively of the events the BSU organized. No comparable class-focused student organization was present for lower-income students. Years before, students had organized a group called FACE (Financial and Class Equality) to address the concerns of lower-income students on campus, but the group had not been able to sustain itself over time.

Black students had other resources in place that were not present for lower-income white students—the Black Studies Department and the Charles Drew Black Cultural House, one of a number of residential "theme" houses available to students. While the Charles Drew Black Cultural House was open to students of all races, its residents were almost entirely black. Black student organizations and black studies departments at the nearby University of Massachusetts and at other neighboring liberal arts colleges invited Amherst's black students to social events and to hear speakers. Trina took advantage of these resources. She became a black studies and neuroscience major, lived for two years in the Charles Drew Black Cultural House, and attended black-sponsored events on the other campuses.

The Broad Challenges of Class

After dealing with the initial settling in, students faced unavoidable challenges over the next four years because of differences in class and obstacles embedded in their lives at the college. How, for instance, did students handle eating out, taking spring break trips, and making plans for graduation celebrations when some friends could not afford to pay? What were the challenges of dating someone from a very different class background? What class issues had to be addressed, and what options were possible? How did students respond to their class privilege, or to others' privilege, when it came to having connections for preprofessional jobs and internships, or having parental support to take unpaid jobs or internships over the summer or after graduation? How did affluent students handle the negative stereotypes about the wealthy that they encountered and wished to avoid? These were some of the broad challenges of class that are discussed below.

To begin, though, it is important to note certain aspects of campus life that worked to diminish distinctions by class. Casual dress was the norm, meals were prepaid and eaten in a common dining hall, freshmen were prohibited from bringing cars to the college, events on campus were free (a policy of the student government), and college trips were subsidized. That said, there was no single agreed-on perception among the study participants of the role social class played in the social life of the college. "It's wonderful not to be at all aware of people's class status," remarked Lauren, an affluent white student who grew up in Manhattan's West Village and attended high school at Dalton, an elite private high school. "That's something that I'm grateful for about Amherst." She noted that although some people may dress nicer than others, suggesting they might be wealthier, "I don't think it's a particular attitude that most people carry around like a badge of honor if you have money. . . . I think that in the Amherst culture, at least the people I surround myself with, you don't really care how much money you come from." Contrast that experience and perception with those of Brianna, a lower-income black student from Houston who had stayed in a homeless shelter at age four when her mom could not support two children on her own. "I wouldn't say there's a day I wake up and I'm not aware of [social class]. . . . Race and class relationships affect every aspect at an elite college. Whether it's said or not, it's definitely there." For her, an "unspoken tension" existed between students from different socioeconomic backgrounds; she was aware of "misunderstandings and assumptions on both sides that create this friction." Brianna's experience of class at Amherst, though, was not typical of most of her black classmates. A quarter of black students in the study as seniors reported thinking about class differences a lot.[1] Most were more focused on issues of race (41 percent thought about their race a lot).[2]

It is worth noting that a subgroup of *extremely* wealthy students existed within the student body whose family names might grace campus buildings and who grew up in the rarified air of penthouses and estates and of second and third homes. Lower-income students were aware of these classmates and were aware, too, of cliques that were composed of them. But being in those cliques was not an aspiration that lower-income participants reported having. "I feel excluded, but I also wouldn't want to feel included. It's not who I'm friends with, and it's not like I feel the need to be involved with that group of people," said Kayla, a lower-income white student who grew up on Staten Island in "not a great neighborhood" but had tested into Hunter College High School. Carl, a lower-income black student, had attended a private school, had rubbed shoulders with students from extremely wealthy backgrounds, and had come to view some of those on campus as "too into the prep-style life and the money and all [that] those things involved. Do I need to be a part of it? No, not at all."

A number of affluent students, too, reported having no dealings with the cliques of the extremely wealthy. Katelyn, a white student, explained, "I can't relate to them or their world at all, so I have avoided those people. . . . I've just felt I have nothing in common, and I can't understand them, and they probably couldn't understand me." This remark was typical of some of her wealthy classmates. That affluent students distanced themselves from cliques of the most affluent reflected the changes that had come to Amherst, as a social position that once held great allure was now disdained by many students. Matthew, the Deerfield graduate who arrived on campus intent on making connections, was blindsided by the changes, from the casualness of dress to the underlying values that change reflected. This was not his dad's Amherst or his uncle's Amherst.

Making Choices

Choices and complexities abound when it comes to having limited discretionary money. Not having to worry about money, but having friends who must, means needing to make choices. And choices often come with feelings. A group of friends of mixed means gathers to make a plan—Do we go out for dinner or eat at Val prepaid? If we go out, where do we go (how expensive or inexpensive a restaurant)? There's a great concert off campus. Do we attend? Spring break is approaching. Where should we go? How should we get there? Where will we stay? A lower-income student weighs spending money to join in the activity. She could decide not to join in or to participate in a limited way. Or she could opt to join fully, knowing it would mean having to work extra hours to make up for the expenditure or having to forgo something. Her wealthier friends weigh going ahead with the activity and thus possibly excluding her, or scaling back the plan to something less desirable but less costly, or covering the expense for their friend so that she can join in the outing. Should they opt for the latter, she, in turn, must then decide how she feels about accepting this generosity. Her wealthier friends may come to resent not getting paid back or may feel taken advantage of—feelings that may be hard to express.

Amherst students reflected on their experiences dealing with these situations from their different positions on the spectrum of wealth. Emily, the lower-income student from the South Dakota farm, speaking in the fall of her freshman year, said, "Socially it's been hard to find a niche." She had come, she said, "from an area where everyone is the same status. All of my friends, we were the same." Emily and her friends at home, she continued, "found different ways to be creatively entertained not going out and spending money. Here I noticed it's a lot of 'Well, let's go to the movies. There's nothing going on.' Or 'Let's do this,' and 'Let's do that.' And I'm thinking, my fifty-dollar budget for the month is not going to be stretched very far." Problems arose over basic issues like "stocking [the] fridge." "I feel bad," Emily explained, "because my roommate is very generous and very just like, 'Oh, you can have anything you want of mine.' And I'm thinking, 'You know, I feel like I can't repay her.' . . . So I'm very careful of what I use." It was important to Emily to be "taking care of [her]self."

For Kristen, a lower-income white student from Pennsylvania, questions about whether to spend money on anything more than the basics were moot. She simply could not afford to. "My financial aid has allowed me to attend Amherst. I have very little money, and all the money I have goes to medical bills and other pressing expenses. . . . I have some larger medical bills that were partially covered by insurance that I'm still paying off the deductible for." Amy, another lower-income white student, noted that if something came up and she was unable to get her hours working at the Writing Center in during the week, "then, no, I can't go out for dinner that weekend, and I know that." Asked if she ever felt excluded from group activities because of her financial straits, she responded, "Sometimes I make those decisions like 'No, I'm not going to do that,' but I don't really usually feel excluded because I just know that that's part of the choices I have to make." And even if the money was there, questions might arise about whether a fun activity was the wisest use of funds. Brandi, a lower-income black Prep for Prep student, explained, "[There were] plenty of times where I would've loved to go out to eat, or go out to Springfield and go bowling or something. It's like you have the money, but you've got to think twice—should I really be spending this, or should I be saving it?"

Some affluent students had an issue as well with having sufficient discretionary funds. Megan, an affluent black student, said her family just missed qualifying for financial aid. "So that leaves me with not a lot of pocket money. I work off campus [at a local bookstore]. I've worked off campus all four years of being in college. Everyone's like, 'You have a job?' and generally expect that it's not going to be my priority. I do that, and I'm an RC [resident counselor]. I can't afford to give up either. There are people who just don't really understand that."

Eating Out and Other Activities

Perhaps the activity that most often confronted students directly and unavoidably with issues of class was eating out. A great deal of thought might go into a lower-income student's decision to go to a restaurant with friends. For Emily, who worked long hours to be of help to her family back in South Dakota, the considerations she weighed left her feeling "a little strained" at times. On the one hand, she did not feel she should be spending money on going out to eat. But on the other hand, she said, "I want to see my friends. I want to be a part of that. I know if I said, 'Let's just go to Val tonight,' they would." But she did not want to feel like "the bad friend" who was making them eat in the dining hall when they wanted to go out. Like 40 percent of the participants in the study, affluent and lower income, black and white, Emily at times spent money in order to be part of an activity with her friendship group, however much she might regret it later.[3] There were other times when Emily would simply say, "'I don't want to tonight.' And they don't ask; they don't press."

In his senior year at Amherst, Robert looked back on another situation in which fitting in was at issue, the times in his first couple of years at the college when "all the guys were going out for a big expensive dinner—40, 50 bucks—when you're making 125 bucks every two weeks working as an RC or whatever." He continued, "So that's half your budget. You really should not be spending it on one meal. But if you're in that situation, and the whole group is doing it, you don't want to be the one guy that doesn't do it." So he tended to go to those dinners, but in the back of his mind he was thinking, "Geez, this is probably a waste of money." At the end of his senior year Robert reported, "I had a great internship last summer. . . . For the first time in four years, this year I actually have some funds." Now he could say to his friends, "Yeah, let's go [out] for dinner tonight." He did not have to think about it as much.

The choices, then, that students short on discretionary funds could make unilaterally were whether to join their friends on the outing and, if they did, whether to scrimp. Rebecca, a lower-income white student, talked about the problem posed by birthday celebrations, which were often occasions when groups of friends went out to eat together. "Whoever's birthday it was would choose what restaurant to go out to, and all the friends would go, and we would all chip in for the birthday person. So if someone chose Judie's [Restaurant], I would be thinking in my head, 'Oh, man, that's going to be an expensive dinner, with my food and their food and tip and everything.' But even though I knew that it would be expensive, I would still go along. I just tried to order a less expensive meal or something. . . . But I would still go along so as to be included." She was not alone. Other lower-income students said they might join friends but "have something small." They said, "I know the people I eat out with are not concerned about my socioeconomic status. They're my friends." Or "'I'll go with you, but maybe I'll just get an appetizer.' With my close friends, they understand that, and so it's not uncomfortable."

The problems of eating out incurred by the disparities of wealth lent themselves to other solutions that involved those who *had* funds as well as those who did not. Changing plans was an oft-cited option, with three out of four students reporting that they and their friends had changed plans in order to include others who could not pay.[4] Students might end up at the college dining hall and "just go with the no-pay option" if friends could not pay, or if a less affluent friend was coming, they would just pick a cheaper restaurant and go "where everyone was most comfortable." Similarly, going out to the movies could at times be financially burdensome, and if that were the case for someone in a group of friends, the group might "stay in and get a movie and hang out instead."

Alternatively, there were the offers to pay. Almost three-quarters of the lower-income students reported offers by other students to pay for them in order to include them in some activity such as eating out. This was more likely to be true for lower-income black than white students.[5] Andrea, an affluent black student, told a friend who did not have the money to join a group for dinner, "I'll pay for it; don't worry. We just want you there." Monica, an affluent black student, had a friendship circle in which, "if people say, 'Oh, I really can't afford to do that right now; I can't afford to go see a movie with you,' others would say, 'It's not a problem. We'll pay for you.'" Sometimes the offers were made with reimbursement in mind, with remarks such as "You can pay me back later." Or "I'll pay for you this time, and next time we can go out to ice cream and maybe you can treat me."

But there were times when groups of friends went ahead with plans, leaving their lower-income compatriots behind. Two out of three lower-income students felt their financial circumstances had at times resulted in their exclusion from activities.[6] It simply was not possible to do everything. Marissa, an affluent black student, spoke of one of her friends "who never comes out with us because she very carefully budgets everything that she does and understandably so."

Travel
Offers to pay could extend far beyond places to eat in town. Julian, a wealthy black student, explained, "I invited some friends to come to Hawaii with me over winter break [freshman year], and some [were] like, 'Well, I don't know if I can afford it or not,' and my dad was like, 'Well if they can't, then we can help.'" For many affluent students, travel had been an important part of their lives growing up. Now in college, many of the affluent students looked forward to taking trips with friends over breaks. In the spring of his senior year, Matthew, the Deerfield grad, noted, "Spring break trips are quite expensive." And that can lead to conundrums: "A couple friends and I were planning on going to the Bahamas, and then a couple kids who were planning on going said, 'I'm sorry, but I just can't.' And then you have to decide—do you want to go to the Bahamas, or do you want to be with your friends in who-knows-where? We all decided unanimously we wanted to be with our friends in who-knows-where, so we're not going to the Bahamas anymore."

The opportunities for enrichment that students from wealthy backgrounds could take advantage of became apparent to Trina, the lower-income black student from Brooklyn, when she studied in Africa in her junior year: "So many of the students were doing all these extravagant things abroad. By 'extravagant things,' I mean after the program was over, going and spending a month in Tanzania or going to spend a month in Senegal.

After six months abroad, I'm out of money. I need to go home. That made me conscious of what people do at Amherst."

For most lower-income students, the trips being planned by affluent students (e.g., to India, to Europe, to the Caribbean, to the Bahamas, or within the continental United States) were never an option. It was nice to be invited on such trips, but going was never a choice. Many lower-income students simply accepted the reality of their situation. When friends planned a spring break trip to Colorado, Kayla, a lower-income white student, did not feel excluded: "I knew it wasn't going to happen, so I never really worried about it." Alisa, a lower-income black student, had a similar response: "I don't feel excluded." There were spring break trips she could have gone on, but, she said, "I would have to foot the bill, and it wouldn't be worth it to me," so she chose not to go.

Who Pays?

Being paid for with no prospects of reciprocating was not an option for some lower-income students. The position was too uncomfortable. "If I was in the situation where I knew I probably couldn't afford it, then I would make sure that I didn't go because I wouldn't want someone to pick up the check for me," remarked Amy, a lower-income white student. Matthew mulled over an instance in which a seeming act of generosity did not have its intended effect. Plans were afoot to go bowling, and "one person said, 'Look, I'm embarrassed about this, but I just can't afford to go.'" He continued, "While she may have felt that that excluded her, we all said, 'Well, that's ridiculous. We're gonna chip in.' But then she feels bad about it so, yeah, there are situations where it's not . . . good." Lower-income students often helped one another out if someone was short on cash, with the expectation that the favor would be returned and things would balance out over time.

At times affluent students reported feeling taken advantage of by lower-income students—of going out with friends and having less-well-off students simply make the assumption "Oh, I won't have to buy drinks tonight" because the wealthy kid "is just going to buy everything." Matthew found going out to dinner "very dicey" when students ordered a lot of things. "[We are] planning on just splitting the check five ways, and then one person is like, 'Well, I don't have that.'" Matthew felt torn at those times when he found himself "the wealthiest in the room or in the top portion." He explained, "Sometimes you want to tone it down because you don't want to be footing the bill for everything. . . . How do you fairly subsidize kids who aren't able to pay? A certain level of subsidization is great, but when it becomes a huge burden and then when the people who can't afford to pay start taking advantage of you, that's when it becomes an issue."

Steven, an affluent black student, talked of a friend who he felt was always using him for money. "He would take advantage of my kindness. I would pay for him for something. He would be like, 'I don't have any money right now, but I'll pay you when we get back to the house.' I would pay for him, and when we got back, he just wouldn't say anything. If we both forgot about it, then he wouldn't say anything. It wasn't like I was paying for him and not expecting him to pay me back." In trying to talk to him about it, Steven said his friend "was always so defensive about it and would argue" with him. Eventually, he had to end their relationship because his friend would not change.

Cross-Class Dating

The question of who pays and what feelings are engendered by how the question is decided had particular salience to dating couples from different classes. There was no finessing the situation; it was ongoing, and many couples needed to develop ways of addressing class differences. Over half of the students in the study reported having dated someone from a very different class.[7] This broke down to nearly two-thirds of the affluent black, affluent white, and lower-income white students and just over a third of the lower-income black students.

For Marc, the lower-income black student from Hartford, the issue of who pays had the added complexity of his gender role expectations. He carried with him a traditional male role model in relation to his girlfriend—he wanted to be "providing for her." But "she could get anything she wanted for herself" and was in a better financial position to do so. The "struggle within" himself about who he wanted to be and the realities of his economic situation spilled out into the relationship when he had to tell her, "I can only do so much as far as extra spending and going on dates and buying things." He "was always self-conscious."

Andrea, the affluent black student from Jamaica Estates, dated someone much wealthier than she was. The traditional female role of having a man "providing for her" clashed with the more modern model of a woman as independent and self-reliant. Her white boyfriend "held true to the whole 'the man pays for things.' And he could afford to pay for everything." She continued, "I told him eventually that I needed him to stop saying that and that it wasn't because I didn't want him to pay for things and take me out and show me a good time. It was just I didn't know how to act or feel about it." Their talking led them to agree that he would pay to take her to dinner, but "every now and then" she could pay.

Alicia, a lower-income black student from Vermont, had, like Andrea, dated someone wealthier than she, but the discrepancy was greater than that between Andrea and her boyfriend. Alicia, too, had had to reconcile the traditional gender role expectations of her partner with her own values, and they reached a slightly different resolution than Andrea and her partner did. Alicia's boyfriend was from "a whole different world. Really wealthy. Beautiful house. Nanny." She "had never been around people who had a nanny." She said, "[He] would pay for everything, which I had a lot of issues with, just on many different levels. I was brought up 'you go half and you each pay half.'" But her boyfriend was "of the old tradition where the man pays for everything." And he could. "I let him. . . . It was hard for the first little bit. But then I got used to it."

For students who dated classmates less affluent than themselves, allowances might have to be made to accommodate their partners' financial circumstances. Benjamin, an affluent white student from Hastings, was used to taking family trips. His parents were both physicians. His mother's research had led to family travel abroad to conferences at which she gave papers. Benjamin met and started dating a woman "quite a bit less wealthy" on a study abroad program. "She definitely had much less spending money than I did, which limited our options in terms of travel that we could do while we were abroad." Challenges arose for Lauren when she drove across the country with her less-affluent boyfriend, who preferred to sleep on the side of the road and save the expense of a hotel. "I had to negotiate with him, like, 'Please, can we just split a hotel room or something, so it's safe?'"

In talking about her experience dating a less-affluent man at Amherst, Sarah, an affluent white student, noted, "You end up being more frugal because you can't go out to dinner; you can't do things like that." In that relationship, frugality was not the only issue that Sarah dealt with as a result of class differences. "It was sometimes difficult, because it felt like he was blaming me for my [privileged] background." In a similar vein, Marissa, an affluent black student who dated someone with less means, noted, "One of the problems in our relationship was that he would draw attention [negatively] to the amount of money that he felt or believed my family had." Lower-income students could feel awkward and uncomfortable about their family situations as well. The parents of someone Tanya, a lower-income white student, dated were both doctors. "My dad is a super and my mom works in a pharmacy in the neighborhood that I live in. I'm very aware that I come from a different place." She reported, "It's not a *big* deal, but it can be a little uncomfortable."

Summers

As summer approached, those students who were thinking seriously of making a career in finance, law, medicine or biological research, or other professions were aware that it would be advantageous get exposure to, and experience in, their chosen field, to build their resumes and to be better positioned for desired jobs or further schooling once they graduated. For many students, preprofessional jobs or internships were seen as vital steps, with two out of three taking such positions during two or three of their college summers.[8] The chances of securing those positions were not even. Being perched high in the class structure could hold enormous advantages for students, which those on lower rungs could see and envy. Justin wanted a job in finance. He was well aware that many students who went into finance came from wealthy backgrounds or had a parent in the field to provide them with connections to interviews. From where he, a lower-income white student, stood, the advantages of coming from a wealthier class extended beyond having and making those connections. In his eyes, affluent students were more skilled at handling interviews. He recognized that affluent students "certainly know the language." He continued, "[You] know what to say if you're raised in a household where people speak about the markets or they speak about deals that they're working on. I think that gives [these] people a huge leg up." Justin was aware that he was not "cultured or socialized for that" and felt it would have been really helpful to know "how to behave" during interviews. Carl's parents had emigrated here from Kenya and had achieved a great deal of success, educationally and career-wise. He saw himself as middle class, which, he believed, may have provided him with "some of the opportunities but not all of them." He explained, "There are definitely kids [here] that are getting doors opened because of their social class, because they're upper social class." Those doors opened to internships and jobs. "They have a greater access to the tools that would probably make them more successful in the future."

Many affluent students were aware of their advantage in attaining internships or preprofessional jobs. Geoffrey was an affluent white student from the Boston suburb of Wellesley whose parents were both doctors. Like his parents, Geoffrey had a long-standing interest in science and medicine. With his parents' help, he had gained two years of research experience during high school. That experience gave him an advantage during interviews for summer jobs in college. As he put it, "You're always one step ahead." In those job interviews he had another advantage—the people he interviewed with knew his parents. "It's hard to know if [the researchers] ever would have just taken me had they not known my parents, just based on my own merit."

Lower-income students faced another disadvantage when it came to preprofessional internships—they needed to make money over the summer. Brandi, a lower-income black student, noted that affluent students "can do this volunteer work, whereas I need to get a job that makes money because that's going to be where I get my money from." She was not alone. Other lower-income students spoke of being constrained by "the need to find a paying job."

Graduation Traditions

Colleges develop traditions over time that may be problematic as the student body changes. The Amherst tradition for "senior week," the week between the end of final exams and graduation weekend, is for students to celebrate, which many do by taking trips together to popular destinations such as Myrtle Beach, the Bahamas, the Caribbean, or Cape Cod. On graduation weekend, friendship groups traditionally host catered receptions and dinners under tents on the lawns outside their dorms for family, friends, and, sometimes, professors. But trips and "tent parties" are costly—not something many lower-income students can afford. With friendship groups that spanned different class backgrounds, planning for senior week and tent parties posed complexities that needed to be addressed. Students talked of not going for the "nicer house" at Myrtle Beach in order to keep costs down and include everyone. But even toned-down plans are expensive if you have little money to spare. Tanya, a lower-income white study participant, related an instance of adaptation and accommodation: "One of my friends got really big into planning for senior week. And he was really super pumped about it, and we were going to get a house somewhere." But a bunch of her friends "were like, 'Um, that's going to cost money.'" As a result, she said, "there was a big planning thing about it. In the end we decided that we would just go visit a friend's place in Connecticut because we can do that for free."

Benjamin, the affluent white student from Hastings, had a couple of friends who were planning on going to the Bahamas for senior week:

[This] would have been at least [an] eight-hundred-dollar trip, which was probably more money than I would have felt comfortable spending, because I don't have much in my personal bank account at the moment. But had all my friends gone, I would have gone and just bit the bullet. But I had a group of friends who simply didn't have that money at all. So ultimately, we're going to Myrtle Beach, which is the standard thing to do, which will be a couple hundred dollars. That was a concession to people who couldn't afford the trip. The two kids who are advocating the Bahamas, I think they realized on their own that they would be excluding people.

Parental Support after Graduation

As graduating seniors, students faced a difficult job market, and the different prospects ahead for affluent and lower-income students made class differences salient. Benjamin recognized the role social class played in determining the types of jobs students could accept. He had friends "for whom salary held a bigger concern" than it was for him. He continued, "I have friends who are in so desperate need of work that they're going to become janitors or whatever—not to disparage janitors." Benjamin noted that affluent students could afford to go to graduate school, to take unpaid internships, and to travel abroad, while for lower-income students, "the salary they're going to receive is a much more important thing." As others noted, affluent students had "more they can fall back on." Many lower-income students had no guarantee they could be supported by parents after graduation,[9] and for them it was "a lot more imperative to really start finding a job."

Downplaying or Hiding Class Differences

One way students responded to the tensions that arose from class differences was to downplay their circumstances or hide information about their class backgrounds. The affluent white students most keenly felt that desire. Half of the wealthy white students reported that, when asked directly, there were times when they wanted to hide their class origins, two to three times as many as in the other three groups.[10] These affluent white students were responding largely to their own discomfort with their relative advantages and/or to the negative stereotypes that existed about the wealthy. Attempts to downplay their class might entail avoiding saying they came from Greenwich or from the Upper East Side of Manhattan. Exeter or Deerfield prep school experiences could go unmentioned. Sarah volunteered that part of the reason she did not say she attended high school in Greenwich, Connecticut, was because "it carries a certain connotation, and if people hear 'Greenwich,' they're going to think 'snob.'" She worried that students would think of her as "this person" she does not think she is.

Benjamin, the affluent student from Hastings, spoke of his particular discomfort with his privileged status, of feeling almost embarrassed sometimes:

> [For example,] there are situations when I can do things, I can go on trips that other people might not be able to go on. That's really not fair. I don't have any more personal merit than anybody else here, really. . . . Through no virtue of my own, I have opportunities that other people don't necessarily have. I'm pretty frugal myself. Part of that is the desire to minimize the resources that are behind me, because I do feel like a little bit uncomfortable that there are opportunities open to me that aren't open to other people.

Benjamin's awareness of his unearned privilege could have been achieved only through his exposure to those who were equally deserving but less fortunate—to the diversity all around him.

Geoffrey, another affluent white student, had similar feelings: "I come from a more wealthy background, which always slightly bothers me because I feel weird when I can afford something but my friends can't. It's a strange situation because I didn't do anything to be able to afford that, and they didn't do anything not to be able to afford it." Lauren's parents paid for her books, but she was well aware that for "some people [the cost] is a huge problem." She said, "So I don't really like talking about how much my books cost because I feel guilty [that] they cost so much money."

At times, comments from lower-income students about class advantages contributed to affluent students' feelings of guilt about their wealth. Sarah, as noted above, had a former boyfriend who came from a much lower social class and made her feel "uncomfortable" about her wealth: "I felt guilty about that." Rachel, a white student from Chicago, had a friend who had "made comments" to her about her family's resources. She explained, "And [he] has made comments as if I was snobbish about it, which I always try not to be. He's made comments about the car I drive or my clothes sometimes." Not surprisingly, then, affluent white students were most likely to feel put down or dismissed because of their social class, with 25 percent reporting having that feeling, versus an average of just 7 percent for the other three groups, thus explaining in part their much greater desire to hide their class.[11]

Discussion

We have seen the complexities students faced as they addressed their class differences. We can gain different understandings of students' class-related experiences by approaching the topic from different perspectives. Let us begin by looking at institutional cultures. The culture at a predominantly white, elite college is that of the dominant group on campus—the affluent white majority. Daryl Smith, a professor of education and psychology, describes the effect that institutional culture is likely to have: "When an individual's identities align significantly with the cultural identity of an institution, there is usually a sense of comfort and a lack of awareness of certain salient features of institutional culture. Institutional and societal norms are taken for granted. The institution can appear to be a neutral, cultureless place whose values and practices are simply the way 'one does business' and where 'individuals are treated as individuals.'"[12]

It is not surprising, then, that affluent students in the study found themselves for the most part fitting in easily with the prevalent values and practices of life on campus. To them, the culture was familiar, normal. That culture had become familiar, too, for the lower-income black students who had gone to elite, largely white prep schools. Those few lower-income white students who, through scholarships, had opportunities to attend private school or enrichment programs had also been exposed to the world the affluent inhabited. Yet there were many lower-income students for whom the Amherst culture was unfamiliar, disorienting, and even alienating. Lower-income students whose parents had not gone to college, or had not attended a college like Amherst, could not turn to their parents for guidance on how to navigate this new culture.[13] They were on their own, facing greater challenges than their more affluent classmates in finding their way on campus.

Another way to think about the challenges lower-income students faced is to consider sociologist Pierre Bourdieu's concepts of cultural, social, and economic capital.[14] Each social class transmits distinctive *cultural* capital. The cultural capital of the affluent has come to refer to many things—to educational qualifications and credentials; linguistic competencies; knowledge of highbrow aesthetic culture (e.g., opera, ballet); cultural goods (e.g., books, dictionaries, paintings); styles of dress and speech; manners;

tastes and preferences; levels of confidence, certainty, and entitlement; and skills, competencies, and abilities to gain access to scarce rewards.[15] It is the cultural capital of the *affluent* students that is valued at an institution like Amherst. Upon their arrival at this elite college, many lower-income students came to realize they lacked that cultural capital that made fitting in socially and in the classroom easier for their affluent classmates.

Lower-income students also lacked the *social* capital of their affluent peers. Many affluent students came to campus with preexisting connections to classmates through their high schools or the summer camps and the enrichment programs they had attended, which gave them immediate entrée into friendship groups. They also had networks and connections through parents and parents' friends that could be used for professional gain (e.g., procuring preprofessional summer jobs).[16]

Finally, as discussed in this chapter, lower-income students lacked the *economic* capital to join in some taken-for-granted parts of social life—eating out, going to movies and concerts, and going on spring break trips. Many affluent students generously offered to pay for lower-income students to include them in activities, for which lower-income students were appreciative. But being the recipient of generosity in a one-sided exchange can arouse negative feelings—embarrassment, indebtedness, dependence, inferiority, and obligation.[17] Overall, the lack of cultural, social, and economic capital marked lower-income students as different from their affluent peers and posed challenges to their day-to-day lives on campus as well as to their social and academic success.

The class issues at Amherst were in many instances different for lower-income black students than for their lower-income white classmates in what might at first seem a counterintuitive way. In our society, being a white person is generally associated with privilege, which would suggest that lower-income white students would have an advantage. But that was not the case. Lower-income black and white students were situated differently when they entered college. As academically talented minority students, many of the lower-income black students in this study had had access to scholarship programs that prepared them for and enabled them to attend private day schools and prep schools. Two-thirds of lower-income black participants in this study had attended private high schools where they were introduced to institutional cultures of affluence similar to what they encountered at Amherst. They arrived on campus with more cultural capital than many of their lower-income white classmates, who had not had the same opportunities to attend these types of private high schools.

Researchers have documented the challenges black high school students face at predominantly white prep schools and private schools.[18] Black students have found themselves caught between the two cultures of home and school, and they are on the margins of social life at their private high schools. But over the course of high school, lower-income black students learn to manage the social, emotional, and psychological challenges of their new environments. They form ties to white classmates, thus enhancing their social capital. They familiarize themselves with a culture of affluence and acquire new forms of cultural capital, gaining the knowledge and skills valuable to succeeding in their new cultural context. By the time they enter Amherst, they are familiar with the culture. As a consequence, many lower-income black participants found little that was shocking. In contrast, almost all lower-income white students in this study came to Amherst from public schools where they had little to no exposure to wealthy students and their lifestyles or to students of color. The culture shock that many lower-income white participants encountered made their transition to an elite college more difficult than it was for many lower-income black students.

A number of researchers and writers have focused on the class-related difficulties lower-income students face in coming to college.[19] However, the seismic change in the makeup of the Amherst College student body has brought with it challenges for *all* students on campus. Researchers have not explored the challenges faced by affluent students as the economic backgrounds of students on campus become more diverse. In this study we look at the situation from the perspective of the affluent students as well, revealing that they, too, are faced with new challenges as a result of the changes in the composition of the student body. The large disparities in wealth between students made class salient for affluent as well as lower-income students.[20] As affluent students formed cross-class friendship groups and dating relationships, they came to see the world from the perspective of others outside their class, acquiring a greater consciousness of class. Both affluent and lower-income students gained a greater awareness of social class over their four years at college.[21] As noted in this chapter, many of the affluent students came to recognize that involvement in various aspects of the social life and the culture at the college was not class neutral.[22] They became more aware of their privilege, understanding that activities they had taken for granted—eating out with friends or going on spring break trips, for example—required economic capital that some friends did not have. What had always been normal and natural was now seen through a new lens, leading some affluent students to feel discomfort with their relative advantages and unearned privilege and to attempt to bridge differences. In addition, wealthy students had to respond to an unexpected backlash against them—the many negative stereotypes students held about the rich—which often caused them to downplay or hide their class backgrounds. For some affluent students, the need to address class tensions led to important insights, deepening their understanding of class inequalities.

A discrepancy existed between the many class-based challenges that students faced on campus and the amount of built-in programming that the college offered to help students handle the day-to-day issues created by class inequalities. Relatively few forums were held to discuss class-related issues. For the most part, students were left to themselves to figure out ways to address class tensions. They could benefit from programming to help them more fully understand and address these issues.

From here we move to another class challenge lower-income students faced. As they adjusted to the college and established a home and friendships on campus, they found that they had a foothold in two very different worlds—the world on campus and their home communities. We look next at the challenges that arose in bridging those two worlds.

3

Bridging Two Worlds

Some distances cannot be measured in miles. There are affluent students in this study who traveled far to come to Amherst but who felt no great distance or disconnect between the world they left at home and the one they lived in on campus. The students who had spent their previous four years boarding at prep schools were old hands at much of what was offered by and expected at Amherst. Those affluent students who had gone to private day schools or wealthy public schools out in leafy suburbs brought with them knowledge that smoothed their transition and later experiences. They were well supplied by their families and communities with cultural capital and exposure to the dominant values; classroom expectations; and ways of speech, dress, and behavior integral to Amherst. To varying degrees, these students, too, were familiar with the wealth that suffused the college.

No great feats of imagination were needed for the parents of the affluent students to picture their children's lives. At least one parent had graduated from college and in most cases both, and for the white parents, all but one had graduated from selective schools like Amherst. Advanced degrees were common.[1] The students themselves were unlikely to have much awareness of just how comfortable and familiar their surroundings were. They had always lived in a well-educated world of privilege.

Affluent students may well have taken for granted the smooth connectedness between family, community, and the college, which stands in sharp contrast to what lower-income students were, in general, experiencing. So much of the exposure was different from what they had known—the wealth; the resources; and the diverse ethnicities, lifestyles, beliefs, values, orientations, and ideas. Even for those lower-income black students who had entered the world of private schools and prep schools on scholarships, a gulf often existed between their families and home communities and the world of Amherst. Many lower-income students had to climb a steep learning curve to find their place at Amherst—a climb their families and communities were not making. Some lower-income students could not afford to go home during breaks in the academic year. For them, the incalculable distance between home and school increased, unbridged. In fact, the distance between home and school increased over time for the *majority* of lower-income students in the study. At the end of their first year, one in three of these students felt that they were juggling two different worlds or cultures. By the end of four years, that number had nearly doubled.[2]

Family

Economic realities made it difficult for many lower-income students to go home for family visits and occasions, while such visits home were much easier for their affluent classmates.[3] It was equally financially impossible for the parents of many of the lower-income students to come spend time on campus with their children, to get to see and share in that world—something that the parents of many of their affluent classmates did often.[4] Faced with limited family resources, Amy, a lower-income white student from Florida, had her dad's help in moving her belongings out of the dorm a couple times over her years at the college but no real visits. Amy described her father's pickups: "It's thirty-six hours, quick turnaround time that he can rent a van and we can put my stuff in storage. But it never feels like he really gets what it's about here because everyone's moving out. . . . I think my mom would have really liked to be able to see my a cappella group. She's a singer, and I'm proud of the group, the Sabrinas. She can't afford to come up here." For a third of lower-income students, the only times their parents had been to campus were to drop them off or pick them up. No affluent students reported their only parental visits to be pickups or drop-offs.

Although Marc lived in Hartford, only an hour's drive from campus, visits from his mom and dad were "few and far between." He said, "They mostly visited when I had concerts for glee club freshmen year." He was a varsity athlete, but his parents had been unable to watch his competitions. "The distance and the driving all add up, especially because my mom has to work on weekends, and she has two jobs now. So that makes it really tough to visit. But when they do visit, it's nice." Marc was not alone in savoring the rare visits. Nicole, a lower-income white student from rural Illinois, had one visit from her family over her years at Amherst. Nicole was excited that her parents were able to meet all her friends. She elaborated, "It was really great to have them, because they'd heard a lot about my friends, and my friends had obviously heard a lot about my family. So to have my two worlds come together, it was nice."

For various reasons some lower-income students were much less comfortable having their parents on campus. Tanya feared the costs they would incur should they visit. She noted about visits by parents of affluent students, "They'll make a big deal out of taking everyone out to dinner, and it will be a big thing." Tanya was sure her parents, immigrants from Moldova, "would be willing to take a few people out to dinner," but she knew they did not have as much money as some of the other parents, and she did not feel comfortable putting them in that position. "It's one of the reasons that I would almost rather my family didn't visit. They don't." Another reason for Tanya's reluctance was her concern that the culture of the college would be foreign and off-putting to her parents. She gave as an example what she envisioned as her parents' probable reaction to attending an a cappella concert at which students intersperse humorous skits with the songs. "They're not going to have fun. They're not going to get most of the jokes. It will just be frustrating."

At the start of her freshman year, Alisa, a lower-income black student, and her parents drove up to campus from their home in Mississippi. Neither of her parents was employed at the time. Her parents stayed for only three hours before getting in the car and making the thirty-six-hour trip back to Mississippi, but those three hours were not an easy time. From their conservative religious perspective, the culture her parents encountered on their short visit was upsetting. Causes of concern were the posters with sexual content that the Student Health Educators had placed on walls. Alisa reported, "My parents took those down. And they were really concerned about the condoms in the bathroom."

Over the next four years, her parents did not return to campus, but they planned to come for graduation. Alisa had worries, both for them and about them. There would be a lot of alcohol around, and her parents, given their religious beliefs and affiliation, "hadn't experienced that." Her parents were not used to the profane language they might well hear from her friends. "I feel like I'd have to prep my friends for graduation, and then I'll have to prep my parents for what they'll see and what to expect." She worried, too, about the awkwardness created by the vast differences between her parents and her friends' parents. Her father was now employed, working for the local gas station. Her mother had gotten a job in town at Walgreen's. Alisa felt she would have to instruct her parents to "not talk about money or class issues" because her friends "will probably be on the upper end." She continued, "Because Dad talks about his store. He works at a gas station, so he'll probably have stories about that." She wanted her parents to be aware that her friends' "parents are investment bankers, professors, or lawyers." When asked directly whether the changes she had experienced since coming to Amherst had brought her closer to her family or more distant, she stated, "I'm more distant from my family." But Alisa believed that distance might change. Drawing back to look at herself and her life, she remarked, "I feel like once I get on my own I'll probably be closer to them because I'll just be living based on the things that they've taught me. Here, I live based on the environment itself."

As noted previously, students from wealthy backgrounds generally had a good deal of contact with their parents on campus. Close to two-thirds of the wealthy students reported that their parents came to campus a few times each year for visits.[5] Some parents made extended stays. When Marissa, an affluent black student, got very ill her sophomore year, her mom flew in for two weeks. Megan, another affluent black student, remained on campus over the summer to work on her thesis, and her mom "came up for a couple of days," staying with Megan in her dorm room. Students expressed an appreciation for the connection between home and school that these visits forged, thankful that their parents got to see what they were up to and meet their friends and got to experience "how things really are" so that they understood what their children had been talking about.

Because the world of the college could be so different from their world at home, lower-income students were much more likely than affluent students (43 percent versus 12 percent) to report that they could not share aspects of their college experience with their parents, deepening the gulf between them.[6] They often chose not to talk about the books they were reading, the papers they were writing, the problem sets they were working on, or the changes they were undergoing because family members did not seem to be interested. "I don't tell [my parents] that there are actually coed bathrooms on campus," Alisa reported. "And all of my friends take birth control. I would never even mention it." As mentioned previously, many of their parents had little or no college experience, and, if they did, they had not attended an elite liberal arts college like Amherst.[7] Jeremy, a lower-income white student who grew up in northern Vermont, was guarded in what he shared with his parents. His dad had gone to college for two or three years but did not finish, and his mom never went. "My parents are by no means intellectuals. They're interested in talking to me about things if I bring them up, but I don't bring them up that often. . . . With my family, I sometimes feel like I hide some intellectual interests; I keep that separate. I close my door when I need to do that kind of thing." Tanya spoke of things that she "would rather not share" because her family would find them "kind of dumb." She noted, "I'll tell my mom that I'm doing The Vagina Monologues, and she'll laugh and be like, 'That's ridiculous. That sounds kind of dumb.'" Tanya recognized that her desire to share something new and meaningful in her life had to be tempered, because experience had taught her that she ran the risk of "feel[ing] bad for having shared it."

Many lower-income students developed friendships with classmates from groups that might not be approved of and accepted by their families and home communities—gays, Jews, and black people if they were white.

Emily, the student from rural South Dakota, said it is "hard when your family members are racist or hold values that are so different from your own." She found discussing politics with them "a really eye-opening experience actually," because she "hadn't ever had that conversation" with her parents before. An example was, she continued, "hearing the things that my dad said and having to just go, 'Wow, my dad is kind of a racist.'" Tanya, the student whose parents characterized some of her new interests as "dumb," also faced the dawning realization that her parents were not "the most accepting people." She elaborated, "They're not horrifically racist—we're not talking Klansmen here. But they make generalizations and assumptions about people based on race a lot of the time." Alicia, a lower-income black student, also had to reappraise her family's attitudes toward differences. She grew up in rural Vermont but had moved to Brattleboro, "the liberal pocket of Vermont." She reported telling her mother, "My two roommates are lesbians, and they're wonderful." She continued, "And just seeing her reaction, not negative, but kind of, 'Oh, okay,' like working it through in her head. I would never have thought she would have had that reaction. I would have thought she would have been unfazed." And it was not just her family's attitude that she had come to reassess. Alicia had always thought of people in her community as "really, really liberal." She continued, "And now I don't think they're quite as liberal as I thought they were growing up."

"I think that I've definitely become a lot more politically liberal since being here," noted Larry, a lower-income white student from Colorado. That change, coupled with other changes in values and lifestyle, created a chasm between himself and his father, a "very politically conservative and very strongly evangelical Christian." He said, "I would never tell him that I drink at parties on weekends and things like that." Larry performed with an improvisation group and knew "the content of the improv shows would be pretty offensive to him, actually." He said it has made him "more distant." Larry had not found a way to bridge the differences with his dad, whose "social life revolves so much around the church that he's in, and things like that." He explained, "I'm not actively involved in the church right now. I can't really relate to them."

A few affluent students who came from wealthy Republican families or communities also felt a growing gap between their beliefs and those of folks at home. Nathaniel came from Manhasset, New York, "a wealthy suburban town" on the north shore of Long Island. Nathaniel described people at home as thinking "George Bush is God, and they think that Obama is a terrorist." He came to feel that people in his home community "need to be more educated." He believed "Amherst would be good for them." Sarah, an affluent white study participant, grew up in a predominantly white, Jewish suburban community in Westchester County, New York. "My father is a Republican, and that always causes a lot of tension, but I've learned that when talking about politics or identity politics or things that I'm interested in, all these other things, I just don't talk about them at home because I feel like they'll just say, 'Oh, Sarah, you're so politically correct.'"

Trina, the lower-income black New Yorker, had wider views about gender roles for women than her immigrant Jamaican family did. Her mother was most focused on Trina's getting married. "When I'm at home with my mom, I think she's worried about my biological clock. . . . She's like, 'So, when is it going to happen?' Trina noted that in Jamaican culture, "a man won't want to marry you unless you're unbelievably tidy or a great cook." Trina struggled with her family's expectations but could not completely dismiss them. "I'm expected to be this household maven. How do I balance that with being an intellectual, being a professional? I don't want to lose the femininity associated with being this household goddess, but I'm an intellectual."

"You're acting white. You're acting better than us." This was, in part, Brianna's family's response to her having gone off to college. Brianna, the lower-income black student from Houston, was the first in her family to graduate from high school and go to college. Her family saw going to college as a "white" goal. When accused of acting white, Brianna would respond, "No. I'm actually more conscious that I'm acting black at Amherst College than you are in Houston, surrounded by black people." Should she "start going too much into the theoretical or philosophical with them," she again faced the accusation "You're acting white."She explained, "I think engaging in theoretical, philosophical conversations is definitely a college thing. My family engages more in realistic conversations." So around her family, she said, "I revert back to how I grew up with them, where they feel comfortable."

Some lower-income students were now on career paths that their parents found difficult to understand or relate to. Amy, the lower-income white student from Orlando, Florida, had parents who were in the arts and were uninformed about academics. "So, especially now, with dealing with thesis and job applications, they just don't get it. And it's incredibly frustrating to try to explain to them. Even in moments where I'm telling them something because I want them to be really proud that I did really well on a thesis section and [my thesis adviser] was really, really happy with it, my mom's like, 'But you're not done with it, right?' I'm just like, 'No, you don't get it. It doesn't matter.'"

Justin, a lower-income white student, aspired to be an investment banker. "I talk to my parents a lot about what I want to do after college, what I'm planning. They don't really know a lot about the companies that I want to work for or what these different types of jobs are." Justin had worked for a stockbroker at Morgan Stanley near his home. His parents noted, "He really likes you. He takes you under his wing." Justin explained, "He hoped I would go back and work for him and he could pass his business on to me. That was the vibe that I got. Yet to me, that was the last thing that I wanted to do. I would never do that. But to them it seems like a good job."

Kristen, a lower-income white student, grew up in a suburban Pennsylvania community. Her mother had started college but had dropped out and had only recently returned. "My mother has been in low-paying job to low-paying job," she explained. Her dad never went to college. "He's been working the same job he hates for twenty-five years. My understanding of jobs is get one because you need to have one, and then you stay there unless you for some reason have to leave. And generally, when you get a job it's because it was available, not for any other particular reason." Talking about her father's life, she recounted, "My dad goes to work from 7:00 A.M. to 3:30 P.M. and then comes home and does something, takes a nap, and then, I don't know, goes to bed. It's not like there's this teeming, bubbling stuff that's going on." That life path stood in stark contrast to her world at Amherst, where for her the atmosphere was "strive, achieve, reach."

Kristen had a formative experience in her freshman year when she took introductory geology and developed a close relationship with her female geology professor. That professor inspired her to apply to graduate school in geology. Kristen had come to feel that "you can reach for your dreams." Talking to her geology professor and seeing her teach, she said, "I've come to understand more of the long view of 'You don't need to make a hundred thousand dollars right out of the gate. You can go to school, and you can be poor and in school until you're thirty-five and still be okay.'" However, Kristen felt that she had to work to explain things to her father: Discussing "things about school or complex things I'm thinking about, either my future or this set of choices in front of me, [my father] doesn't get it right away, and so I have to start again, or explain it again, or explain it a different way."

Out in South Dakota, Emily found herself growing apart from her younger sister, who now had two children. Around the time of the 2008 presidential election, it had been difficult for Emily hearing her sister say that "she wasn't going to vote for Obama because 'he's Muslim,'" a viewpoint that students on campus mocked. Emily's sister wanted to get a job. "She said she really just wanted to work at Subway. She thought that that would be the best job for her." For Emily, who aspired to go to law school, hearing her sister talk made her realize how different their lives were. She noted, "It just makes me realize even more how great this opportunity has been." For Brianna, the black student from Houston, the sense of growing apart from her family, discussed previously, included increasing distance from her sister as well. She said, "With my sister, I can't really talk to her about most things at Amherst College because she has two children. She didn't graduate from high school, didn't go to college."

Communities Back Home

Over the course of college most students developed ways to fit into both their home communities and the world of Amherst, adapting to whichever environment they were in. As might be assumed, for many affluent students, little adaptation was necessary, as both worlds had much in common. Politics could be source of a tension, as Nathanial noted, with the world of Amherst pulling some students away from what they felt were the prevailing conservative attitudes of their wealthy communities.

For many lower-income students, the task was more demanding and, in some instances, impossible. Dana grew up in an immigrant Haitian community in Queens. The families in her community were "immigrants from the seventies, who came to New York and found jobs." Dana experienced a sharp contrast between her worlds at home and at school. She explained, "I can't even imagine joining Amherst and my church life because at church I only speak Creole. It's a much different community than being at Amherst." Asked how she bridged those two worlds, she responded, "I guess I don't really bridge them. I treat them as two separate worlds." However, two young members in her church had attended elite colleges like Amherst, and Dana felt she could share her experiences with them. The three of them "would talk about how it's just a different world." She described her church as "incredibly homophobic" and felt "really uncomfortable at home when people start making jokes, saying, like, 'faggot.'" She went on, "Sometimes I'll ask them not to do that, and they'll just look at me weird." Spending time with people at Amherst who had different sexual orientations made the views of members of her church seem "ridiculous."

Marc's comment, reported in Chapter 1, bears repeating. He noted that it was difficult "bringing Amherst back to Hartford because it's a place that doesn't change and isn't as accepting." "The only way I feel like the gap would ever be bridged," he explained, "is to just keep rubbing those two worlds up against each other until something gives." Tanya, the daughter of Russian immigrants living in Brooklyn, described her adaptation to the two worlds in this way: "I have this thing where wherever I'm going is the place that I call home. When I am leaving Amherst to go to New York, New York is home. But when I'm leaving New York to go to Amherst, Amherst is home. And I feel I have two homes. And they are both very different. And when I'm at one home, I'll forget about the other home, and I'll lose touch with the people there for a while. But then when I get back to that home, I'll just pick back up like I never left."

Almost two out of three lower-income students reported that they had come to see their communities differently over time.[8] Those new views were not uniform in their direction. Some students acquired a more critical perspective. For Jeremy, that change came quickly. When he returned home to Burlington, Vermont, over January intersession in his freshman year, he "noticed the 'country-bumpkin' people" whom he found to be "ignorant in their opinions." He explained, "They're not knowledgeable. That wasn't something I noticed before. I knew I was from a place like that, but I hadn't felt it so strongly. It didn't make me feel good, how much I noticed the difference. . . . For a while, like the first week I was home, I was really uncomfortable being in that community. I was worried that [Amherst] was changing me too much."

Other students had critical perspectives on their home communities before coming to Amherst but with distance were now able to see positive qualities. Ambivalence reared its head. At the outset, Nicole was purely delighted to have left her small, rural farming town in Illinois behind. "I wanted to get out so badly. I couldn't stand it then. I felt like it was a very close-minded, very insular community that didn't accept outside view-points, didn't even recognize that there were. It was a very conservative, very constraining, small rural community." But like many other lower-income students, by the end of four years, she had quite mixed feelings about her home community. She appreciated it more: "I see more of the virtues in the small community than I did when I was there because I'm now not stuck there. So I can see that there was something nice about growing up in a place where I knew most people and where it was a comfortable community instead of elsewhere. So I see more virtues I couldn't see when I was there and yearning to get out."

Tanya, the daughter of Russian émigrés, disliked and was eager to leave her community, Brighton Beach, Brooklyn. But over her years at the college, she noted:

I've come to appreciate my community more. . . . Part of me still doesn't really like Brighton Beach. But it's a very special place because it's got all these very ethnic quirks to it. You can go to the ridiculous Russian bookstore and get these very Russian romance novels and these very Russian knickknacks. It's very refreshing to see the signs but see them in two languages. I miss that. I don't like the place, and I don't want to live there, but I really appreciate it when I get to be there.

Marie expressed ambivalence about her home community in West Virginia and the racial prejudice present there:

I'm more bothered, when I go home, by ignorant racist comments that are common in West Virginia. And just being here has made that so totally unacceptable that I go home and I'm like, "What are you saying?" . . . I think I always noticed it, and it always irritated me a little bit, but now it's a lot more stark a contrast between there and here. . . . But I'm also more willing to make excuses for people at home, in part because West Virginia has extraordinarily little racial diversity, so a lot of it is ignorance. . . . But I think if a black family moved next door to some of the people who make these comments, they would make a couple rude jokes at home and then bake them a cake and decide they're actually nice people. And [at Amherst] people have had plenty of opportunities to move beyond.

When asked whether her views generally had gotten further away from those left behind, Marie, surprisingly, said they had "actually moved closer." She went on, "Just because while I'm here, a lot of times I end up defending the values of people from home, which just forces me to think about it more and see where people are coming from more because I'll be bothered when somebody who's not part of the community feels comfortable putting my people down."

Like Marie, Emily was both more critical and more understanding of her South Dakota farming community. When she first arrived at Amherst, she expressed pride in her community and "the way that they got by and could make things work and didn't have a lot of outside help." That pride had devolved over time to dismay at how "closed-minded" and "judgmental" they were of other people. One reason Emily chose to come to Amherst was that she "wanted to be able to meet people of different races." She noted, "But I didn't think I realized how much *not* having that experience really allows for racism and things to continue in the outside world." By the time she was a senior, Emily had come to feel highly ambivalent about her community. Her college experience, she said, "definitely made me think less of the people that I grew up with." At times she thought her hometown "should just be wiped off the face of the planet." The racism and homophobia in her community meant she could never bring her gay or black friends home, creating "a very strong disconnect with the town . . . and the people in it." But at other times she was more understanding and thought her hometown was no different from Amherst—"it's just that people don't hide their racism." In that isolated town, she knew "those people are going to live and die there, so [their racism's] not affecting anyone else."

Friends from Home

The intellectual interests of some of the lower-income students had already separated them from friends during high school, and their greater involvement in the intellectual world at Amherst deepened that rift.[9] Robert, the lower-income white recruited athlete whose entry into college was described in Chapter 2, was "always a little bit of an outsider." Going to athletic competitions with teammates in the years before Amherst, he said, "I'd be the guy in the front of the bus reading, and they'd be throwing stuff at me. . . . It wasn't cool to read a book on the bus." As a senior at Amherst, speaking of his connection with friends back home, Robert noted, "I have less in common with them now than I ever did." He recognized that his interests and values had "changed quite a bit." Going back home, he said, "I can still get along with [my friends], but I want to be in that environment less." Half of his friends, like a lot of people from his town, had "stuck around. Not too many people move on." He explained, he could "go back and have beers, but in general, most of the kids I have very little in common with now. . . . I just wouldn't have a lot of these academic conversations with any of my friends. It just wouldn't come up. And if I brought it up, I don't think any many of them would be too interested."

Given that lower-income white students felt the most alien when they arrived on campus, it may be of little surprise that those students were almost twice as likely as students from the other three groups to report that they could not share aspects of their college experience with friends from home.[10] Speaking about her friends back in West Virginia, Marie vouched that it was hard to connect with them. She explained, "We've been doing such different things. I only want to hear so many minutes of talk about their baby. And they only want to hear so many minutes of talk about my classes. . . . There's not really that much common ground anymore."

Emily would try to explain to her friends back in South Dakota what her college experience was like, but, she said, "I don't think they understand. They see my pictures, and they think, 'Wow, you have lots of black friends.' They're mystified by the whole thing. I try to tell them about the outside world, and it's a great place, and you should leave home, and you can do other things besides this." She had come to see her old friends as "more closed-minded," and she no longer saw herself as "being one of them." "They're going to follow their parents and maybe work on the farm." It made her sad to realize that "a lot of them are smart kids who will work on a farm the rest of their lives" but that their lives *could* have turned out differently if they had had access to a broader education:

When I go back or when I talk to them, it's a lot of talking about the past and the old days. And when I'm [at Amherst], it's talking about the future. . . . I have so many choices in front of me at this point. A lot of them are in relationships, and they're probably going to get married soon. I've gone to several of my [high school] classmates' weddings. Seeing that a lot of their choices have already ended, it's hard. I feel like in five years I probably won't be friends with a lot of those people because we'll just be in two totally different places in our lives.

Some lower-income students in the study reported a distance that arose over time between themselves and their friends who also attended colleges, but colleges very different from Amherst. Amy, the white Orlando student, had grown apart from her friends back home who went to large universities where "they really haven't had to grow academically." College was easy— watching lectures online and taking "maybe one multiple-choice exam." She said, "They don't really get what I'm doing here, and sometimes that's frustrating." She came to view her friends as "slackers," though she had never thought of them like that before. And she saw them as "small-minded"—perhaps because she "just had more experiences" than a lot of her family and friends had had.

The lack of connection Amy described was not confined to white lower-income students. When speaking of his friends from his neighborhood, Marc, the lower-income black student from Hartford, noted, "A lot of them either went to community colleges in Connecticut or in the Hartford area, to be specific, or they didn't go on to college. . . . Being at Amherst is very different from being at one of the community colleges. Whenever I try to relate the experiences that I'm having, it's a disconnect between me and my friends just because they don't have the same [experiences]."

Other lower-income students, both black and white, talked of old friends from home now viewing them as outsiders. They no longer "fit in." They were met with sarcastic greetings like "Oh, *college* boy's home." They might be labeled now as a "New Englander," or "one of *those* people now," or as a person who thinks he or she is "better than all of them." References were made to the "fancy school" they went to, and questions were raised for some black students about whether they were "staying true to [their] race."

A number of lower-income black students at Amherst had gone to prep school and had experienced changes in interests and values, made new friends, and lost touch with old neighborhood peers. Brandon grew up Newark but had left home for boarding school at age thirteen. Looking back as an Amherst senior on his social connections to his old neighborhood, he reported, "To be honest with you, I don't really have any friends from my neighborhood." Carl, a lower-income black student, was raised in Plainsboro, New Jersey, and had gone off to board at Middlesex School in Concord, Massachusetts. Speaking of neighborhood friends, he said, "They're just different from people [at Amherst]—public school kids, their experiences are totally different. They probably won't be going into the same fields we are, won't be in the same crowds." With friends at home, Carl said he would never talk about anything that made him different: "I never talk about Amherst."

The Hopes and Dreams of Others

Close to three-quarters of the lower-income students spoke of people at home living vicariously through them. In contrast, only a third of the affluent white and half the affluent black students felt that way.[11] While it is not possible to know for sure what accounts for this disparity, the educational backgrounds of the students' parents may shed some light. Almost all the affluent white participants had a parent who had attended an elite college and had completed a graduate degree. These parents had made their own journey through the world that their children were now experiencing. In sharp contrast, half of the lower-income students came from families in which neither parent had graduated from college, and almost none of those parents attended an elite college like Amherst. Half of the lower-income students who had a college-educated parent also had a parent who had not gone past high school. For the parents of many lower-income students, the exciting and unprecedented opportunity their children were experiencing may help explain the vicarious involvement and strong identification they felt with their children's college lives.

The upside of that strong identification at home that so many lower-income students felt was the support they got from and the pleasure they gave to their families. This was especially true for the half of the lower-income students in this study who were poised to become the first ones in their families to get a college degree. Their impending achievement was a special source of pride, pleasure, and anticipation for those families. Students talked of their parents' eagerness for them to "be successful," of family members being "proud" and "really excited" about what they were accomplishing, and of people "pulling for you"; "they really want to see you do well." Brandon, the lower-income black student from Newark, felt his parents, uncles, and aunts took vicarious pleasure in his accomplishments and in the expectation that he would "graduate, get a great job, get married, and just live the life of an elite." As a college athlete, Brandon had an additional, special means of bringing pleasure to a particular person in his family—his stepfather, who attended his games. His stepfather "didn't get a chance to play college sports. He was a highly recruited athlete, but he never got a chance, so he's always at the games." Brandon noted, "And he's always talking about me to his friends, and when he goes to work, he shows pictures. And he gives everybody a link to the website. When I meet people or things like that, they already know so much about me."

The downside of having family members heavily identifying with their experiences was the pressure and the onus of the expectations they carried. Trina felt "everybody" was vicariously living through her. "Especially coming from an immigrant background, a lot of my family who came to the States struggled so much to get here. I remember my cousin drove me up here. She came to America when she was eighteen. She's thirty-five now. She was like, 'You must see how blessed you are.' It's a little bit burdensome, but it's more often reassuring." Trina went on, "My family would be devastated if I didn't become a doctor. If I told my mom that I didn't want to be a doctor anymore, I don't know what she would do. . . . I still want to be a doctor, but I don't know." She worried about the possibility of getting rejected from medical school. "It would crush my family, and it would crush me."

Brianna's family, too, was invested in her becoming a doctor. In her initial interview in the fall of her freshman year, she explained, "If I don't become this world-renowned doctor, then I feel I didn't meet [my family's] expectations because that's what they wanted me to do." This expectation is of particular interest in that it sheds light on the crosscurrents some high-achieving, lower-income students could be exposed to at home. Recall that it was Brianna who also reported she was accused of "acting white" by family members for even going to college. Over time, numerous family members weighed in with their own unrealized aspirations, but by the end of college, with her goals changed, Brianna was able to distance herself from those pressures. "I wanted to be a doctor when I first came to Amherst. I don't actually like adults. I like children a lot better. . . . My interests are community service; working with children; working with animals; and, ideally, a job that combines all of those together." The pressures were still there, but Brianna had changed, as had her response to them: "The last three years I've gotten to the point where I don't care. I ignore them—aunts, grandmas. . . . My view on it now is that if I ask you for advice, give it to me. If I don't ask you for advice, don't give it to me. And even the other day, I hung up on one of my aunts." The aunt had taken fifteen minutes to tell Brianna what to do with her life.

According to Dana, her mother, a New York immigrant from Haiti, "has always pressured everyone in our family to go to medical school, to be a doctor just because that's what *she* really wanted to do when she was younger and never got the chance to. But none of us are interested in science at all. My sister went down that path. She was premed, and she absolutely hated it." Dana's sister supported her in doing what *she* wanted to do; she told her "to try not to listen to parental pressure and to get the most out of college."

Tanya experienced a variant of the pressure Dana felt to fulfill a mother's dreams. Back in the former Soviet Union, Tanya's mother was unable to finish pharmacy school because she was Jewish. Tanya explained:

> She also wanted me to do pharmacy, but that was not going to happen. So the next best thing would have been [a] doctor. And every so often it's the "Jew guilt" thing. She'll try to do that. She'll be like, "You know, back in the Soviet Union I couldn't finish pharmacy school because I was Jewish." And I'll go, "That's really bad; that's really sad for you." But I would hate to tell my children that I couldn't finish graduate school in whatever it is that I wanted to do because my mom was pressuring me. . . . So I had to teach myself to ignore the nagging guilt and just go with it.

Kayla, a lower-income white student who grew up on Staten Island, said her parents were eager for her and her siblings to "go off to big colleges and get fancy jobs." She explained, "That's the goal, to be better off than your parents were. And because my two older siblings didn't go off to fancy schools—my brother stayed to be an electrician, and my sister was going to the local community college—I was aware of the pressure." Justin, another lower-income white study participant, said his dad stressed that "'you have to work really hard and try to be the best you can at what you do.' It seems very simple, but the bar is set really high." The setting of the bar for one lower-income student was "go to graduate school and have an advanced degree, or become a professional." He was not alone feeling the pressure of family members' expectations. In addition, lower-income students could put pressure on themselves to succeed. As Rebecca, a lower-income white student, put it, she felt she owed a debt to her parents, who had "pretty much sacrificed as much as they possibly could" for her success. She was left with the feeling that she had "to return them the favor by being successful."

Affluent students were not necessarily spared parental pressure to be successful. But no lower-income student reported being told simply, "Do what makes you happy. . . . Do whatever you want," as Katherine, the daughter of affluent white New Jersey parents, was told. When asked about his parents' career advice, Nathaniel, the affluent white student from Long Island's north shore, reported, "They're kind of open. My mom doesn't really have much input. She just wants me to be happy and wants me to be on my own and do whatever. My dad's kind of deterred me from going into finance a bit." As for her parents' advice, Andrea, the daughter of a wealthy black couple from New York, stated, "They support whatever I want, really. You know, my mom didn't go to college, so she just is happy that I went and I have that solid background. I've never felt pressure from my parents to be in a certain career."

"The preeminent message is 'Do something that you'd enjoy doing.'" This was the message Benjamin, the affluent white student from Hastings, got from his parents. "I think they would say, 'You know, all we care about is that you're happy. And it doesn't have to be successful in terms of monetary but that you do something and do really well at it.' That's a pressure." Benjamin's parents were both doctors, and his mother was "one of the foremost people in her field. . . . She's one of the more sought-after lecturers." By "really well," Benjamin felt his parents wanted him to experience a similar level of achievement in whatever endeavor he undertook. Geoffrey's parents were also physicians. He said, "I've put a lot of high expectations on myself because I feel like I have to live up to my parents. I always feel like I'm [in] my father's shadow, and it's very hard to ever surpass that." Geoffrey was often identified not as "Geoffrey" but as his father's son. The pressures, internal and external, that Benjamin and Geoffrey experienced as the offspring of extremely high-achieving parents were a special form of parental pressure that lower-income students were spared.

Assisting Family

Some lower-income students found themselves in the complicated position of having discretionary money to spend because they were receiving financial aid, while members of their families were strapped for funds. Nearly half of the lower-income students reported using some of their money from the college to pay various family expenses when they were at home—in particular, gas and groceries.[12] A small group of students (one white, three black) also spoke of sending money home. Emily worked over twenty hours a week. She explained, "I work to help my family, too, not just to support myself. . . . My sister is nineteen, and she just had her second child, and she does all right, but she [has] needs for my niece." The financial help Emily provided was not restricted to the money she sent her sister every month. "When I go home I'll buy her [my niece] clothes and stuff. And they had a birthday party for her, and I got her cake and things like that." Emily was well aware that working extra hours to send money home had taken time away from her academic work and her social involvement at school. Her concerns for her family took an emotional toll as well: "Just having to stay in that world and having to help my sister out and having to talk to Medicaid people and things like that—it keeps me between the two worlds and not fully in this one."

Students also spoke of buying a parent a new phone or shoes; of paying a vet bill because the cat was theirs, too; and of paying for college applications or housing fees for siblings. Often parents gave assurances that they would be paid back, but often that failed to occur. Kristen's mom would say, "I'll reimburse you, I'll reimburse you," but she would not. Kristen elaborated, "Our grandmother's coming, and she needs to stay in a hotel. I'll at least put the hotel on my credit card, and it will get paid back at some undetermined date long in the future—maybe never."

Beyond any monetary contribution they made, lower-income students offered other types of assistance to their families and in so doing were pulled away, both physically and emotionally, from academic and extracurricular pursuits. When family illnesses or fresh financial difficulties arose, many of the lower-income students, black and white, as well as the affluent black students, served as important sources of support for their families. Frequent trips home to help with family crises meant missing classes and falling behind in school work. Any emotional preoccupation with home interfered with completing work when they were on campus. Nearly half of the lower-income students, both black and white, and almost half the affluent black students reported that family issues and problems had interfered with their academic performance. This was in striking contrast to the single affluent white student who made such a report.[13]

As many lower-income students looked ahead, they felt they would, in time, be financially responsible for their parents. With little put away for retirement, these parents were counting on their upwardly mobile children to help them out. Two-thirds of the lower-income students said they expected to or would like to be able to support their parents. This was true for only 11 percent of the affluent students.[14] These numbers help explain why, in choosing a major, lower-income students in general gave more weight than affluent students to the financial opportunities their major would provide. As Rebecca put it, "Part of the reason I'm a bio major and looking to be in the health field is because I know that I'm almost guaranteed to have a job." She was eager to contribute to taking care of parents who had sacrificed so much for her.

Amy, the lower-income white student from Orlando, had accepted a one-year internship for the year after graduation, a position that did not pay much. She discussed this with her family, and they were "not happy at all." She elaborated, "My sister wants to be an elementary school teacher, and my brother is a musician, and so, unless he hits it big, I plan on going to law school. I'll probably be the one who has to take care of my parents because they don't have really *any* retirement plans. They're just working on living *now*. I know I have to figure something out so I can make enough money to put a lot away [for my parents]." Other lower-income students realized, like Amy, that their siblings were not going to be in a position to take care of their parents, so the expectation was that they, with their Amherst degrees, would be responsible—although "maybe not right away."

But aside from feeling obligated, many students wanted to help their parents out. Many voiced an awareness of the sacrifices their parents had made for them. Their parents had "given up a lot of money" to support their education, had "made a lot of sacrifices," and had put their education first. In return, students spoke of giving parents "back some of all they've given" them and of finding a career to "make enough money to help" their families. Corey, a lower-income black student from New Bedford, Massachusetts, planned to support his parents: "That's one of my goals because they've supported me for the last twenty-one years. My dad always reminds me how he used to change my 'shitty diapers'—direct quote. He doesn't let me forget that. So I guess I'll have to change his or at least pay someone to."

Other lower-income students spoke not of the sacrifices their parents had made but simply of the desire to better their parents' lives. Brandon planned to move back to his home community of Newark. "I would see myself helping my family. I want to give them support because I would be able to work full time." Delight was in the voices of some students as they talked of ways they might eventually be in a position to give something to their parents; perhaps they could help immigrant parents return to the home country they so missed and help them finish building their house there, or help pay for trips to visit relatives, or make it possible for them to "live out their retirement years in the most comfortable fashion."

In contrast, most of the affluent students could count on continued support *from* family, should they need it.[15] Katherine, an affluent white student from Montclair, New Jersey, serves as a good example. She explained, "I don't have to go right into the workforce, and I don't have to worry too much about how much an intro-level job will make." Katherine's parents wanted her, she said, to "feel comfortable that I don't have to focus on making money now." She had chosen psychology and sociology as her two majors solely because of her interest in and enjoyment of the subjects. She also had the good fortune to have grandparents who had put aside money should she decide at some point to go on to graduate school.

The few affluent students who expected to help support their parents came from families whose financial situations had deteriorated with the severe economic recession that began in 2008. Their parents had lost jobs, or had businesses that had failed, or had seen their retirement accounts diminish severely.

Missing Voices

While 70 percent of lower-income students struggled to bridge two different worlds, 30 percent did not. The experiences described in this chapter are representative of most but not all of the lower-income students. Some *were* able to maintain close ties to family, despite the changes they had undergone, reporting, for example, "I've changed my perspective, but I think we're just as close as we were before"; "I feel being at Amherst has made me a lot closer to my family"; and "[Being at Amherst] made me appreciate my family a lot more."

Some students credited their increased maturity for helping them bridge the gulf with parents. Nicole, the student from rural Illinois, said she felt "just as close, or perhaps closer, to my family—just because I have grown, and so I'm not as combative, argumentative with my mother. And my sister and I can appreciate the support system between the two of us more as we've grown older." Brandon, the Newark student, noted a change in perspective that had brought him closer to his family. He explained, "I feel like as I've gotten older, I have matured, and I've just heard from people's experiences and in classes and things of that sort. I've attached more value to family relationships than I would say I previously did. And I would say I put more effort into keeping touch than I previously would have before."

Dana, the daughter of Haitian immigrants, attributed the closeness she felt for home to having always been in a tight-knit family. The feeling just continued through her years at college. "I speak to my dad pretty much every day; my mom, not so much. I don't really understand students who speak to their parents only on vacations. That doesn't translate to me, just because I was raised in a really tight family."

Over much of her time at Amherst, Brianna had tended to keep a distance from her family in Houston, but in her senior interview she reported, "I have been talking to them more about some stuff that's going on with me. So it's brought me closer to them, to certain people, probably my mom." Brianna had also become "more appreciative" of her friends from home. She went on, "They're really like my true friends, and they get me. I think here [at Amherst] I'm very misunderstood. People aren't familiar with me, don't know my background, haven't seen my home life, haven't met my family. They don't understand a lot of my actions or comments. And because of that, they make assumptions."

Discussion

When elite colleges and universities extend offers of admission with generous financial aid to lower-income students, they justifiably take pride in the incredible opportunities for learning and future success that they are offering. A college education broadens students' opportunities for self-development and employment.[16] Often less appreciated are the challenges lower-income students face in adjusting to the great distances between their homes and college—distances that go well beyond the miles. So much of what lower-income students in this study were exposed to at Amherst was different from what they had known—diverse ethnicities, lifestyles, beliefs, values, tastes, orientations, and ideas. That exposure, and the attendant learning, led to changes in many of the lower-income students. The changes, in turn, created a gulf between many of those students and their families, friends, and home communities—a gap that, in some instances, widened over their four years at the college. For them, the incredible opportunities offered at Amherst entailed an unforeseen loss; they changed so much and traveled such a distance that they no longer felt "at home" back home. That world was no longer their world.

Many researchers have documented the pain, ambivalence, and alienation that lower-income students may experience regarding home, feelings that can accompany their higher education and their upward social mobility.[17] Apart from the changing feelings about their "old" worlds and relationships with the people who still inhabit them, these students may also have to deal with "significant effects on their sense of self."[18] To cope successfully can entail assimilating into the new world and leaving the old world behind. Students whose identities and sense of authenticity are rooted in a working-class past may struggle with both the desire to fit into their new world and the desire to maintain authenticity.[19] And their responses to these opposing pulls vary—an aspect that fewer researchers have explored.

Among the working-class students she interviewed at a large public university, sociologist Allison Hurst found three distinct responses to college.[20] One group of students, a group she labeled "renegades," aspired to membership in the middle class, sought to acquire cultural capital, and chose to assimilate to the new ways of their affluent peers. Their family relationships became more troubled and draining, and in time, the families and communities left behind became "them," not "us." Students in the second group, labeled "double agents," were chameleonlike, making no clear choice of class identification. These students became adept at moving between the two worlds of home and college, changing themselves to fit each social group and setting. They had pride in their families yet were interested in moving beyond them. A third group, labeled the "loyalists," resisted assimilation and remained tied to their home families and communities. They saw their working-class families and communities as "us" and their middle-class peers and their middle-class world as "them." They did not hold the same aspirations as students in the other two groups and were less ambitious.[21] With one possible exception, the lower-income students in this study at Amherst fell into Hurst's "renegades" and "double agents" categories.

In an interview study of white, first-generation, working-class college students, sociologist Jenny Stuber determined that half the students, those whom she labeled "integrated persisters," had adjusted well to college, were integrated into college life, and had not felt alienated or disengaged.[22] A quarter of the students she interviewed experienced debilitating feelings of marginality and were unable to adjust to campus life. These "alienated persisters" *were* disengaged, socially and academically, matching the depiction of working-class and first-generation college students often put forth in the research literature. But another quarter, whom she saw as "resilient and motivated persisters," initially experienced feelings of marginality and disengagement but overcame them and found a place for themselves on campus, becoming integrated into that world. Almost all of lower-income students in this study fit Stuber's depiction of "integrated persisters" and "resilient and motivated persisters."

To fully understand the challenges that lower-income students faced in choosing to attend an elite college, race must also be taken into consideration. For some lower-income black students, exposure and possible assimilation to the dominant affluent white culture was accompanied by feelings of alienation from their communities, and some of their lower-income white classmates shared these feelings. But for some black students, difficult feelings brought on by class mobility were in some instances compounded by sadness and guilt about what they were losing with respect to race. They were moving into a new world, a largely white world, away from not only their lower-income communities but also, in many cases, lower-income *black* communities, their *black* neighborhood friends, and possibly their own families. These internal struggles could be further compounded by accusations from folks at home of not "staying true" to their race, of betraying their roots and their people.[23]

We move now to examine challenges of race at Amherst. We look at students' perceptions of racial offenses, either intentional or unintentional, that occurred in face-to-face encounters and in anonymous posts in online forums and at students' responses to them. In Chapter 5 we look at the challenges that black students faced within the black community on campus.

4

Racial Insults

As in our society as a whole, the issues concerning race at Amherst College are complex, as are students' responses. It may be tempting to state that black or white students at Amherst College feel a particular way about a racial issue, but that would be simplistic and misleading, as responses in both groups vary greatly. Take, as an example, students' reactions to an attempt at humor in the *Indicator*, a student-run journal of social and political thought, referring to a widely publicized racial incident. In the wee hours of the morning of November 25, 2006, five officers from the New York Police Department shot Sean Bell, an unarmed twenty-three-year-old black man, fifty times as he sat in his car after leaving a party in celebration of his impending marriage, set for later that day. Two weeks after the shooting, a satiric item about Bell appeared in the *Indicator*'s "Report Card"; it read, "I'll bet he has cold feet now."

An uproar ensued on campus. The Black Student Union (BSU) expressed outrage. The *Indicator* staff wrote an open letter to the Amherst College community that offered an apology to any members of the community "whom we have offended in this and past issues of the magazine."[1] On a Facebook site, Black Students of Amherst, a student wrote, "For *The Indicator* to not only make light of a sick reality for many people, but to disrespect a murdered man, crosses too many lines for any insincere apology to make amends." A campus-wide forum was held.

To some students, the anger and indignation voiced by black students was uncalled for. Jeremy, a lower-income white student, viewed the item as "insensitive," but he did not think it was "racial" because it was not "making fun of a race." Benjamin, the affluent white student from Hastings, noted critically that the stance "the *Indicator* took, and some other kids around campus took, was that the BSU was much too sensitive. Definitely one of the things I heard subtly ingrained in a lot of conversation was that blacks are almost too alert for signs of discrimination against them." Jason, an affluent black student, discerned similar feelings: "There's definitely the assumption that we're all very militant, looking for the most trivial instances of racism under every stone."

Some black students were dismayed that they were expected to tolerate what they saw as racial insults and accept the pain they engendered. Brianna, the lower-income black student from Houston, was dismayed and upset to hear students react by saying, "The *Indicator* makes fun of everyone, and you should just accept it." She explained, "My reasoning on it is [that] just because they do it to everyone doesn't make it right. It's not justified because you treat *everybody* equally badly." Trina, the Prep for Prep student from Brooklyn, found the *Indicator*'s humor "so hurtful, *personally* hurtful. This is an extra burden [of] being at Amherst that white students don't have to face."

Although the campus controversy was depicted as between black and white students, neither all the black students nor all the white students saw the *Indicator*'s "humorous" treatment of Bell's death in the same way. Angela, a lower-income black student from the South, had this take on the "Report Card" remark: "I'm sure that was huge to a lot of people. It was smaller to me because I don't think that people meant it to be malicious." Julian, an affluent black student from Baltimore, also held that "it wasn't racist" and objected to making "a big deal" about an attempt at humor that "most people probably wouldn't have even thought was racist until you said it was racist."

While many white students viewed the BSU as overly sensitive, other white classmates, like David, an affluent student from Washington, D.C., had a different perspective. David had dated an African American woman for their four years in high school. He said, "[That relationship] had a big impact on the way I think about race and the way I think about being white. It is something that I've done a lot of either introspection or formal work [on], working with other white people about what it means to be white and then talking in mixed-race groups about race and what it means to be the race you are in this country." In regard to the *Indicator* controversy, David saw many white students as "not wanting to confront the possibility of racism." Nicole, the lower-income white student from rural Illinois, knew students who wrote cartoons for the *Indicator*. Nicole took a nuanced stance: "In the same way my friends and I all make joking references to our own backgrounds, the people writing the cartoons do the same to their own." For her, the mistake they made was joking about someone of *another* race, which she found to be a "problem" and "offensive."

How widespread and pronounced is racism at Amherst? That is hard to assess, since what different students saw and experienced was so varied. Not all students read the two anonymous online forums that existed on campus (discussed below), which were replete with extremely racist comments. Black students were more likely to perceive racism on campus than their white classmates. Perceiving racism was reported by over three in four black students in the study, as opposed to just over half of the white participants.[2] Researchers elsewhere have also found that students of color perceive more racial conflict and discrimination on campus than white students.[3] It was not merely the perception of behaviors directed at *others* that black students were noting. As seniors, over half of the black participants in the study spoke of having personally felt left out, put down, dismissed, or excluded at some point during their four years because of their race.[4] The perception of racism becomes more complicated when class background is taken into consideration. Lower-income black students were more likely to perceive racism than affluent black students (92 percent versus 64 percent). What is difficult to tease out is whether this was purely perceptual.

An additional complexity for those black students who perceived racial slights is that they might be made to question their own perceptions. When black and white students talked about particular incidents and shared perspectives, some black study participants came to question whether what they perceived as racism could be interpreted in a different way. Conversations with her white friends gave Andrea, the affluent black student from Jamaica Estates, a chance to hear those friends' views as they contrasted with her own. Where she might have seen something as "hostile or aggressive" toward her or heard "a racial comment" she might have found "offensive," she came to see through the eyes of her friends that perhaps the offending students "didn't mean it that way; it just came out wrong." She continued, "Maybe I shouldn't take offense to that. Maybe they just don't understand." But how was she to tell? Whitney, an affluent black student, found herself struggling with perception when white classmates "consciously say, 'I'm not racist; I'm not treating you differently'—but you are."

During their four years at the college, 40 percent of black study participants reported having heard what they perceived to be racially offensive comments in the classroom.[5] These comments were seen by some, like Devon, an affluent black student, as rooted in ignorance, based on "something the student saw on TV maybe, or some weird source. Or it's been a viewpoint that has been taken for granted by the student that he or she may not realize is totally wrong or prejudiced." To these participants, the offending comment could be seen as the result of a poor choice of words or perhaps an overgeneralization. Kevin, a wealthy black student from Orange County, a suburb of Los Angeles, explained:

> There are times when people misspeak, and things are said that the students or professors that say them don't even mean to come out

that way. Just because you're talking about such a volatile issue to some people, words can come out the wrong way. People in black studies classes are quick to remind people, "You might want to rephrase what you just said." . . . People overgeneralize when they are talking in class, and people will remind them, "You can't say that about *all* people of a certain color or a certain race." Someone will say, "All the blacks are poor, and they're on welfare," and someone will come back and say, "That's not true. That's factually incorrect."

The word "nigger" was used readily in the anonymous online forums but appeared infrequently in face-to-face speech. Two black students in the study had the following reactions to hearing students refer to them or other members of their race as "niggers": "[People] drop the n-word accidentally, not in an aggressive manner, in speech. They say, 'Oops, sorry.' And it's very uncomfortable and offensive, but I wouldn't call them racists." "At parties, when alcohol was involved, you might hear the n-word. Does it happen often? No. I've seldom had people coming up to me and call me the n-word."

These last two students' remarks illustrate a way that some black students have come to live with what psychologist Derald Sue and his colleagues call microaggressions,[6] defined as brief, commonplace, intentional, or unintentional hostile slights and insults based on race.[7] They coped by downplaying the intent or importance of these insults to remove the sting. Microaggressions can often come from well-intentioned white people who believe in racial equality but inadvertently engage in these behaviors. While any one slight might seem insignificant to some, to others it could be devastating, and the cumulative effects of such slights can be even more so. Microaggressions can affect the mental and physical health of their targets, create a hostile and invalidating climate on campus, and disrupt problem-solving abilities.[8]

Stereotypes and Their Effects

Psychologists Samuel Gaertner and John Dovidio have found that growing up in a racist society, white people unavoidably internalize negative feelings and beliefs about those who are black.[9] But Gaertner and Dovidio argue that racism in America has undergone change, becoming more subtle and disguised—becoming what they term "aversive" racism. White people may endorse egalitarian, nonprejudiced principles and still hold *implicit* negative stereotypes of black people that may lie outside of their awareness and conscious control. This makes racism today more difficult to identify and acknowledge. Well-intentioned white people may fail to perceive instances of racism or may minimize the experience for those who are black, regarding them as overly sensitive and themselves as unprejudiced.

It should not be surprising, then, that racial stereotypes made their way to Amherst and that black students were confronted with incorrect and often pejorative assumptions about them and others of their race. Three of four black students in the study reported feeling that incorrect assumptions about them were based on their race.[10] What follows are some of those assumptions.

Perception of Black People as Threatening, Violent, and Criminal

"If it's late at night and you're walking—maybe somebody crosses the street instead of walking on the same side [as you]. . . . You're a black guy, and black men have this intimidating demeanor and reputation, not only at Amherst, but it's just the way it is in the U.S.," said Brandon, the lower-income black student from Newark. Carl, too, felt he was perceived at times as a threat. Raised in a racially mixed suburban community near Princeton Junction and schooled at a Connecticut prep school, he described himself as "larger than the 'normal' black male" and observed that because of his appearance, "some people might be afraid—definitely that happens."

Black students reported hearing assumptions that black people are "hyperaggressive or are going to harm whoever," are "really confrontational," are "rowdy or loud or violent," and are "very militant" and that if "a black man's walking down the street, we should cross the street." Following the stabbing of a black male by another black male from another college at a campus party, black participants heard classmates say it was "no surprise at a BSU party," because a black male was "more likely to be violent in an intoxicated situation, or a scary person," and "a white student isn't capable of attacking someone."

Perception of Black People as Less Intelligent

Black students reported hearing that students of their race "have lower intelligence" than white students. They were seen to be "taking lower science classes or need[ing] to really catch up more with white students" and as "not qualified to be here." In the eyes of some students, as an elite college, Amherst needed elite students, and assumptions were made that black students did not deserve their spots at the college and did not "have that ability to meet that standard." Black students were "admitted just for diversity"; they were "all part of this affirmative action movement." They had been "given some kind of unfair advantage in the admissions process" and were "here because [the college president] wants more black kids." Approximately two out of three lower-income black students and one out of three affluent black students believed their classmates assumed they got into Amherst because they were black and not on the basis of their merit. The issues concerning admissions are complicated by the fact that underrepresented minority students *do* have an advantage in the admission process.[11]

Trina, the Prep for Prep student from Brooklyn, felt that white students had "preconceived notions" about what she knew. "I don't think people are ever going to stop thinking that my SAT scores are lower than theirs or they're ever going to stop thinking that my GPA in high school is lower." In a class discussion about affirmative action, a comment sent Trina "into a tailspin," and she blurted out, "I would've gotten into Amherst College if I was green. I'm qualified to be here." She went on, "You should've seen everybody's face—not surprised that I was having a tantrum but surprised like, 'You really think you would've gotten into Amherst if you were green?' I feel if I weren't black, I wouldn't need to give examples. My SAT scores were really good."

Benjamin believed that among some students "the implicit assumption is that a lot of the ethnic diversity, and particularly the black kids at this campus, are here because of some diversity initiative." Jeremy, a lower-income white student, noted, "A lot of people think that black students here aren't as academically strong as the other students." Some black students shared that belief. Much to his discomfort, Christopher, an affluent black student, felt judgmental of black friends who had not performed well academically: "I almost feel like judging them the same way. 'How did you get in here? It must have been because you're black.' It sounds [like a] really, really terrible thing to say, but I think it's interesting that even if, as an African American myself, if I'm able to judge someone like that, I can only imagine what other kids say."

While some black students sensed that many white professors and students questioned their intelligence, they found it impossible to know that for sure. They could not, however, avoid the pain that came with that demeaning perception. Some also felt pressure to do well academically to prove they merited the opportunity to be at Amherst. Kevin, an affluent black student, recounted, "I just had to prove myself that I was able to handle the material and the class." Trina had strong concerns about fulfilling the negative stereotype that black people are less intelligent. As a consequence, she never raised her hand to respond to a question in a science class unless she was 100 percent sure of the answer. When she and her black lab partners were struggling in biochemistry lab, she worried, "Oh my gosh, we're the only black group in here, and we're struggling, and everybody's looking at us. But everybody else is struggling, too. Everybody else's mitochondria are dying, too. Why is it that we feel particularly bad?" She went to her professors for help with questions during their office hours because she did not want classmates to think it was the black girl who did not understand. White students could ask "dumb" questions and not worry about someone thinking less of people of their race as a consequence. Not so for Trina. Many students got extensions on their assignments. Trina had never done so. "I always turn an assignment in on time because I don't want to be that black girl whose assignments are late."

Doubts about the intelligence of black people could be expressed in many ways. Black students, both affluent and lower-income, perceived a subtext in comments to them such as these: "Oh my gosh, you speak so well." "You are so articulate." Or, more directly, "You're the smartest black kid I ever met." Jason, an affluent black student, noted, "As an African American you have to do something positive to get the professor to take you seriously when you make a comment or write a paper. . . . With some professors it's a level of basic respect that, if you're black, you've got to earn, where everybody else gets it via the benefit of the doubt."

Perception of Black People as Poor

The widespread stereotype existed on campus that black students were poor and white students were rich. Many black students found that classmates just assumed most students of their race are "urban, inner-city black poor," are "on welfare," "live in run-down neighborhoods," "live around a lot of violence and poverty," are "exposed to more crime and violence," and are on "especially high amounts of financial aid." As one affluent black student put it, "[Students] feel I shouldn't live in the neighborhood I do; I shouldn't be in the social class that I am." Trina drew attention to the value she saw in having "students of color here that aren't extremely poor and aren't living in the ghettos that you see on 20/20 that are on public assistance." She said, "I think it changes people's perspectives on what it means to be a student of color."

Some black students encountered professors who took as a given that they were raised in disadvantaged circumstances and, as a consequence of that assumption, responded to them differently than they did to white students. Dana, the lower-income black student who grew up in the Haitian community in New York, said, "[Professors] assume that I come from a troubled background. So, if I send them an e-mail to ask for an extension, they'll be much more likely to say yes to me."

One of Whitney's professors "made it seem like Amherst was twenty steps above" her high school, assuming she had gone to an inner-city public high school. In fact, Whitney was attending Amherst with no financial assistance and had gone to prep school. Brandon, the lower-income black student from inner-city Newark, felt professors did not have "as high expectations from [black students] as maybe other, white students." He explained, "I just feel like some have assumed that you don't come from as great a school system so you're not as prepared as some of the other more wealthy students." In fact, Brandon had boarded at a Pennsylvania prep school, which he described as "one of the top in the country."

Knowledge of Black Culture and Heritage

Stereotypes of urban black culture, promoted by the media, abound in our society, and many students at Amherst arrived on campus with little knowledge of black people beyond those stereotypes. To Alicia, a lower-income black student, the stereotypes included "being interested in hip-hop and driving certain cars and living in certain areas. . . . There's metal in your mouth, and there's all this jewelry, and the guys are all wearing really baggy clothes, and the girls are all wearing bikinis. And you're all supposed to be able to dance."

Many black students in the study, both affluent and lower-income, felt that white classmates assumed black students were knowledgeable about urban black culture. Black participants talked about being asked, for example, the words to hip-hop songs or how to do a hip-hop dance. One black student spoke of a classmate coming up to him and saying, "You must really love that new Lil Wayne song, huh? It's great!" It was a song he had never heard. Megan, an affluent black music major from the outskirts of Trenton, New Jersey, had grown up in a largely white environment and had attended Princeton Day School. She described herself as "predominately white in terms of culture." When it came to racial stereotypes, Megan said, "I fulfill approximately 0 percent of them." Megan had professors who turned to her "for confirmation about African American music." She elaborated, "I'm like, 'Frankly, you probably know more about it than I do.'" She went on to recount, "Once some white girl asked me to braid her hair. I was like, 'I have no idea how to do that.'"

Assumptions were made that people who were black were not only all culturally the same but were also all African American. Brandi, a Caribbean black student, reported, "Everyone assumes that being a black in America [means] you're an African American and, because you're perceived to be an African American, that you're to know everything about 'blackness.'" Trina, too, reported, "People just assume that I'm African American, and not just that *I'm* African American. They just see *all* black people as being the same culturally. And actually, I'm a first-generation [Jamaican] immigrant."

Three out of four black participants said they felt they were regarded as representatives of their race.[12] This was something that occurred frequently in the classroom. Looking back over their four years, half the black students felt they had been regarded at some point as representatives of their race by professors and/or other students.[13] They were assumed to be knowledgeable about black people and Africa and were looked to for "the black perspective," as if there were a single black perspective. In one class a student turned to Trina and asked, "How does the black community feel?" Trina's reaction: "I'm a first-generation immigrant. I have no idea." As representatives of their race, black students were also presumed to have the same opinions about issues such as affirmative action. Dana, a lower-income black student, said, "[Students] assume that I automatically support affirmative action or black universities, which I do, but they make the assumption that I do. I know a lot of black students on campus who are anti–affirmative action, and they really don't appreciate it when people make those assumptions about them."

In a black studies course, Andrea, an affluent black student, was assumed to be knowledgeable about Africa because she was African American.

As noted in Chapter 1, she said students "just assumed that I knew more than they did when it came to Africa." Similarly, Kimberly, another affluent black student, felt her views were given extra weight—"as if what I have to say should be representative in some way, or in some way have more validity or truth-value because I am African American." Two lower-income black students talked about professors turning to them for their responses in discussions about slavery. Marc said, "I feel I almost have to give a stereotypical answer. But I am not an *African* American. My parents are Jamaican, and they came over from Jamaica twenty-something years [ago], so we've never been slaves. So I don't know how a slave feels. I don't have that connection." Brandi had responded, "'Professor, honestly, we get tired of being the angry black people. We get tired of talking about race. We get tired of saying, "Slavery was wrong. The white man is bad."' You just get tired of being a representative of your race."

Managing Stereotypes through Humor

One way that students managed the sting of racial stereotypes was by making those stereotypes the focus of joking with cross-race friends. Four out of five students said they engaged in joking about race.[14] To someone new to campus, such joking might seem offensive, but between friends it was an indication of closeness. White friends might joke with a black student, "Oh, fried chicken day at Val. We were thinking about you." They might say to black friends, "I'll bring the watermelon if you guys bring the mac and cheese." One form of joking was to call someone by the name of another person of their race, making fun of the stereotype that all people of the same race are alike. Martin, a lower-income black student from Oakland, California, had a racially diverse roommate group that joked about race. "We call my other roommate Obama. They call me Obama sometimes. Again, we're very open about race and joke around a lot."

The playful use of stereotypes could be directed both ways. Julian, who played football, took to calling a white friend on the team "White Trash." His white teammate called him "Darkness," and Julian would call him "WT." "It's very affectionate," he explained. They got to the point of hurling "random racist" slurs at each other—using "a different one every time." Julian could be called the "n-word," or "Blacky," and Julian might yell back, "Honky" or say, "Oh, hey, cracker," as they tried to "trump the meanness of the other one."

Four out of five students, black and white, found the racial joking on campus to be humorous, affectionate, and nonoffensive overall among good friends.[15] Eighty-five percent of the students, however, reported that they had heard racist comments framed as jokes.[16] "You only got in here because you're black" or words to that effect would be lightly tossed off. Was the remark to be laughed off, as though the speaker and you both knew you merited being at Amherst? Or was it a put-down, a way of giving vent to feelings that could be aired only in the guise of humor? Again, how was one to tell? A black student referred to a friend as "the queen of saying derogatory comments in a joking manner." Because "there might be deeper meaning" to jokes, you had to know "when to say them and who you're around when you're saying them." With her friends, Talia, an affluent black student from Brooklyn, had an understanding "that it's all jokes." But she noted, "Every once in a while, we'll step over the line. But for the most part, it's humor."

Marc had heard friends joke, "Oh, well, you're black, so you must play basketball." Or "Oh, you're black, so you've probably stolen something." Marc said he chose to laugh it off more often than he ridiculed them for saying it. He continued, "But I'll definitely say, 'That's pretty offensive.' . . . I think over the years I have grown to tolerate a lot, just 'cause for me it's easier to not have confrontation. But I want them to understand that the things they're saying could be very hurtful to someone who's sensitive about their race."

Anonymous Online Forums

Black students were confronted with racial insults on the two online forums at Amherst, the Daily Jolt and the Amherst Confessional, which, according to students, were filled with "a lot of gross stuff." Seventy percent of black participants had read offensive racial posts on these forums.[17] Talia, an affluent black student, had searing recollections of postings "using the n-word." She elaborated, "Calling us stupid, calling us lazy, saying we didn't deserve to be here . . . every type of racial slur you could imagine against black people." As another black student put it, they were rife with familiar "angry, ugly stereotypes." Some of the posts were devoted to "badmouthing black women, saying that white women were better and here are all the reasons why," with one stating simply, "I would never date a black girl."

Black students had varied responses to these racist posts. Some students chose to never read the forums. Others, like Devon, an affluent black student, eventually stopped visiting the sites, having realized, "I don't want to read ignorant, nasty stuff." One way that some black participants reported buffering themselves against these insults was to view them as a sad but unavoidable reality of the online world. As Jason, a wealthy black student from the Bay Area, saw it, 99 percent of the comments likely came from "trolls. . . . A 'troll' is somebody who will post deliberately inflammatory comments to try to get horrified, shocked responses. You just see people use all sorts of ridiculous racial slurs and what not. It's so over the top, you think they can't really be serious. They're just trying to get a rise out of somebody." Christopher, an affluent Long Islander, had similar feelings. He considered himself an "Internet generation kid" who was "used to all this silliness and garbage" online. As a result, he stated, "Personally,

I just don't get offended by it." William, raised in an exclusive enclave in Potomac, Maryland, did feel "a little offended [and] a little bit frustrated" that students would make such posts, but he said, "This person's probably putting it up just for attention, really. So I had to let them do that and not really get worked up over it." He went on to note that when students posted angry rebukes, the original writer "would respond in one sentence like 'Nigger' or something ridiculous. And people would get worked up again, and that person would just have fun poking at people." William had learned not to take the bait.

Carl, the lower-income black student from Princeton Junction, agreed that the comments were meant "to get a rise out of the campus." He believed that the students who made such posts did not necessarily believe what they said but were having fun getting a war started, that they "enjoy[ed] arguments and drama," and that they liked to get people "riled up." While in the past he might have been drawn into the drama, speaking as a senior, he felt "mature and older now, and most things are just water under the bridge." He no longer read the online forums. His attitude had become "Who cares?"

Trina, the lower-income Prep for Prep student from Brooklyn, *did* respond to a post she found racially offensive. She received a two-page response to her post from another student stating his belief that she was "just being overly sensitive." The student wrote, "I'm Jewish, and I've never experienced discrimination on this campus." Trina felt her experience as a black student at Amherst was being negated and dismissed. She did not write back.

Along the lines of Trina's thinking, some other black students, affluent and lower-income, saw classmates who made racist posts as "really, really ignorant" or "really immature," choosing to characterize the comments not as "hate induced" but rather as "dumb posts." For others, as offensive as the characterizations were, they were unexceptional, an ugly aspect of living in a racist society. This perspective provided a level of detachment. The insults were seen as "just life": "Anywhere you go, there are ignorant people. I'm not surprised"; "People are people, and it's like that everywhere." One student embedded the offending posts in the immediate surroundings: "I accept it as part of Amherst culture."

While some black students were able to shrug off the racial attacks, others were truly shaken reading what some of their classmates might really be thinking about them. The posts made them wary and uncomfortable and caused them to think, "Probably I know someone who wrote something offensive." Marissa, an affluent black student from Chicago, had believed that there was no one on campus who would use such offensive racial language. But when she learned of the racist online comments, she doubted her previous beliefs: "It made me question and wonder who really goes to school here. . . . I've realized there *are* people here who've discriminated against people of my race. Just because I haven't had clear, distinct experience with it doesn't mean that it hasn't happened." Brandon, the lower-income black student from Newark, had never heard comments like this within his own group of friends. He was taken aback. "It makes me wonder what people are like in little groups, what people are like among their friends. If you're willing to say something like that anonymously, what do you say with your close group?"

When the Confessional came online in her junior year, Talia recalled, "it made me so angry. . . . I had never experienced such blatant racism until I saw that stuff on the Confessional. That changed the way I saw things." She viewed the writers of those incendiary comments as "cowardly" in their choosing not to "say it to [her] face." She continued, "They hid behind a computer. That pissed me off." Her interactions with white classmates became a struggle. With white students she had to work hard to take race out of the picture and "look at the person as a person," because if she looked at a person as a "white" person, she found that her "anger at that time would be projected onto them, which isn't fair." Talia arrived at a perspective that allowed her to move on with her head held high: "People can say whatever they want, and they can make these comments. It's rude, and it's hurtful, but it doesn't take away from what I've accomplished here. The people that I know here genuinely are not like that. So to hell with everyone else. Plus, I feel like you wouldn't really say these things and go so far out of your way to insult someone unless you were threatened by them—because otherwise, why bother?"

For Trina, the online forums were a reminder that the college was not "this racial utopia." She took the posts to be a sad reflection of what some unknown number of students really felt. Since people posted to the online forums midday, "you know they're not drunk":

> They didn't say something because they're inebriated and can't use that as an excuse. . . . This really occurred to somebody. This is not a joke. This is the way they really think, and anonymity allows them to say it. I'm like, "So you're in class with me, and I repulse you. You would never say anything to me because it's not politically correct." Political correctness, to me, is the number-one obstacle to overcoming racism, because people don't get rid of their racism; they just don't talk about it. The fact that the Daily Jolt allows people to say what they're really thinking I think is good, but [it's also] bad because it doesn't encourage a real dialogue where you're held accountable for what you're saying.

The racist comments posted on the forums generated a range of feelings for white students as well. To some it was "horrifying that there are people who hold these opinions and will express them—even though they won't do it in public." One white student worried about students having "all those attitudes and [about] what that means for black and nonblack people in larger society," concerns that were accompanied by feeling "ashamed, almost, that other people on the campus felt that way and were expressing it." David, the affluent white student from Washington, D.C., found the posts hard to read. He had never heard such comments from students he surrounded himself with, and it was sobering to him to learn that "there are still very pervasive views that are racist, and people don't even necessarily connect them to racism. They think that's just funny, or they think that it's a joke. . . . It's even weirder to not know where that exists. You can't even confront it. You can't even have a conversation about it." For Emily, who came from a rural South Dakota community where black people were routinely referred to as "niggers," the racist online comments on the Daily Jolt were the kinds of things "people back home would say" and that she "would be embarrassed about." From Emily's perspective, it was one thing for folks who had no direct exposure to black people to be "ignorant," but how was she to understand her fellow students and their hurtful words? She came to see that "Amherst in many ways has a lot of the same faults as the outside world." Students may use "PC language" and be "articulate people, but that doesn't mean that they don't carry the same beliefs."

Continuous exposure to racist remarks in the online forums had the effect for some white students of eroding their upset and concern. As one student put it, "They don't affect me as much because I'm used to them." The online forums came to be seen as "just a ridiculous cesspool of absurd statements," written by "jerks" or "one or two people that are being total assholes." The forums were simply a place where people "say inflammatory things to be saying inflammatory things," where someone was "trying to start an argument . . . instead of actually saying something real or of substance." One affluent white student saw the Amherst Confessional as "a pretty racist forum, and that was upsetting." Her coping strategy became simply "If you didn't want to look at it, you didn't have to look at it." Students and the college administration were powerless to shut down the anonymous online forums. Legally, students had a right to free speech.

Face-to-Face Interactions

There were, however, some racially offensive remarks that could not be avoided—those that came up in face-to-face encounters. How were black students to handle these offenses? In the freshman-year interviews, black students mentioned three types of responses to perceived racist remarks: angry confrontation, masking feelings, and becoming the educator. Four years later, students were asked specifically whether they used any or all of these three responses or had other ways of handling these difficult situations. The original three emerged again as the major responses. Each had its merits; none was ideal.

Confrontation

One possible response to a perceived racial offense was confrontation—getting angry at the speaker and letting him or her know that the comment was racist, offensive, and hurtful. Of the three possible responses, this was the least frequently used. Only one-third of lower-income black students and half that many affluent black students said they responded at times in that way.[18]

Black students saw several problems with confronting white classmates who said something racially insulting. They worried that in doing so they were fulfilling the stereotype of "the angry black person," that they were like "Malcolm X" or "a militant Black Panther," which they wished to avoid being. Marc, the black student from inner-city Hartford, felt that racist comments needed to be challenged, but he said, "I don't think getting angry is the best way to go about it." Such a confrontation with the offending student only "supports the stereotype." Confrontation was referred to by one student as "the nuclear option," to be avoided because it "didn't end up well for anybody." Other students concurred, stating, "It's not a good way of dealing with conflict in general"; "It never ends well"; and "[The results are] always even more negative." Talia said, "[I hate] shouting or yelling to get my point across. . . . It doesn't mean that I'm not angry. I just don't think anything productive comes from screaming and yelling at people. When you say things when you're angry, you say things you don't mean, that aren't effective. You're just insulting them right back."

Like many other students of her race, Trina found herself using confrontation less over time. "Anger was the first tool in my arsenal before, but as a pseudo grown-up now, I look further." She went on to say that when hearing something offensive now, "I wouldn't stop myself from saying something that was really important, but I would frame it in a way that I thought was more conducive to the conversation." She mentioned an incident in which, she said, "at first I was going to get really angry. Then I was like, 'No, I'm not going to do that because that's not going to help them. They'll just be like, 'Another angry black girl.' So I went to my friends and vented."

Brandon, the lower-income black student from Newark, also saw himself as having changed in his response to racist remarks. "When I was younger, it would probably be completely anger—like, 'You shouldn't have said that. It's offensive, and I take offense to it.' It would probably be in a very angry manner." But over time, his education and reflections had brought about change: "[By] learning more about my history and about black culture . . . and developing my own theories and ideas, I'm more comfortable and confident defending in those situations in an *academic* manner." Brianna, the lower-income black student from Houston, said she had *always* responded to racist remarks with some sort of comment, but what changed was how much anger she showed when she made the comment.

Depending on what was said, and whether she could understand the reasoning behind it, Brianna's level of anger would vary: The level might range from "not at all annoyed to mildly annoyed to very annoyed, depending on where I start and how adamant or how offensive I feel you are being. . . . When I actually get very angry, there's more of a loud, reactionary response from me, whereas when I'm annoyed, I will debate with you. And then, if it's not going anywhere, I just won't talk to you."

Masking Feelings

The second response black students reported having to racial offenses, and a much more prevalent one, was to mask their feelings in order to keep the interaction on a positive footing. Just over half the black participants reported using this response.[19] Some students would later vent their frustrations to a black or racially mixed group of friends, seeking support and understanding. For black students who did not respond, unbeknownst to the white students involved, a wall had gone up, and trust had broken down. Those black students were likely to write off those relationships as ones that could go no deeper than acquaintanceships. White students who committed the offenses would not know they had done anything to offend and thus might repeat them; masking had its problems.

William, an affluent black student from a wealthy Washington suburb, often covered up his feelings in response to a racial offense. In such a situation, he noted, "I've made a judgment about that person. So it'll be at least some type of wall that's gone up a little bit. I wouldn't hate the person per se, but we'll be a little less close from that point on. . . . The problem I always had [with this response] is that it gives people the impression that that sort of thing is totally okay, wonderful behavior." Faced with racist remarks, Corey, the lower-income black student from New Bedford, also chose silence. Anything he might say he felt "would put up a wall just as much as keeping quiet." He continued, "If that tension is going to be there anyway, I'd rather just keep quiet. . . . I think as soon as a white person makes those comments, that's the wall; that's not my choice."

Some students masked their feelings because they were so taken aback by the incident that they did not know how to respond. Marissa, the affluent black student from Chicago, spoke of an instance in which her friend's roommate "used a racial epithet" around her. She elaborated, "I left the room because I didn't know what to do. I just assumed that it's common knowledge that you can't [do that]. I don't even use it colloquially amongst [other] black people—I'm that uncomfortable with the word. . . . That was an instance where I was unequipped to deal with it completely."

After being targets of racial offenses, some black participants reported that they tried to manage their feelings internally and did not discuss them with friends. Whitney, a varsity athlete, said her most frequent response was "not even sharing with black friends, just bottling it up, venting in my head." She recounted an incident in which a former assistant coach said that she "should go to the back of the bus like Rosa Parks did." She continued, "And it was a joke. I didn't tell any of my black friends or other black people I knew. She could potentially get fired for that, or a big deal could've been made about it, and I didn't want to make a big deal out of it or other people to make a big deal out of it. So at the time I just sat there and zoned out."

Being the Educator

The third option that black students described was to step back from their emotions and attempt to educate those white classmates who made the racially offensive remarks.[20] This required considerable maturity, calling on black students to be, as one student put it, "the bigger person." Some black study participants called this "the Martin Luther King approach." Almost half the black participants reported using it. Others wished they did, as it was held out by many as the most desirable response. Kimberly, an affluent black student, spoke ruefully when she noted, "I'd like to say that I'd go the 'educate' route because it seems like it's the most effective, right thing to do. But honestly, I probably would say nothing and vent to someone later, unless it was something really horrible."

Brandon felt it was important "to educate people about blackness and being black so that the negative stereotypes that they may see because they don't have direct interaction with black people are proved to be negative and not true." His preferred response was "definitely trying to just educate the person and let them know why their comment is racist and offensive." If he opted not to make the attempt, he would "vent with other black students just because it could be something that frustrates you." He spoke of an incident in which a white student was using "nigger" in a rap, and black students were offended. The student "tried to justify it because it was in the rap song that they were singing." In that instance Brandon chose to engage the student, to create awareness "about the word and why it's a sensitive subject and it would be best not to use it."

Upon hearing offensive comments, Brianna said, "[I would] challenge your position to the point only to where I think I can make an effective change. But if you are still at the point where you want to believe what you want to believe, I'll just stop talking to you. I'm not gonna waste my time talking."

For some black students, educating white classmates was less about presenting facts or increasing white students' general awareness and more about letting those students hear personal reactions to offensive remarks. Talia, the affluent black student from Brooklyn, assumed a certain level of awareness in white students. She saw little point in trying to edify more generally. She explained, "I do think that, although there are some really sheltered people who honestly don't know, I mean, come on, unless you're living under a rock, you have to have some concept of race. Black people are everywhere. I'm not going to sit there and preach about why it's wrong for you to say something racist, but you'll know that it offended me and that I have a problem with it." She went on to give her view on the futility of talk at times. "If someone is just racist, I could preach to them until I'm blue in the face. It's probably not going to change their opinion of black people. So what can you do but just let them know that it's an issue, and you shouldn't say that to people. And if they choose to continue saying that, I feel sorry for them when they run into someone who doesn't mind speaking with their fists."

The role of educator could have its desired effect. In talking about his chosen response, Marc stated, "Usually I'll opt for the educational route. . . . I hope it's made a difference. It's easier to tell [if it has] with people who are closer to me and that I'll talk to again on a daily basis, because more often than not, something else will come up that follows up the point." If the person's response has changed, Marc knows "the person took something away from that last conversation." But the work of educating others can prove onerous. "Every now and again, because I get tired of doing the educational thing, I probably opt to the second option, just keeping it inside and later venting. . . . I always feel there's the third option, education, but I hate feeling that's my role. I don't want to feel I necessarily have to explain to people what it means to be black or why something is offensive or whatever. . . . I don't want to feel that's my reason for being at Amherst."

Marc was not alone in wanting at times to shuck the role of educator. Other black students, regardless of class, reported finding it "tiresome"; they did not want to "stand [t]here and preach to you [about] why what you just said was so offensive. You should know why that was offensive." When Anthony, a lower-income black student from upstate New York, was younger, he felt he "had to educate people": "'No, I don't come from the projects just because I'm black.' But as you get older, it's like, 'If you don't know by now, then I feel sorry for you more than anything. It's not me. I'm not going to educate you.'" Kevin, an affluent black student, found educating people "an asinine way of going about solving a problem. If the person is also twenty-two years old, and they haven't figured out racism, . . . you're not going to be able to sit down with them and educate them about racism at this point." He did not want to have to point out that "you shouldn't have put that Confederate flag sticker on the back of your truck because it's representative of the slavery in the South." Putting himself in the offender's shoes, Kevin imagined that being given "a history lesson [about] the Confederate flag would aggravate me and would make me want to put more Confederate flag stickers on the back of my truck." The most effective response in that situation he now felt was to state flatly, "I don't really appreciate that sticker. You can do whatever you want with it, but I find it pretty offensive."

Choosing between Options

Some students used all three options, depending on "what mood I'm in," "who says it, why they say it, and what they said," "how much I care about the person," "how blatant the racism may seem or how intentional it is to be racist," and "how offensive it was, how important it was to me." While having seemingly just dismissed the educational approach, Kevin went on to describe a more complicated response: "It really depends on the situation. If I'm at dinner with a bunch of adults that I don't know, and I'm just there, and I hear something, I just bite my tongue. But if I'm with a group of peers, then I'll say something about it."

Discussion

Colleges and universities are more racially and ethnically diverse today than they have ever been. But bringing underrepresented minority students to campus does not guarantee a more comfortable, less hostile racial climate for minority students.[21] Scholars have documented the difficulties underrepresented minority students have faced on predominantly white campuses.[22] Sociologist Joe Feagin and his colleagues, for example, found that the overwhelming majority of black students at a predominantly white university experienced incidents of racial discrimination on campus.[23] Black students have encountered attitudes, perceptions, behaviors, and expectations about race, ethnicity, and diversity that were less than accepting. Researchers have found that when black students perceive a "chilly" racial climate, they are likely to feel alienated and less likely to reach out to form relationships with diverse classmates. A hostile racial climate also interferes with academic success.[24]

Racist attitudes and behaviors are considered to be politically incorrect on most college campuses nowadays. Racism appears as microaggressions, which, according to Derald Sue, take three forms—microassaults, microinsults, and microinvalidations. Overt expressions of racism in the form of microassaults—that is, *deliberate* explicit racial derogations meant to hurt the target—occur less frequently today on campus than in the past. Unfortunately, we saw examples of microassaults in this study at Amherst—racial slurs and hostile put-downs posted in online forums under the protection of anonymity as well as occasional face-to-face occurrences.

As opposed to overt racism, the racism in the white community at Amherst was more likely to be "aversive racism,"[25] discussed previously in this chapter. Aversive racism manifested in microinsults (i.e., insensitivity, rudeness, communications that demean, stereotyping) and in microinvalidations (i.e., communications that exclude or that negate thoughts and feelings).[26] Examples include the demeaning stereotypes of black students as less intelligent than white students and as undeserving of their place at the college and the negations of black students' perceptions of racism. Some scholars have argued that microaggressions are minor and trivial or, as one puts it, "pure nonsense."[27] Calling them into question can be construed as another instance of black people's thoughts and feelings being negated. While a single insult or invalidation may have minimal impact, the cumulative effect of repeated occurrences can be quite detrimental.[28]

Many white students at Amherst may well have shared the view of Matthew, the affluent white Amherst legacy, that it did not seem that "at Amherst, race is that big a deal." Beyond Amherst, researchers have found that white students generally are not aware of what it is like for black students to live in an environment in which, even if only on occasion, they hear racist joking, racist epithets, and racial insults; in which they are told they do not merit their place at the college; and in which they do not receive full respect.[29] Minority students tend to perceive more differential treatment based on race and to view campus climates as more hostile and racist and as less accepting and more discriminatory than white students do.[30]

At Amherst, what impeded a greater awareness by white students of the racial discrimination and prejudice around them, which they may have been contributing to? It may be that some white students simply lacked an understanding of the ways implicit racial prejudices might have been influencing their and other classmates' behavior toward black classmates. It may be because, upon hearing racial offenses, black students often chose to mask their feelings, making it difficult for white students to recognize that racial offenses had occurred and for them to understand the feelings those offenses evoked in black students. Awareness may have been impeded by the lack of direct talk between black and white students about how they each experienced race. Thus the hurt, angry, pained, and frustrated feelings of some black participants in this study in response to racial slurs and hostile put-downs went unheard by many white classmates.

Considerable variability existed among the black students in the study in their responses to the microaggressions they were exposed to. Some black students were able shrug them off or find ways to buffer themselves against them. Others were not. What seemed like small slights to some black students were perceived more often and with greater upset and hurt by others.

The occurrence and consequences of microaggressions on campuses can be countered only if those racial offenses are recognized and their meanings decoded. By failing to promote dialogue to educate students around racial issues such as these, colleges and universities reinforce the status quo. They enable white students to continue to wittingly or unwittingly insult and hurt black students and invalidate their perceptions, and they send a message to black students that combating racism is not a priority.

When black people are insulted and their feelings are invalidated by those who are white, they turn for support and confirmation to one another—to people who might understand their perspective, argues Beverly Tatum, president of Spelman College.[31] Black students need "safe spaces to retreat to and regroup in the process of dealing with the daily stress of campus racism."[32] These safe spaces can be tables of black students sitting together in the dining hall or black student unions and cultural centers— places where they can be heard and understood and that help black students deal with stereotyping and build positive identities. The benefits and costs of "safe spaces" are discussed in Chapter 9.

5

Black on Black

"We have a barbecue for the incoming freshmen every year. At that point, all the upperclassmen are introduced to the lowerclassmen, and they get to talk to each other." Welcome to Amherst College. The "we" in this quote is the Black Student Union (BSU); the speaker is Dana, the lower-income daughter of Haitian immigrants who chaired the BSU for a year during her Amherst career. The welcome party is an instance of the support that black students entering Amherst received from those black classmates already on campus. That support included offers of assistance regarding course choices and just "getting acclimated to Amherst." As freshmen, black students got to know one another simply because "you stand out to each other." Jason, an affluent black student, described the black community as "not that big, but it's very tight-knit."

In their senior interviews, black study participants continued to note "the camaraderie amongst black people. . . . We help each other out." Marissa, the affluent student from Chicago, offered her view of the way the black social network develops: "I think that once you meet someone who's black at Amherst, you start meeting people, and most people know each other or know of each other. I think there is that familiarity . . . even with people who are three years younger than me, who've only been at the school for one year. And you still get to know them, because you stand out to each other." "Once you get tagged as a minority," Marc noted, "you get inundated with tons of e-mails about minority issues and events happening on campus and things like that.

And I think it's important that at least the opportunity to go to those things is being constantly presented."

The presence of black peers at predominantly white institutions has important consequences for black students. Higher education researcher Shaun Harper found that black males cite the encouragement, support, and validation they received from same-race peers as essential to their success in college.[1] Psychologist Beverly Tatum, president of Spelman College, contends that living in a racist society, it is immensely helpful for black students "to share their experiences with others who have lived it."[2]

While the sense of community was a part of what many black participants noted in their interviews, that was not the whole story. Seen from a distance, the black world on campus might have appeared to be homogeneous. The BSU sponsored events on campus throughout the year and organized two major cultural events annually. Black students could be seen walking together across campus or sitting together at large tables centrally located in Valentine dining hall. But any generalization about "the black students at Amherst" is going to miss the mark—unless it is that generalizations cannot be made. There was too much variability on numerous characteristics, ranging from the apparent, such as skin tone and gender, to the less immediately obvious, such as social class, cultural background, the saliency of race to identity, or immigrant status. These differences might go undetected by those who were not black and who might assume homogeneity among black students that did not exist. The differences could also cause tensions among black students themselves that those outside the black student community might be unaware of. The following brief profiles of two black women in the study are intended to give a sense of this variability.

Megan and Brianna

"Since I grew up in a predominately white environment, I'm predominately 'white' in terms of culture, if you could put it that way. My parents are always making fun of me because I don't do things the 'black' way. . . . I would say that most of my friends here so far are probably white, and I guess that's kind of an unconscious choice that I made." These were some of Megan's reflections in her freshman fall interview. Before coming to Amherst, Megan, whose family lives on the outskirts of Trenton, New Jersey, had spent twelve years at Princeton Day School, a private preparatory school. There were four other black students in her class of eighty. Megan's parents both had master's degrees and both worked in administration at the College of New Jersey. Megan received no financial aid from Amherst; her parents earned just over the maximum to qualify. She considered herself "solidly middle class," while acknowledging that, having "spent a long time tiptoeing around the rich white kids," she had been "socialized into the wealthy elite." Even so, Megan worked off campus at a bookstore all four years while at Amherst and was a resident counselor for her last three, for which she received financial compensation. When asked in her interview in the spring of her senior year if she wished she had had more conversations than she did about class over her years at Amherst, she replied, "No. I don't really care." When asked the same question in regard to conversations about *race*, she responded, "I don't care." Megan's focus was on music, her major. She played piano and composed and had a won a statewide composition contest in her junior year of high school. Her sense of identity was rooted in music.

Houston, Texas, Brianna's hometown, is fifteen hundred miles from Princeton. Her upbringing, concerns, and attitudes were also far from Megan's. In stark contrast to Megan, Brianna saw the world through the lenses of race and class. When she was asked whether she wished there had been more conversations about race at the college, she responded, "Yeah, I love 'em. They're great." She wanted to have had more conversations around class issues, too. "I feel in the country that we're in, we tend to try and not talk about class, and Amherst College is a direct replication of that. . . . Race and class relationships affect every aspect at an elite college. Whether it's said or not, it's definitely there. Being a black female that's low income and from the South, I feel like 'the other' in a lot of cases. It's really nonnegotiable for me to feel those feelings and to voice my opinion about [the tension around race and class] and let others know about it."

Brianna's childhood included living in a homeless shelter, having parents who spent time in prison and struggled with drug problems, living with a middle-class aunt in Illinois for three years, and achieving stellar academic performance at a small, largely black and Hispanic charter high school back in Houston. She is the youngest of five siblings and the first in her extended Houston family to go to college. Unlike Megan, once at Amherst Brianna got very involved in black affinity groups, eventually taking executive positions in both the BSU and the Black Women's Group. Along with her strong racial identification, Brianna also had a keen interest in Hispanic culture and eventually became the president for a year of La Causa, the Hispanic affinity group.

The discrepancy in how important race was in defining them led Megan and Brianna to make very different choices about whom to eat with in Valentine. On any given day you might well have seen Brianna at one of the "black" tables in the central area. In her view, sitting at one of those tables was "not self-segregating." "My white friends come sit with me all the time," she explained. "You can come sit in the middle section; it's not like I'm going to haze them." She noted, too, "People [are] always complaining how blacks and Latinos sit together, and it shouldn't be awkward to integrate. If you want to sit with us, you can sit with us. I'm not gonna tell you that you can't sit with us. But don't expect the burden to be on black, international, [and] Latino students to get up from where we feel comfortable and . . . sit with you so that you can feel better about your situation."

One person you would not have seen seated at the "black" tables was Megan. When asked her view of those tables, Megan replied, "Terrifying. Forgive me—I have a penchant for dramatizing. It's not 'terrifying.' I don't make eye contact when I walk by. It's not purposely. It's that I know who's sitting over there, and I know that if I go over there, people are going to be like, "What the f—— are you doing here?" At another point she noted the following about students eating at the "black" tables: "I would not sit with them because I would not feel comfortable, and when I do sit over there, I'm stressed out." Megan's feelings about sitting at a table of *white* students stood in sharp contrast to Brianna's. She commented that she had an "abundance of white friends," most from the same middle- to upper-middle class that she came from. Because she was so accustomed to being the only black person in the room, she noted, she did not "really feel excluded by a white group of people." "It's never stopped me from trying to be friends with them," she added. Megan had friends of different races, but her largely white world led her to be viewed askance by some black classmates at the college. "There's definitely one girl I can think of who loathed me because I just did not spend time with black kids. I'm not necessarily inclined to seek out black people because they're black. I'm inclined to seek out people because they're people. I've learned to differentiate that. At this point, frankly, in terms of people I consider to be my friends, there's one black person."

Brianna expressed a similar view about race in choosing friends; she did not tend to acknowledge race, she stated, "[as] being a critical part of how I choose my friends. It's really their personality and their values and ideals that I tend to judge them on." Class, however, played a large role in friendship choices for Brianna, and that was true for Megan, too. While both had friends from different classes, both noted that most of their friends were from the same social class as them. Brianna explained, "I'm drawn to similar people because they understand me on a level that someone from a different socioeconomic background wouldn't be able to understand." At the end of her freshman year, Megan, too, reported that she was "more inclined to be friends" with more people of her social and economic class. This inclination remained true to the end of her senior year, when she reflected, "I find that we also gravitate toward each other—birds of a feather, you know."

As for dating, specifically interracial dating, there was an enormous difference between what Megan and what Brianna experienced. Megan had dated only white students. She reported, "I've never in my life so much as kissed a black person." Although it was not said directly to her, her sense was that "the black community on campus is always like, 'God, what are you doing? Why you always got to be dating all these white folk?'" Brianna, on the other hand, dated only black and Hispanic students—that is, until the spring of her junior year, when she dated the first of two white classmates she went out with while at Amherst.

The lives and worlds of Megan and Brianna illuminate some of the many differences that exist among the black students at Amherst. In trying to convey a sense of that variability, one black student noted, "There are the southern black students, and then there are the black students from New York. There are black students who don't talk to other black students, because they're from a different class." The differences helped create a vibrant black community on campus but also created tensions within that community. Those differences and tensions are the subject of the remaining sections of this chapter.

Self-Definition

When given a list of preset racial categories on the college application, all the black students in the study had identified themselves as "African American, black." In their fall freshman interviews, however, free to describe themselves racially as they chose, black students gave more varied responses. Students used terms such as "mulatto" and "biracial," or phrases such as "a mix of African American and white," "African American and Persian." Some students identified themselves as Caribbean American and others more specifically as Jamaican or Haitian, on the basis of their families' countries of origin. Students who were born in the Caribbean and had immigrated were more likely to identify as Caribbean American, whereas those whose parents were Caribbean and had immigrated before they were born were more likely to identify themselves as African American.

Both an African American and a Caribbean community existed on campus, with differences at times standing between students from these two communities. Whitney, an affluent black student from the Midwest, found that it was not easy for her to make friends with many of her black classmates, as many of them were "black immigrants, coming from the West Indies or western Africa, and that's different from African American." She said, "I'm African American." She did not share the same culture or history and noted, "[Black students on campus] sometimes segregate themselves from other black people based on the way they grew up." Indeed, Trina, a Caribbean immigrant, found that she missed "hanging around with people who are from the same neighborhood" as her, and she sought out and grouped together "with people that are from Haiti or Trinidad or Vincentia" because they were "culturally similar."

Tensions also existed among black students of Caribbean descent. The split between Caribbean immigrants and those born here but of Caribbean parents was a cause of tension. Talia, an affluent black student born in the United States, identified as "half Jamaican." Her grandparents had lived in Jamaica and immigrated with her father and her sister. She was raised with these family members, who imbued her with an awareness of Caribbean and, more specifically, Jamaican culture. She had friends on campus who had immigrated from the Caribbean who would, she said, "Be like, 'Oh, well, how would you know? You're not even really Jamaican.' 'Oh, you don't act Jamaican. You act so American.' 'You act so white sometimes— you sound like a white girl.'" She felt that one Jamaican friend looked down on her because she is only half Jamaican. She continued, "[My friends would use] a Caribbean saying. And they'll be like, 'Do you even know what that means?' And I'm like, 'Yes. Just because I don't say it doesn't mean I don't understand it.'"

Black students at Amherst varied in the extent to which race was important to their identities. Devon, an affluent black female, placed great importance on race in her self-definition. She associated blackness "with having black consciousness." She was eager to build a strong black community on campus, and she made race a focus of not only her social world but her academic studies as well, choosing black studies as one of her two majors. But Devon encountered a lot of black classmates "who choose not to acknowledge [the importance of their race]. They feel it's not as significant as other things." She questioned the blackness of these students. She felt that it "hurt[s] other black people when people don't make race relations, in this nation and internationally, a priority. That's really detrimental to other people of their same race who are at disadvantages because of that lack of discussion."

Devon described a friend on campus who was "very into her blackness" and had "Black Power" tattooed on her wrist and "Africa" tattooed on her back. A large gulf existed between black students like Devon and her friend and those black students like Marissa, for whom race was not as central in defining themselves. Marissa, the affluent black student from Chicago, had identified herself on the admission form as black "because my family's black." Her maternal grandmother was Swedish, but Marissa did not know anything about her grandmother's culture or history. While Marissa had identified as "black," she noted in her freshman fall interview, "I don't say that I completely identify with all black culture." She continued, "In terms of how people perceive black people, I don't think that I fit in with that." Marissa had mostly white friends in high school; she explained, "People didn't see me as a 'real' black person. Might be because of my skin tone or because of the way I talk, the music that I listen to, how I dress. I actually don't fit what they thought [a] black looks like or should be like." Marissa had many experiences both in high school and, to a lesser extent, at Amherst of having her blackness questioned by other black students— "'Are you black enough?' 'Do you act black?' 'Is the way you speak, the way you dress, black?'"

Over her four years at Amherst, Marissa came to feel less vulnerable to black classmates who questioned her blackness. She did not need to be, she said, "the kind of person they think I should be." She was "not in their group"; they did not see her as being "the same as them," but in her words, they were "nice." She explained, "They don't treat me badly or anything like that." The role of race in Marissa's thinking had also undergone change, with a new focus on issues of race. "My interests gravitate toward race and how that affects literature, education, politics, everything. It's definitely saturated my life since I've been here." Her social world also transformed. Back in her freshman year, Marissa was critical of black students who hung out primarily with other black students: "I just don't like that. I don't like just hanging out with people just all of any race 'cause I just don't think that's fun. I like to meet all different people, and I think sticking to your race is normally close-minded about making friends." By the end of her senior year, though, when asked about the "black tables" in Val, she reported that for a while she had sat there "all the time" and that currently she did "sometimes." She noted, "But it depends. I do different things every day." In that same interview, she gave an answer to a question about friends on campus that would have been hard to predict when she first arrived four years earlier: "I would say my immediate friend group is mostly black." Her increasing involvement with black classmates did not exclude her dating those outside her race, as she went out with white men and one Hispanic man during her years at Amherst. Although she felt some subtle pressure from home to eventually marry a black man, she held strong feelings on the issue of dating outside one's race: "I wouldn't be here if there wasn't such a thing as interracial dating."

Social Class

Potential obstacles existed for relationships between black students from families with wealth and social standing and those from families with less financial means. For William, an affluent black student from Potomac, Maryland, the obstacles were more than potential. "From age nine to eighteen, I lived in a wealthy neighborhood, two acres per lot, something like that, people with pools and tennis courts in their backyards." He had attended a small, private, all-boys school. William had expected that, as an African American, he would "have a lot in common with African Americans in general." But he discovered at college "that class is important. . . . Making friends with certain lower-class African Americans is a little complicated because some of them will say, like, 'sellout.'"

Some affluent black students, like William, found it easier and more comfortable to be friends with white students on campus with whom they shared a "similar background" or "upbringing," or with other affluent black classmates. Andrea, the wealthy black student from New York City who was profiled in Chapter 1, grew up "in a very white neighborhood." "I went to a high school where I can count the black people on my hand," she said. At Amherst she noted "obvious differences" in the way she "dressed, spoke, acted" when compared to many black students on campus. "I don't really hang out with too many black people. But the people that I do are pretty much from the same exact social class; they would define themselves as middle to upper class, too."

Some black students at the other end of the class spectrum spoke of their difficulty connecting to affluent black classmates. Brandon, who grew up in inner-city Newark, noted that it was hard for him to find common ground. Over his years at the college he had at times been "at the same places hanging out" with affluent black classmates, but he had not "been close friends" with them. He found it hard to relate to black students who were not from the "urban culture" because, he said, "we're not really similar. We like different things." Brianna, the lower-income black student from Houston, used the term "sididdy" to describe a view she held about wealthy black classmates when she first encountered them at Amherst. "Sididdy," Brianna explained, was "an urban colloquial term that meant 'acting very elitist and better than you.'"

Acting White and Having Blackness Questioned

The stereotypes of black people as portrayed in much of the media are based on urban cultural images. Anthony, a lower-income black student, spoke about perceived blackness or whiteness: "The closer you get to a stereotypical black person (listening to rap or having baggy jeans, etc., etc.) or the closer you get to the stereotypical white person (collared shirt tucked in, boat shoes, playing golf, etc.), the closer you get to one of those sides. Using slang would be seen as 'black,' and talking properly would be seen as 'white.' All those things combined—whichever you're doing more of, you're either acting more white or more black."

About 60 percent of black participants in the study reported having their blackness questioned or being accused of "acting white" while at Amherst.[3] Examples, given in the interviews, of behaviors that might incur that accusation included "following soccer and football more than . . . basketball [or] . . . playing volleyball"; dressing up "really, really nice"; wearing "khakis with a button-up shirt"; listening to "mostly rock music or not what stereotypically black people should listen to"; not identifying with "hip-hop culture"; "not spend[ing] time with black kids"; and having "all white friends." One student explained, "It could be because of your socioeconomic status. It could be because of the way you dress, because of the car you have, because of friends you keep." Black students reported hearing comments like "He's black, but he acts white"; "Oreo"; "You're not black really; you're more white than you are black"; and "That guy who forgot he's black."

The study's black participants had different reactions to, and different characterizations of, these accusations. Brandon, the lower-income black student from Newark, saw the references to "acting white" as merely descriptive and not a real questioning of a person's blackness. He had attended an almost all-black school through eighth grade before going off to a preparatory boarding school in Pennsylvania that exposed him to "white" culture. To Brandon, when black students who grew up in an all-white environment and had all-white friends were perceived as acting white, "it's not necessarily a negative thing. It's just common knowledge to associate 'white' and 'black' with two different cultures. And when someone who isn't white is associated with that white culture, you don't question their blackness."

But some participants felt their claim to be "black" under attack. They were offended and angered by accusations of not being "black enough" or "true to their race." One student experienced some comments as "very vitriolic." Alicia, the lower-income black student from Burlington, Vermont, had her blackness questioned because of her speech. "It's an uncomfortable situation to be told that part of you is not what it is, to be told that you're not black. That's a horrible thing to have told to you, that your identity is not good enough." She was made to feel that "if you don't have the proper speech of a black person, then you're not black—you don't fit the black mold." She added, "And I have never used slang like that in my entire life." Marc, the black student from Hartford, said, "Just because I listen to a different music than I'm *supposed to* listen to, or that I dress differently than I'm *supposed to*, or something like that, doesn't necessarily mean that I'm less black or that I'm less sympathetic toward blacks or that I don't go through the same struggles as different blacks. I feel like dress in anything and people *still* see the color of your skin. You can't hide that."

Perception That Black Students Should Stick Together

Some black students felt that an expectation existed on campus among some others of their race that they should "stick together," join the black community on campus, sit at the "black" tables, become a member of the BSU, and go to BSU parties on weekends. A BSU member might ask, "Why don't you come to the [BSU] meetings?" E-mails were sent to black students from the BSU about events and parties the organization sponsored. To some black students, implicit in those questions and e-mails was the assumption that they *should* spend time with black classmates. Whether the pressure was external or externalized was not always clear. Kevin, an affluent black student from Orange County, outside of Los Angeles, worried about other black students' perception of the fact that his social world was not centered on students of his own race. He *assumed* they wondered why he did not hang out more with black students. "It's never been explicitly said to my face. . . . I've had students ask me why I didn't come back to the BSU or something like that but never aggressively in my face about it. I think it's just my own insecurity."

Half of the black students, both affluent and lower-income, reported feeling some pressure to hang out with black classmates, but there were shifts for some black students in their perception of that pressure and/or their response to it over their four years at the college.[4] Before coming to Amherst, Brandi, a lower-income student who chose not to have her background identified, had to deal with comments about her "speaking like a white person" and about her thinking she was better than others in her all-black church and black community because of the way she spoke or because she went to school with white people. So when Brandi came to Amherst, she thought, "All right. Let me not give anyone else a reason to think I think I'm better than them. Maybe I should sit with these black people over here so people don't think I'm trying to be white or something." Looking back in her senior-year interview, she reflected, "[As a freshman], you're really paranoid—like 'Oh, my gosh! There are people looking at me.' . . . You get older, and when you reach my age, you don't even care [what others think]." And as to whom you choose to sit with? "I don't think *anyone* really cares."

Andrea, the wealthy student from New York City, had vacillated as to how to respond to expectations to spend time with black classmates. Other black students in her largely white high school had expected her to hang out with them, join the Ebony Club, do "these black things with these black people." When she arrived at Amherst, something shifted: "I was like, 'Okay, I had enough of that.'" But during her freshman year, she felt "similar pressure again." She said, "And I struggled with it. And then I had to make that decision to ignore those pressures."

Black Tables in the Dining Hall

Why are all the black kids sitting together in the cafeteria? Beverly Tatum asks this question in her book by the same title, in which she explores the phenomenon of black students self-segregating in high schools. She argues that black adolescents seek each other out at cafeteria tables because of a developmental need "to explore the meaning of one's identity with others who are engaged in a similar process."[5] In line with Tatum's observation, a casual observer likely would have noticed black students sitting together at Valentine dining hall, with its centrally located cluster of tables of black students in clear view. But as Megan's expressed discomfort about those tables indicated, there were black students at Amherst for whom the tables were not in the least a desirable place to eat a meal. Forty-one percent of the black participants in the study reported that they *never* ate at the "black tables."[6] Only two black students, one affluent and one lower-income, said they ate at those tables frequently. Sociologists Sandra Smith and Mignon Moore found similar differences in whether black students chose to eat at the "black tables" in the dining hall at a predominantly white university.[7] In our study, because some black friends at Amherst did choose to eat together at the same tables most days and others did so from time to time, those black students were taken by some classmates as representing black students more generally, and the tables themselves were referred to by some as "the black hole."

Half of the black participants (62 percent of lower-income black and 43 percent of affluent black students) reported that they ate at the "black tables" occasionally and had no fixed pattern as to where they sat in the dining hall, or that their pattern changed from one year to the next. What was the draw? Marc, the lower-income black student from Hartford, and one of those students who occasionally ate at the tables, gave his take: "Friends sit with friends, and some people like to make their friends among their race. It's not necessarily [that] the black students want to sit by themselves but just that they're sitting with their friends, and their friends happen to be black." Numerous other reasons were given by other students. One student described the tables as "convenient. They're right next to the trays. It's not like you've got to go searching for a little round table. They're long tables." If you were a black student and came to lunch alone, it was easy to "find somebody to eat with"; you did not have to worry "about meeting up with a friend." The tables provided a measure of social security: "If I go by myself, I just sit [at one of the black tables] because I know I'll find someone I know. It's kind of comforting"; "I wouldn't feel uncomfortable sitting at that table with new people and getting to know them, because we're from the same group of friends." Because the students at the tables were black, some black students assumed them to be like-minded: "People who think the same way I think. [I'm] tired of being ridiculed. [I] want to be around people who like the same things, have the same experiences."

The seemingly simple act of eating with friends at a table provides another instance of the variability and complexity of black students' experiences at Amherst While Brianna, as noted previously, was sitting at the black tables with no compunction about the perception of self-segregating, other black students at those tables felt self-conscious about playing into a stereotype of black people keeping to themselves. Brandi had heard a first-year black student say, "I feel bad when I sit with my friends [at one of the black tables] because I feel everyone's like, 'Well, how come those black people only sit with each other?'" One more level of complexity existed: While some black students had concerns about self-segregating, others struggled with an inner imperative to sit with other members of their race, as explained by William, the affluent black student from Potomac, Maryland. He said, "At first I felt pressure. I felt like I *should*. It made me a little anxious. . . . It made me like, 'Should I be sitting there? Should I be trying to make friends? Because they're black, *should* they be my friends?' But I got away from that." As a senior, he noted, "I sit with my friends—who I *want* to sit with."

There were, in fact, students at Amherst, black as well as white, who did view the black students sitting at black tables as self-segregating. No mention was made of the many white students sitting together at tables in the dining room—that did not seem to be seen as self-segregating. Julian, an affluent black student, grew up in a predominantly white neighborhood in Baltimore and attended a private school at which he was one of a small number of black students in his class. When asked how he felt about the black tables, he responded, "I hate 'em. . . . I think they make black people too cliquey. I understand the need or the desire to be around your own people and culture groups. At the same time, I think it's limiting to keep yourself in one group of friends, especially as the minority." For him, it was important that black students interact with white classmates and develop greater understanding between the races, and thus his attitude toward sitting at the tables—"I'm not a fan of it at all." Andrea, too, was upset that students at the black tables were, in her view, extremely "cliquey" and "not very open to letting other people sit and eat there and be comfortable there. If a group sits there that's not black or doesn't know someone there, they get dirty looks."

Many black students talked about making different seating choices different days. Corey, a lower-income black student from New Bedford, Massachusetts, noted that for him it was not "a conscious decision, like 'Today I'm sitting with the black people.'" Most black students had friends of different races, and where they ate depended on who was around or where their friends were sitting. Like Megan, some black students in the study never ate at the tables. They gave a variety of reasons for their decision: "I don't really think about [the black tables]"; "I'm just not friends with the people who sit there"; "I always dined with my roommates or a bunch of people from my floor"; and "I sit with the athletes." Just as some black students chose to sit at the black tables because they were comfortable, others purposefully avoided the tables because, like Megan, they would not feel at ease there. As Monica, an affluent black student from Maine, stated, "I'm mixed; I'm black and white. I would feel out of place in that group. . . . There's just this feeling it would be weird to sit there if you weren't a part of their group." Some black students did not eat there specifically "because it's considered the 'black section' at Val," and they hated "being looked at only because of [their] race." Another student, considering options, stated, "Race is the secondary thing. . . . I'd sit with my friends first before I'd sit with [black classmates]."

At the far extreme, some black students found the behavior of the students at the black tables upsetting. They viewed those who ate there as reinforcing "the stereotype that all black people are loud." Martin, a lower-income black student from Oakland, California, said:

> To be blunt about it, they act like caricatures of black people. It really disturbs me. They're just really loud. I think most black people who have gotten to this point, gotten to Amherst College, have two ways of talking to people—there's how you speak to kids in your neighborhood who happen to be black, and then there's how you speak to professors in class and that kind of thing. It's people pretending to be really loud, really obnoxious, and just always looking

for confrontation, especially girls. It makes sitting over there really miserable.

Skin Tone

Three in four black students in the study reported hearing derogatory comments made by others of their race about skin tone.[8] Often the remarks came in the guise of joking. Black students could be put down either for being "so black" or for being "practically white." Facebook groups existed for people of different skin tones (e.g., one for "dark chocolate" and one for "mocha"). Students asked one another, "Which one do you belong to?" and there was talk about "who *should* be in what group—like you're not as light as you think you are, or you're dark." Trina noted, "Black people are shadist in general. . . . At Amherst, in more shallow conversation, you hear a lot of shadism," a term used to describe judgments about a person because of their skin tone.

For a woman, it could feel problematic to be dark skinned. Dana, the daughter of Haitian immigrants, noted, "In general, the 'beautiful' black women on campus are perceived to be the lighter ones. There used to be one general 'hot' list on the Daily Jolt. . . . Then people started requesting hot lists for the different races. So it was the top ten 'hot' black women on campus. If you looked at the list, everyone who was a part of it was considerably light." Some black women with dark skin felt that black classmates found lighter-skinned black women students more attractive and were not interested in them because they were "too dark." A black female student with dark skin commented, "It's better to be dark skinned if you're a guy and light skinned if you're a girl."

But lighter-skinned black women could also have issues. Some recounted hurtful remarks made by darker-skinned friends about their being "too light," and these remarks were difficult to respond to because they were often said in a joking manner. For Alicia, a lower-income black student who identified as African American and Caucasian, her light skin color contributed to her decision to leave the BSU. She had joined as a freshman, thinking it would be "one big social opportunity. They're a *huge* part of the campus life." She left the BSU before her first year ended. She explained, "I [felt like I] am not the right shade of black to be in BSU. And there is a definite air in all the affinity groups on campus that you have to be a certain way. . . . I just didn't quite fit in with that. So I think in that sense [having light skin] has closed down some opportunities." Her skin tone was not the sole reason for her leaving. She felt she did not know "how to speak a certain way, feed into being the black, BET [Black Entertainment Television] stereotype."

There were instances of lighter-skinned black students being made to feel that they could not legitimately claim their "blackness" and that their light skin tone had led them to experience race differently. Marissa, the affluent black student from Chicago whose grandmother was Swedish, was herself light skinned. She had a friend with darker skin who insisted that Marissa could not truly understand what it is like to be a black person in this society, that, Marissa said, "because my skin was lighter than hers, I couldn't have the same experience or know any of the same things." Andrea had light skin and had heard people say things such as "Oh, she's *black*? She's *really* light." Or "Oh, you're not so black, because your skin isn't really, really dark." At these times Andrea felt that her blackness was being called into question, and she found it offensive to be told she was "not black because [of her] skin." She concluded, "Skin tone's a really touchy subject for me."

Brianna talked of a black friend of hers who was "lighter" than she was. She said, "She's probably like *honey* brown. But because I'm so dark, and 'cause most of the people I see and encounter when I go back home [to Houston] are dark skinned, I consider her light skinned. And she considers herself brown skinned and someone that's really, *really* light skinned as *light* skinned." Brianna's friend would insist she was "*brown* skinned," but Brianna would object. "No, you're *light* skinned." Brianna did not see herself as engaging in "mean-hearted teasing" but rather giving "a difference of opinion." Her friend, however, "takes it as a derogatory comment . . . a put-down, so she fights against it."

Talia, an affluent black student from Brooklyn, had two good friends, both light skinned, who went to a party hosted by a third friend, who was dark skinned. When they arrived, their hostess told the two friends, "You have to be at least my complexion to get in. You're too light." Though said in a joking manner, the greeting left her friends "pissed off about it because that's *hurtful*." One of those two friends is biracial, and "people forget she's black—so she gets very defensive." In discussions among black classmates about being a black person or about a "black" movie, she might be challenged: "'Oh, what do *you* know about that?' And she's like, 'I'm black, too.'"

Gender Issues

While black men and black women on campus faced many of the same challenges, some were distinct to their sex. Given her race and gender, a black woman could be seen to carry "more of a burden" than a black man, who "gets some privileges based on being a man." Kimberly, an affluent black student, felt her comments often went unheard in the classroom. "I'll say something, and then a white guy will say the same thing, basically— maybe a little bit louder. *Then* someone will respond to it, or it'll become something people talk about." Kimberly spoke with a professor about her concerns. As he saw it, the cause of the problem was how Kimberly's comments were made. She needed to be more assertive, more confident. To Kimberly, though, it was unclear whether the issue that led to her ideas being overlooked was simply the way she presented them or whether it was because she is a black woman. She said, "I don't think those things are easily separated."

Trina, the Prep for Prep student from Brooklyn, offered a different take on which sex carried "more of a burden": "Yes, there are stereotypes about black femininity at Amherst, but [they're] not as oppressively determining of who you are on this campus. But black men at Amherst—I think they have it really, really bad. People have this idea [of what black masculinity is], and if you're not like that, then you're a poser, a sellout. I'm like, 'No, you're just being who you are. There's nothing wrong with coming to class on time. There's nothing wrong with doing the reading. There's nothing wrong with not being a jerk.'" It was "devastating" for Trina to see black men "doing what people expect a black man to do." To her, another negative stereotype of black men, that of their dealing drugs, was upsetting, and it was deeply distressing for her to see a black male student at Amherst "fall into the trap of fulfilling it." Trina confronted a student who was selling weed in the Charles Drew House in this manner: "'The fact that white kids only come to the Black Culture House to buy weed from you—why would you *do* that? You're pulling all of us down, making this stereotype of the center of Black Culture House on campus is where you buy weed.' I just thought symbolically it was bad, socially it was bad, and it was just *so insulting* to me."

At least one stereotype of black men was quite positive. As Whitney, an affluent black woman, noted, "Black male athletes are desired more. There's that 'Michael Jordan, Kobe Bryant, always-so-good-at-basketball-or-football-I-want-to-know-him' kind of thing. . . . There's that saying 'Black men have it tough in this world.' It's different here. They're put on a pedestal, in a small sense."

The desirability and paucity of black men caused problems for black women at Amherst. With two all-female colleges in the area, the competition for black men was great. From the perspective of some black women, "the black men on campus tend to have females throwing themselves at them." Black men "are always going off campus, to Mt. Holyoke or to Smith, to find themselves a white girl or to find themselves a hookup with a white girl. They never actually give black women a date." Devon, an affluent black female, said, "I still want to roll my eyes when I see a black guy dating a white girl. But like I said, they don't really date; they just sleep together. So I'm not missing anything."

Indeed, the black men in the study reported dating women of many differences races—as one put it, "all kinds of flavors of women." And Marc, for one, felt no pushback for not dating black women. He had had "multiple and short relationships on campus with whites, with Latinos, with multiple different races. Not with blacks. And it's been positive. It's never been an issue where someone will say, 'Oh, you're dating outside your race. You can't do that.'"

Alisa, a lower-income black student from a town outside Jackson, Mississippi, said, "[I feel like] it's more accepted for a black guy to be with a white girl. It's not equal. White guys can be with white girls. Black guys can be with white girls. But that kind of leaves the black women out, as far as relationships." "A lot of my friends would like to date a black man," Dana noted, "but there aren't a lot of black male–black female relationships on campus." This was not entirely unexpected. She had been told when she first got to Amherst:

> "Oh, there aren't any good black men on campus. They all date white girls. They're not interested in us because we're too dark." I feel like that comes up a lot. A lot of my friends at Amherst have dated people—just not here, not at Amherst. . . . It came up at a BSU forum. We talked about interracial dating. Then it boiled down to dating at Amherst. I know a lot of the guys felt victimized because they felt like the black women were blaming them. [Black male students] were like, "I don't know. It just doesn't happen."

Black women reported looking for partners at the nearby University of Massachusetts or at Hampshire College. Some found boyfriends when visiting friends at more distant schools.

A number of black women felt that the black men at Amherst had low regard for them, saw them as "mean" or "giv[ing] too much mouth" or "just not interested." Black women felt they were seen as "too stuck up" or "not as easy as the other girls." Yet if black women were sexually active, they felt they were demonized automatically as "hos." The general lack of attention paid to black women on campus by black men was "stifling" for Marissa. "It's feeling ignored, in a way. It's feeling put down. In a way, it's feeling invisible." Marissa spoke poignantly of black women on campus sharing their experiences of not being made to feel "beautiful by black men—and all men, all races," of how difficult it was on campus for black women to form romantic attachments, and of having to go home, where "guys actually talk to [her]." She noted, "I feel like people see me there."

Because of the more limited possibilities for black women to find partners at the college, Devon believed black men were happier with their experience at Amherst than black women. While some black women like her appreciated the classes and the opportunities the college offered, as well as the Amherst diploma awaiting them, she said, "it's not like, 'I *really* like my school,' or 'I'm going to miss college.' A lot of the black guys actually are going to miss college. Some of the black girls—I just know they're ready to get out of here. The ones I talk to, they're like, 'Postgraduate life's so much better.'"

Many black men in the study reported being aware that it was harder for a black woman to date a white man than vice versa and were sympathetic to their plight. Martin, the lower-income black student from

Oakland, understood that black women "get really, really frustrated that black men on this campus aren't paying attention to them." He continued, "I feel like it's probably a lot easier to be a black male on the campus than a black female. It's very easy to just not care what people think about you if you're a black male on this campus, or at least not think about it so much. [Black women] feel like they're under a constant microscope by everybody. I don't feel that."

Most black women in the study were not interested in exclusively dating black men. The majority of them had dated nonblack classmates (75 percent of the affluent group and 57 percent of the lower-income group).[9] Of the black women who dated interracially, almost all had dated white men. Several affluent black women reported that they generally dated or dated only white men. And while black women may have felt that black men overlooked them, Andrea, as noted in Chapter 1, felt that black men objected to her dating white men: "I definitely felt negativity from black men."

Just Joking

Despite the differences that existed among black students and the tensions that arose among them, the sense of community described at the opening of this chapter was there, too, affording many black students support, understanding, and friendship. The understanding felt among black classmates and the sense of belonging allowed them to poke fun at each other and put one another down, playing off the racial stereotypes that pervade the larger society. It might well be that this form of joking actually increased the sense of closeness and community. And there was a lot of such joking. Almost every black student reported having joked about race.[10] "It's accepted. You look at a black comedian. They do it all the time. . . . It's become accepted because you watch it every day." Among black students, "we're kidding" was understood. Brandon, the lower-income black student from Newark, said, "Black people make fun of other black people all the time, poke fun at each other. It's something that we do to release tension from being black and the stress from being black."

One stereotypic behavior—that of black people running on CP (colored people's) time—was frequently used for humorous release. Arriving late for dinner, a friend might joke, "You didn't really expect me to be at the dining hall on time. Because black people are *never* on time." Black students were "just playing off the same stereotypes people really do have, a way to offset them [by] using them." Aside from the joking about CP time and always being late, there were jokes about slavery with reference to differences in skin tone. If you were lighter skinned, "*you* probably worked in the [master's] house," whereas if you were darker skinned, "*you* were probably working out in the field." There was humor to be found in stereotypic food choices, Drinking Kool-Aid could draw the response "Oh my God, that is *black* of you."[11]

Discussion

Race is often constructed as a black-white issue. Attention is focused on the relationship between "white" and "black" people as though they were two homogenous groups. This view promotes generalizations about black people and the black experience and is consistent with the more general research finding that people in an in-group (i.e., members of their own group) tend to see people in an out-group as lacking in variability while seeing their own group as more heterogeneous.[11] The unidimensional depiction of black people obscures their diversity and the nature of their relationships with one another.[12]

While having race in common may help bind many black students together, race, however important, is only one of a number of intersecting factors that go into creating their social identities.[13] Some of the more obvious other factors are social class, gender, and physical distinctions, such as skin tone, all of which can help draw black students together or distance them from one another. These factors make an enormous difference in an individual's experiences and sense of self, as borne out by the reflections of the black students in this study. How central race is to a given individual's sense of identity is another important variable that may give rise to tensions among black classmates. To try to distill "the experience of black students" in this study to a single experience would be misguided, missing the heterogeneity among them.[14]

The importance of recognizing this diversity among black people has been addressed by Beverly Tatum, president of Spelman College, which has, by tradition, educated black women from the South. Tatum has said, "I am often asked why I would choose to lead an institution as 'homogenous' as Spelman College. Of course, the question is based on a flawed assumption. Although 97 percent of our students are racially categorized as 'Black,' the student body is quite diverse."[15] Tatum directs our attention beyond the similarities—that Spelman students are black women—and focuses it on the numerous ways these women differ from one another (e.g., in social class, religion, country of origin, region, and sexual orientation). Other educators have stressed the importance of recognizing and appreciating differences in the experiences of members of the same racial group.[16]

Educational researchers Shaun Harper and Andrew Nichols examined the variability among black male undergraduates, exploring how their differences influenced their experiences with one another.[17] The areas of difference noted included their styles of dress; their speech; their cultural interests, including musical preferences; whether they came from predominantly white or black neighborhoods; and what choices of extracurricular activities they opted for (e.g., athletics, black fraternities). Harper and Nichols found that differences impeded communication with and support for one another among the students. The researchers went on to lament the fact that few studies of the experiences of black students on campus "do much to explain how within-group differences impact experiences, dynamics, relationships."[18]

The differences between black students at Amherst mirror divides that have long existed in the larger black community. Tensions arise from these differences, in part, because not all identities are seen or treated as equal. Having wealth or lighter skin color, for example, confers privilege and advantages, while poverty and darker skin bestow disadvantages. Lawrence Otis Graham, author and commentator on race, politics, and class in America, touches on the fault line between the black upper class and an economically marginalized underclass in describing his growing up in that upper class. He knew early on "that there was *us* and there was *them*."[19] There were those black people who had wealth, attended the right colleges, belonged to the right fraternities, had the right family background, and had "good hair" with "nice complexions"—and those who did not.

The issues surrounding skin color discussed earlier in this chapter occur on other college campuses as well. Sociologist Margaret Hunter reports that some darker-skinned black female college students spoke of feelings of jealousy and resentment toward lighter-skinned black peers, whom they perceived to be more attractive to men.[20] Yet she also found that lighter-skinned black students were ostracized in return by darker-skinned peers. As also noted in the Amherst study, some light-skinned black students have their "blackness" called into question, and some feel themselves dismissed by black classmates as not being in a position to understand what it means to be black.

Issues between black classmates based on skin color are long-standing in the larger black community as well. Dark-skinned black people are more likely to experience frequent racial discrimination than those with light skin.[21] Economic disparities in education and income are associated with differences in skin color.[22] Black women with darker skin complete fewer years of education, enter less prestigious occupations, and have lower income than black women with lighter skin.[23] Black people with lighter skin are more likely to make it into the power elite.[24]

We draw attention in the study to the divide among black Caribbean Americans in terms of those born in the United States and those who were raised, at least in part, in the Caribbean and to the cultural divide more generally that separates black Caribbean Americans and African Americans. One reason for the divide between black Caribbean and African Americans that has been discussed in the research literature did not come to light in our interviews with students. First-generation black immigrants from the Caribbean often strive to preserve their "foreign" identities in a belief that West Indians are viewed more positively by white people than African Americans, whose family roots can be traced back to slavery. Black Caribbean immigrants may try to avoid the stigma of being an African American.[25]

As late adolescents/young adults, black students on campus were engaged with the question of how to define themselves, and a part of that definition was establishing their racial identity, or what it means to them to be a black person.[26] This aspect of identity was not one that most of their white classmates gave much thought to, as they tended not to view themselves in racial terms. Black students faced a wide range of choices. How you speak or dress, what music you listen to, what campus groups you join, and who you hang out with all contribute to your sense of self. For some black students, taking black studies courses, in which they learned about black history and culture, was an attempt to help them reach their own sense of black identity. Some black students were drawn to attitudes and behaviors that they felt were "authentically black" and questioned the blackness of classmates who made other identity choices, seeing them as not being "black enough" or as being "too white."[27] For some black students, the choice of whether to sit at the "black tables" in the dining hall reflected an aspect of their racial identity and could be fraught with feelings.[28]

Establishing a secure racial identity for some black students entailed an additional layer of complexity because it was not merely a matter of *self-definition*; it was influenced by the way they were regarded by other people. It can be difficult to feel at peace with your blackness when others question it. The study offers encouraging instances of students who, after four years at the college, saw themselves as having become less concerned about the way they were defined by others, having come to embrace and feel secure in the identities they had fashioned for themselves.

The findings regarding the variability among black classmates along many axes and the many feelings engendered by those differences may be revealing and surprising. This is because, as Beverly Tatum notes, the differences among black people are "often submerged and ignored."[29] She argues that these differences "need to be brought into the open so students can learn to relate as equals across difference."[30] Just as there is a need for black and white classmates to talk to one another if they are to learn about race—about each others' experiences, feelings, beliefs, and attitudes—the need exists for black students to do the same about their differences and the inequalities that divide them. Black students could benefit from structured dialogues to learn more about and from each other, with a focus on gaining greater knowledge and understanding about the issues that divide them and about incorrect racial assumptions they may make about each other. They would, we hope, become closer to one another in the process.[31] The nature and benefits of structured dialogues are described in some detail in Chapter 9.

6
Black and White

Seeing Race Anew

In his classic work *The Nature of Prejudice*, Gordon Allport argues that prejudice stems from a lack of knowledge about, and exposure to, members of another group.[1] Allport goes on to posit optimal conditions that would reduce prejudice. What is needed is for members of the majority and minority groups to interact together cooperatively with equal status in pursuit of common goals. The effects of this intergroup contact would be greatest if the contact was sanctioned by institutional supports and resulted in a perception of "common interests and common humanity between members of the two groups."[2] Fifty years of research have borne out the truth of Allport's claims—such intergroup contact *does* reduce prejudice.[3]

Amherst College is an almost ideal setting to see Allport's beliefs in action. The optimal conditions are in place. Students of different races enter the dorms, the classrooms, the dining hall, and the many extracurricular activities on campus on an equal status basis. They have opportunities to work together toward common goals, be it as teammates; fellow performers; colleagues on class projects; or on any of the many clubs, organizations, and publications at the college. Ample settings and time exist for friendships to develop across racial lines, all within the context of an institution with a strong commitment to diversity. The college has gone to great lengths to create a racially diverse student body, driven in part by the belief that a diverse community offers important learning that cannot be gleaned from books. Does that learning take place? Does living for four years in the Amherst community lead to changes in awareness, understanding, attitudes, and feelings?

Consistent with previous research, these benefits of diversity proved to be present at the college. But research also indicates that even if cross-race interactions occur under the most favorable conditions, learning does not always occur.[4] This, too, was true at Amherst. Some students felt they had learned little about race from living in a racially diverse community. This chapter addresses the extent to which students felt they derived educational benefits from diversity and what the nature of that learning was.

Cross-Race Relationships

Having classmates of different races on campus does not ensure that *meaningful* contact with students of another race will actually take place. A student could conceivably go through Amherst and get to know well only students of his or her own race. Some students did just that. But four of five white students in the study reported that they had gotten to know well two or more black students over their four years at Amherst.[5] All but one black student felt they had gotten to know well at least two white students.[6] Given that white students made up two-thirds of the student body and black students less than 10 percent, the somewhat higher percentage for black students is not all that surprising.

What is surprising, though, is that at the end of *freshman* year, over 90 percent of students in three of the four groups in the study reported having gotten to know well at least two classmates of the other race. In the affluent white group, however, this was true for only 54 percent of the students. But after four years, students in that group showed a 50 percent increase (to 77 percent), bringing their outcomes closer to those of the other three groups. For wealthy white students, continued exposure in different situations over time appears to have led to closer relationships with their black classmates.

Three other indications of the existence of close connections across race emerged from the study. In their senior interviews, 70 percent of the students reported currently having at least one student of another race as a roommate or in their room group.[7] The majority of students reported having dated someone of another race (70 percent of black and 44 percent of white students).[8] And while the majority of the friends of lower-income students and affluent white students were of the same race, a third of those friends were not.[9] For affluent black students, almost three-quarters of their friends were classmates of a different race.

Clearly, a large majority of students at the college had made meaningful cross-race connections. Given the many contacts across race lines that were possible for students during their years at Amherst—be it as close friends, acquaintances in classes and activities, suitemates, or romantic attachments—it is not possible to tease out how much effect any *one* type of connection had on learning. We did, however, explore other questions: What effect did the combinations of connections across race have on students? How many students felt that they had learned something about other races or their own race through the overall experience of living and interacting in a racially diverse community? And how did those numbers change over the four years?

At the end of the *freshman* year, a little more than a third of the study participants reported having learned something about people of other races or their own race.[10] The percentages in all four groups went up from freshman to senior year, demonstrating that learning continued to occur over the course of college. As seniors, a little over half of the students in the study reported having done so.[11] So although continued learning took place, clearly there was more potential for learning than was realized.

A look at the percentage of students, group by group, who reported having learned from the racial diversity and a look at how those percentages changed over time reveal that learning did not occur uniformly and that social class made a big difference in the reported learning for white students. More lower-income white students than affluent white students felt that they learned about race during their freshman year (47 percent versus 21 percent), and this pattern remained true through senior year (53 percent versus 33 percent). It is possible that the lower-income white students had more to learn, as they were less likely to have had contacts with black people or people of other races before coming to Amherst. Strikingly, as was true their freshman year, a lower percentage of affluent white seniors (33 percent) reported learning about race than their cohorts in the other three groups (53 percent of lower-income white, 62 percent of lower-income black, and 57 percent of affluent black participants). This finding is troubling, as affluent white students make up the majority at the college. Also, they are likely to move into positions of some power in our society and may be unlikely to work to address racial inequalities if they do not have an understanding of the impact of racial stereotypes, prejudice, and discrimination.

For black study participants, social class made little difference, in terms of percentage, to their reported learning about race, either as freshmen or as seniors. What is important to note is the *increase* in the percentage of black students, both wealthy and lower-income, who reported learning something about other races or their own over those four years. These percentages increased sharply, from 35 percent freshman year to 59 percent senior year. In fact, at the end of four years, more black than white students (60 percent versus 43 percent) reported having learned from the racial diversity at the college. That difference may result from the fact that black students were more likely to describe having learned something about members of *their own* race than white students were about theirs. The tremendous diversity among the black students on campus, as explored in Chapter 5, makes that quite understandable.

Reduction in Widely Held Stereotypes

Part of what black and white students reported learning from their exposure to one another involved racial stereotypes. Racial stereotypes are widely held in our society, and students on campus were not exempt from holding them or spared being subject to them. Four out of five black students and almost half the white students in the study reported classmates having made inaccurate assumptions about them on the basis of their race.[12]

For many students, commonly held stereotypes decreased over time. "Now I understand that white people are not a monolithic group," stated Trina, the lower-income black student who had gone to Manhattan's elite Trinity High School, where her white classmates came from privileged backgrounds. That skewed exposure led to her "monolithic" view of white people. Her subsequent experiences at Amherst—the close contact she had with white classmates from varied walks of life—opened her eyes. And she was not alone. Through their friendships and acquaintances with white classmates, other black participants in the study came to broaden their views: "There are good white people and bad white people"; "Not all white people have the same views"; "Some [white people] understand where you're coming from and why you hold the views that you do, and some don't." Brianna, the lower-income black student from Houston, realized, "Too often people try to categorize a group of people into one box, like 'If you're black, then you're like this or like that,' and vice versa. But I think my experiences at Amherst have helped me to realize that everything is more on an individual basis." Similarly, some white students came to see that "there's no set behavioral standard for black people"; that "there is a lot of variance, even in culture, within a certain race"; and that "'black' is not a monolithic group."

The Association between Race and Class

A prevailing societal stereotype of black people is that they are poor. Many white students shared that assumption and were taken by surprise when they encountered affluent black students on campus, whose parents were investment bankers, doctors, lawyers, and people who ran businesses. Before college, the black people many students had encountered in their own lives and in the media came from families with little means. Getting to know affluent black students on campus led some white students to realize that their black classmates came from varied class backgrounds. Some gained an appreciation of the special challenges affluent black students faced in having numerous inaccurate assumptions made about them.

Katelyn, an affluent white student from Phoenix, had attended a racially diverse high school in which 85 percent of the students were Hispanic, 5 percent black, and 10 percent white. While Katelyn had been exposed to diverse peers in high school, the school population was low income. She had never met any "upper-class" black people before college. At Amherst she developed a close friendship with an affluent black student who spoke with her about the struggles wealthy black people had with racial stereotypes. Katelyn came to see that "whites don't understand that they're upper class and put all these stereotypes of the lower class on them." She saw, too, that black people of means faced an additional issue, as they were viewed by some in the lower-income black community as "betraying them," as "Oreos."

Like Katelyn, many lower-income black students had little exposure to wealthy black people, and some also gained an appreciation of the special difficulties confronting black students from affluent families. Brianna had attended a charter school in Houston designed to educate "underserved populations." The students were mostly black and Hispanic and had little contact with any affluent students. Looking back on her experience at Amherst as a senior, she reported, "I've definitely gotten a better understanding of the situation that upper-middle-class blacks are in, because they're in a socioeconomic class [that] traditionally has not been reserved for members of their race. But they're in a race that's not traditionally been a part of their socioeconomic class. So they're in this limbo stage where they don't belong to either group, so they tend to form their own group."

The flip side of this stereotype was that being a white person was associated with being wealthy.[13] Some black students had never encountered white classmates who were poor and were unaware of their numbers in society. The white students they had gotten to know at their private high schools were affluent, and many were extremely wealthy. Trina formed a close friendship at Amherst with a white male student from "a very low-income background" in rural Colorado. Trina was totally taken aback to discover his financial situation. "I'm like, 'Wait. All white people aren't rich? You're on financial aid, too?'" This relationship contributed to her realization, noted previously, that white people did not form a monolithic group. Angela, another lower-income black student, met a white classmate at Amherst "from a really poor family, *really poor*." He had had to go to speech class to learn Standard English. She realized that "even though he's a white male Protestant, all those other things, that doesn't automatically equal privilege."

Intelligence

Another widely held societal stereotype heard on campus about black students was that they were less intelligent than their white classmates, and one corollary was that black students were less qualified to be at Amherst College. For some white study participants, experience with black classmates helped dispel these beliefs. Alexander, an affluent white student from a suburb of Washington, D.C., had attended a private school from kindergarten through twelfth grade. He had been exposed to few black students in his classes before coming to Amherst and had found that "it was hard to tell if they were smart or not." He noted, "But here at Amherst you can really tell that there are people from all races that are very smart. I didn't necessarily have the thought that [black students] weren't smart before, but now I really have proof that they are." Jeremy, a lower-income white student, grew up in South Burlington, Vermont, a community that was "very white—some Asian minorities, very few blacks and Latinos." That community and its public high school had given him little exposure to people of other races. Looking back as a senior, Jeremy reported, "I think a lot of people think that black students here aren't as academically strong as the other students. When I first got here, I never would have said it, and I wasn't actively thinking it, but I probably had the same sense. Now I don't. I've had a lot of experiences with minorities in classes that have shown me that that's not true." Aside from the learning that these last two quotes reveal, they also give a sense of how difficult it could be for white students to acknowledge their racial prejudices that made them uncomfortable with themselves.

For some black students who had grown up hearing this pejorative stereotype about members of their race, it was heartening to be in an environment where black students were academically focused and successful and where people did not denigrate the intelligence of members of their race. Brandi, a lower-income black student from New York, spoke to these issues: "Where I am from, most people of a different race think that black people are ignorant, uneducated, and thieves." She felt "proud that there are a lot of black people at Amherst who are leaders, that set great examples. . . . It was nice to be around intellectuals that were black."

Negative Stereotypes of White People

In the eyes of some black students, white people generally "just don't understand, and they're oblivious to the idea of racism. They say there's no racism, but there is racism." More pointedly, they "are always trying to oppress black people" and "don't listen. They don't care. They're unfeeling." One white student was told by black friends that she was "so fundamentally different" from them that she could not understand them. "It was just like, 'Oh, you're white. You have no idea. You can't understand this whatsoever.'" Another white student told of a black friend who would, she said, "always tell our white friends that we could never understand how she felt because we weren't minorities. Maybe she's right."

When a forum about the need to start a multicultural resource center on campus was being organized, Marc noted, "a lot of black people [were] saying, 'White students aren't going to show up . . . because they don't care.'" At the forum, Marc found himself in a room "full of people, not just one race but a very big mix." The presence of many white classmates did not change some black students' belief that white students were not concerned about racial issues. Marc went on to say, "There's always just another step of 'Even if they come, I don't know how much they took away from it.' Or if [white students] *were* there, not enough were there." Stereotypes can be difficult to overcome.

For some black study participants, interactions with white classmates did modify their views. Whitney, an affluent black student, spoke with admiration about a white friend who, in freshman year, stood up to another white student who had told a racist joke. "A lot of [black] people think all white people are racist and that when they're behind closed doors, they just say whatever they want to say about other races. And this experience shows how it's complex; it's not so black and white. . . . I assume that white people make black jokes and laugh and no one ever stands up and says this is *wrong*." But Whitney realized that "there are people who do that." By the end of senior year, Whitney believed that white students were open to discussing racial issues and were "open to change and wanting to be more inclusive, even though they still might make racist, classist, and/or gender bias comments." She went on to say, "People in this region—I am overgeneralizing—have good intentions in seeking change and being more inclusive but, because of the negative aspects of the history of this country, still possess an unconscious temptation to be biased."

Being at the college made Trina realize not all white people are "completely oblivious as to why racism is still a problem in society." Trina formed a close friendship with a white student who was interested in issues of racism. She said, "It made me see that there are white people that do care about issues of race and that they'll never understand what it means to be the victim of racism in America—but that they *care*." In high school Trina had felt that people saw her first and foremost as a black person and not a person. Through her friendships with white classmates at Amherst, though, she came to see that "there are people that don't think that your whole personality is wrapped up in the fact that you're black. . . . People are interested in who *you* are."

For Marc, being with friends of different races allowed him "to see there's support for minority issues. . . . Having white friends who really cared about the issues that are going on on campus and things like that with minorities, people of different races, was important and really nice to see." Brandon, the lower-income black student from inner-city Newark, was greatly moved by students' responses to the election of President Obama: "The reaction on campus really had an astounding effect on me. I was surprised to see so much open support from the white students because the subject of race had been very touchy at times before. So that assured me that there is a diverse white population at Amherst and made me slow to judge white people in the setting of a place like Amherst."

Urban Black Cultural Images

Being black is associated in the media with living in the inner city and with urban black culture, as described in previous chapters. During their years at the college, many white students got to know many black classmates who belied these stereotypes, whose knowledge and interests diverged from the media's presentation and whose speech, dress, and interests did not match those images. White students spoke of black friends who had taken them by surprise because they listened to opera, classical music, or rock music or knew little about rap, or dressed in khaki pants and polo shirts and spoke only Standard English.

Other Racial Assumptions

A number of other racial stereotypes were voiced on campus, though less frequently than those cited above. Black males were assumed to be "better athletes" than their white counterparts, to be "good at sports," to "play basketball," and to be "fast as hell" or "much faster sprinters." Of particular concern to lower-income black women on campus was the depiction of the black woman as "always mad, saying what she wants, and being very confrontational"; "angry"; "sassy"; "really loud, really obnoxious, and just always looking for confrontation"; "loud and opinionated"; and likely to "state her mind and ignore what anybody else will have to say." Some black women thus saw themselves as unfairly put down for being strong and articulate about their beliefs. No evidence surfaced in the interviews indicating a reduction in these stereotypes.

Understanding Race and Racial Privilege

Learning about race encompassed more than a possible reduction in stereotypes and prejudice, and students reported a variety of other types of learning. Some white students came to understand the significance of race in American society. Many white participants in the study grew up in predominantly white communities and had barely thought about race before they arrived at Amherst. To them race was "just a constant," something that was a nonissue in their lives. Looking back as a senior, Sarah, an affluent white student from Westchester, remarked, "Freshman year I didn't see myself as *having* a race. I feel sometimes you do that—you're like, 'Oh, I'm white,' which is an absence of race, which it's not at all." After four years she had come to feel, she said, that "it's almost offensive to think that, but the concept of race didn't really seem a big deal to me at all freshman year, and I remember thinking from the first interview, 'I've never thought of any of this before.'" Over those four years, Sarah came to realize that her race was "instrumental in making me who I am." Similarly, through getting to know and interact with black students on campus, other white participants from upper-middle-class, predominantly white neighborhoods and high schools became "more aware of the fact" that they are *white* and came to "think more openly about race and racism."

Amy, the lower-income white student from Orlando, had explicitly been taught *not* "to think that race even really exists," to see people as people. She had found it "shocking and upsetting" to learn from her biracial friend and classmate that she felt she was treated differently because of her race. That conversation called Amy's color-blind philosophy into question and helped open her eyes to the fact that race "really does [exist], and that is a huge factor affecting experience." Emily, the lower-income white student from South Dakota, also became aware of the importance of race and of how people responded to others differently depending on the color of their skin. She remarked, "[That was not] something that I would have thought about before Amherst—how people automatically will put things on you by your race." If you're a white person, Emily came to realize, "people assume you're a higher status."

At the beginning of college, many white study participants had little understanding that racism not only puts people of color at a disadvantage but also puts white people at an advantage. As entering freshmen, white student after white student reported being oblivious to his or her race and its consequences: "I never had to think about it"; "I don't think that race has had a large impact at all in my life"; "I don't think my race has affected anything"; "I'm sure it has made a difference, but I haven't consciously noticed it"; "I don't think [race has] opened any doors or closed any doors for me." When she entered the college, Ashley, a wealthy white student from an affluent Minneapolis suburb, was not sure if being a white person had made any things easier in her life, although she was dimly aware that she might have faced more challenges had she not been white. "I've probably been helped out a little bit because I'm white, but I don't know. I have no idea."

But coming to know students on campus who did not share their racial privilege changed some white students' perspectives. They came to recognize that not having to think about their race was itself a privileged condition that black people did not share. As one student put it, "What I'm learning is that to [black people] it's a big deal, when to me it doesn't seem like it's a big deal." Another student thought about "white privilege a lot more—things that white people take for granted, that they just don't have to deal with and that they don't realize that they don't have deal with." One white student came to see that "white people have more opportunities than people of other races in the U.S." Another realized that if you were not white, "you might have had to work harder to prove yourself" and that she had an advantage in situations at the college "because it's easiest to walk in as a respectable-looking *white* person." Other white students, too, realized the privilege that accrued to them because of their race. David, the affluent white study participant from Washington, D.C., noted, "Most of my professors are white. Most of the people that interview me for jobs are white. Not that people here are necessarily explicitly racist. But, sure, you can definitely tell that I'm treated differently than some of my other friends are by professors. . . . I can go in professors' offices, and there's a comfort level that even when I've been in professors' offices with friends of different races, the comfort is different."

As noted previously, before college some white students had had little or no direct, personal contact with black people. Many had never heard firsthand accounts from those who had experienced racism and discrimination, concepts that remained largely theoretical to them. Marie, a lower-income white student, grew up in a "pretty rural area" an hour outside of Charleston, West Virginia. Few black families lived there. Marie knew "from an intellectual standpoint that racism exists," but her experience interacting in a diverse community at Amherst "just brings it closer to home a little bit, hearing [a close black friend] talk about it, and it's like, 'Yeah, that really does happen.'" Rebecca, a lower-income white classmate, had never understood "why there was always so much talk about prejudice" because she had never discriminated against anyone and had never felt discriminated against. "I just never saw what the big deal was, maybe because I've never seen it happen." She formed a close relationship with a black friend freshman year:

> Some of the stories that [my black friend] told me kind of opened my eyes. I think that people say that discrimination is still going on, and I think I just had never witnessed it. But when she was telling me stories about how her family is black and things that have happened to them, I was shocked. . . . I had never known a personal example of something like that. What I did realize was that I was unaware that there were still certain prejudiced things going on.

Racial Categorization and Identity

The question of who is "black" in our society is not a simple one. There is no one, single, agreed-on criterion. According to the "one drop rule," anyone with any black ancestry is categorized as black. State statutes differ in making the designation, defining anyone with from one-thirty-second to one-eighth to one-fourth "black blood" as a black person.[14] And how a state or other people categorize someone may not be identical to how that person regards him- or herself. Becoming aware of the complexities around defining a person's race or racial identity led some students to new understandings about race.

Growing up outside Jackson, Mississippi, Alisa, a lower-income black student, had found it easy to categorize people by race. "It was just assumed that if you had lighter skin, you were 'white'; people with darker skin were 'black.'" But Alisa had grown up with a narrower range of people in her home community than she found at Amherst. She came to see that the way she thought of people's race was not necessarily how they identified themselves. "Just by talking to people that I assumed were black, I found out that some preferred to be acknowledged as 'Caribbean American' over being referred to as 'black.' Also, people who are biracial or multiracial tend to want to be considered 'black' instead of being referred to as 'biracial.'"

Further to the point, it is worth noting that some students who were biracial preferred to be identified as "biracial," "mixed," or "black *and* white."

Recognizing Commonalities across Race

One important form of learning that occurred for many students, black and white, was the discovery of greater commonalities across race than they had imagined existed and, along with that, an awareness that the boundaries between racial groups could erode. Some black students had anticipated experiencing difficulties in establishing relationships with white classmates, and they were surprised to find that that was not the case. As a senior, Alisa, the lower-income black student from Mississippi, reported:

> As far as getting to know a person, I don't think race is a factor—not anymore at least. I used to think that people of my own race would understand my experiences better and therefore I would get along with them better. However, I've had good and bad experiences with people of all races during my time at Amherst. Therefore, the diversity of Amherst helped change my mind. Now I believe the attitude of a person matters more than their race.

Dana, the lower-income black student from a largely Caribbean neighborhood in Queens, had also worried about relating to white students. When she entered college, she assumed that if she tried connecting with white students, they "would clash or . . . wouldn't connect well." She said, "I was afraid I wouldn't understand where they were coming from and that I would feel alienated." She had come to feel, however, that she "shouldn't make assumptions about different races." In becoming friends with white classmates, she explained, "[I realized] that race isn't an issue in terms of our friendship. It doesn't have to be, but it can, if you make it. Generally, we're just friends with each other because we like each other." This realization left her in the gratifying position of "not worrying about [race] so much when you first meet somebody."

White and black students reported numerous instances in which they discovered that despite their differences, they had much in common. Before coming to Amherst, Danny, a lower-income white student from a small town in New Jersey, had attended a Catholic school where, he said, "all my peers, all the kids I went to school with, everybody was white. I didn't have much contact with anybody else." He expressed some surprise at the end of his first year when he reported having "friends of all races here." As a senior, Danny's friendships with black classmates had given him a new understanding of racial differences. "I've come to realize that while there are superficial differences in culture and music, whatever—at the same basic level we're all pretty similar. There's not really that much of a difference between us." Other lower-income white students who had not had close black friends until college expressed similar feelings: "You can be friends with whoever you want. . . . It doesn't matter what race your good friend is; they're still going to be your good friend"; "[The college] has definitely opened my eyes to how similar my experiences were to even the [black] people that my parents would have stereotyped."

Along the same lines, Kevin, an affluent black student from Orange County, California, came to believe that black and white people can transcend differences and "come together to create a healthy, productive environment where race is no longer a primary source of social tensions." Carl, the lower-income black student from a racially mixed neighborhood in Plainsboro, New Jersey, discovered that "people are pretty accepting. Sometimes the barriers that exist aren't really that hard to knock down. People are just too hesitant to do it, too hesitant to talk to someone of a different race. Because when they actually do, they have a lot in common and can really be good friends." After dating a white person, Andrea, the affluent black student from New York City, had come to feel that although racism is "as much of a barrier as people think it is—race in the workplace, race in your love life, race in your social life—you find that person, you love that person, there's no racial wall that should be there." She continued, "So that's what I've learned: break down those barriers."

Some black study participants, however, remained more cautious about the ability to move past racial differences. William, the affluent black student from Potomac, Maryland, came from a predominantly white community and had attended a predominantly white, all-boys private school. On the basis of his years of experience living among white people, he had reached this conclusion:

> I've learned that there is a difference between black people and white people. This difference is directed by experience, and it creates a gap between races. I've learned that this gap simply can't be bridged, because empathy can only take you so much into the mind and experiences of someone besides yourself. While this may be scary, and imply some things that are difficult to accept, it is still possible for races to coexist if the difference in experience is acknowledged.

Interracial Dating

Eighty-five percent of the students in the study had positive feelings about dating someone of another race when they arrived at Amherst.[15] For some black students who were biracial, feelings were particularly positive. A few students, both black and white, had already dated people of another race during high school, and, as noted previously, 70 percent of black and 44 percent of white participants engaged in interracial dating during college. After dating someone of another race at Amherst, Alexander, an affluent white student, reported, "I think it's great." The idea of interracial dating had "only improved" in his mind, though he said he was not "negative about it before."

Some students came from families that viewed interracial dating as unacceptable. But living in the Amherst community, away from their families, could lead to changed attitudes and new behaviors for these students. Amy, the lower-income white student from Orlando, reported a change in her feelings about interracial dating. "[It is] probably more fine with me . . . because I'm farther away from my family and my grandparents. It wouldn't be okay with my grandparents if I was dating someone who wasn't white."

Amy was not alone in experiencing change. Before she entered college, Trina said, "[I was] absolutely against interracial dating. . . . I thought it was wrong." Trina's concern focused on black men's attraction to white women and her belief that that attraction was rooted in "the idea that white women are the exceptional 'ideal' of what a woman should be like." After four years at Amherst, Trina saw black men's attractions differently. "You've been with [white classmates] for four years, you've lived in housing with them—why shouldn't you like that person?" She could see that black men who dated white women had come to know these women and genuinely liked *them*, not some ideal.

Increased Understanding

The friendships that developed between black and white students on campus and the talking that took place in the context of those friendships could result in greater understanding of and empathy for one another's perspectives on race and in greater clarity about one's own experiences. "Just hearing someone's personal story, it adds to your own understanding," noted Emily, the South Dakotan. Emily had a biracial friend who had grown up in a "small white town." She explained, "And hearing about how excluded she felt made me think about my own town and definitely made me think less of the people that I grew up with because I think about the other side of it and how she would feel coming back to my hometown. Because my friends [at the college] have been outside of my racial group, it's definitely made me expand my thinking."

From conversations with his black friends at the college, David, the affluent white student from Washington, D.C., got a sense of how difficult they felt it was to try to talk to white people about their feeling that "white people won't interact with black people." And he learned their view on why that might be—that white students "worried about engaging" with black students, feeling that "they don't know how." Amber, a lower-income white student, had a black friend who was concerned that her black identity was being challenged at the college—that she was being pressed to conform to "white" standards. Amber's talks with her friend helped her "understand more where she was coming from and why [a black person] would feel that way." Her friend explained to Amber her sense that the way she "spoke and wrote was being dismissed [in classes], and she had to write or speak a certain way in order to talk to the professor or get a good grade in the class."

"I have relatives from the South. I've spent a fair amount of time there, in the country. I think I've got a pretty fair idea of what it's like to be *black* in the South." This was the perspective on race in the South that Jason, the affluent black student from Oakland, California, had when he entered Amherst. Jason's mother was from Virginia, and his family used to visit there every summer. "I consider it a pretty prejudiced place and not a place I'd prefer to spend any time." Given his summer experiences in Virginia, Jason had developed "a knee-jerk reaction of being leery of white Southerners." In his freshman year, Jason became close friends with a white student from Birmingham, Alabama, and their friendship was based on many shared interests. Jason noted, "[At first] I was kind of leery of him. You know, he's that guy from *Birmingham*. Is there a fire hose in his room?" Jason's friend's perspective was of great interest to him. He explained, "Because I've never really been able to grasp what that's like. It's very interesting, especially when you hear him talk about what his family did or didn't do during the civil rights movement. He talks about one of his uncles who is a doctor and was considered a very, very progressive doctor because he also treated black patients—but they had to come in through the back door." To his surprise, Jason learned that he could form a close friendship with a white Southerner. As for additional learning, Jason noted, "There is a sliding scale between what some people consider 'enlightened' attitudes on the subject of race. If letting blacks in through the back door is uncomfortably, unpleasantly 'progressive,' [that was] a very different standard of 'enlightened' than what I'm used to."

Through his close friendship with John, a wealthy white classmate from Brooklyn, Marc gained an appreciation of a surprising racial issue his friend had had to confront. Like Marc, John had gone to private school, and many of John's black neighborhood friends who went to the local public school gave him "a ton of gaff. . . . He got racist remarks for being white and buying into just like the whole white culture and going to private school. They would always question why he felt he was too good to go to the public school in the area." For Marc, who had had those same taunts directed at him by *his* black neighborhood friends, having those conversations with John led him "to take away that everyone has struggles with race. It doesn't matter if you're white, black, Latino—anything." There can be "racism on all ends. No one is really safe in their skin."

Interested in learning about differences, and feeling he had a grasp on the black issues on campus and more generally, Marc chose not to invest his time in the BSU. "I really wanted to branch out and tackle a tougher problem." With that in mind, in his junior year he joined La Causa, the Latino cultural, political, and service organization on campus. It was a group Marc felt he knew "almost nothing about," and he felt he had a lot to learn from this exposure. The exposure included living in the La Casa Cultural House with students interested in promoting and expressing Latino cultures. For Marc it was "a wonderful experience" that enabled him to find out "what it was like to grow up in a Latino culture and even what it was like coming to America from other, Spanish-speaking countries." "In sum," he said, "a culture that was wholly mysterious to me became something I could not only understand but become a part of, if [only] temporarily. . . . We would stay up late at night sharing stories and having heated discussions, some of which were never emulated in classroom settings."

Andrea's talks with white classmates helped her gain a new perspective on some white behaviors that in the past would have upset her. Through conversations with white friends, she came to realize that some comments she took to be hostile or offensive toward her were not meant in the way she had interpreted them. "So it actually really helped me a lot to talk to people *not* of my own race about this." She underwent change: "I'm not angry constantly. I have more tolerance and patience when people don't understand a certain aspect of black culture. I find that a lot of people around here can be pretty ignorant at times to black culture. So it was really helpful and it definitely made me think about things differently—maybe I shouldn't take offense to that, maybe [white people] just don't understand."

Alicia, the lower-income black student from a predominantly white rural Vermont community, learned something unexpected about some members of her own race over her years at the college. She was light skinned. As noted in Chapter 5, Alicia's blackness was questioned by other black students on campus. She came to view racism as "a multiracial phenomenon, meaning that all races participate in racism against other races and against their own races." She said, "I have encountered racism from both blacks and whites at Amherst. I had never encountered racism from other blacks before I reached Amherst."

Increased Comfort Interacting with Black Students

One last type of learning was reported, and that concerned white students' feelings when interacting with black students. Close to half of the white study participants reported growing increasingly comfortable in those interactions over four years at the college.[16] This was true for more lower-income white than affluent white students (62 percent versus 25 percent). Lower-income white participants had entered the college with less cross-race experience and had more to learn. Only 13 percent of lower-income white students had a mixed-race friendship group before coming to college, as opposed to 31 percent of the affluent white students. With one exception, all the white students left the college after four years reporting that they felt comfortable interacting with black students, and the same held true for black students about their comfort with their white classmates.

These students carry with them what they learned about race and, as a result, are in a better position to help bridge differences in the larger world. As noted in Chapter 1, Emily believed that her experience with friends outside the classroom was going to increase her willingness to engage with people of different races and from different backgrounds. She believed that had she gone straight from South Dakota into the world beyond, "it would have been a lot more difficult." "And Amherst," she added, "has definitely provided a stronger bridge than I could have done on my own."

Classroom Learning

Having looked at the learning students reported from their social world, from living and interacting with people of another race, our focus now shifts to another potentially important source of learning about race—the classroom, with its attendant classroom discussion. Though the college does not require students to take courses on race, 85 percent of students in the study reported taking at least one course that addressed race either as the central topic or as a subtopic.[17] These courses were located in ten departments across the curriculum—in anthropology; black studies; economics; English; history; law, jurisprudence, and social thought; political science; psychology; sociology; and women and gender studies. Fifty percent more black than white students chose to take courses specifically about black people or Africa (74 percent versus 48 percent).[18] Black students were also much more likely than their white classmates to choose black studies as a major (26 percent versus 7 percent).[19]

One benefit of academic coursework on race was that it provided analytical frameworks for understanding race and racism—their history, dynamics, and effects. Students spoke of learning "a different way of looking at our country"; learning about "white hegemony and how white power is the assumption and what that has meant for society"; and learning about the diaspora, the displacement of black people from west and southeast Africa to the Western Hemisphere as slaves. Such knowledge enabled Brandon, the lower-income black student from Newark, to develop "theories and ideas" that helped him feel more comfortable and confident in defending his positions in an academic manner. As a black studies major, Trina felt she had learned "a language that's more conducive to actually affecting people's ways of thinking. And you learn the history of why, in general, white people at Amherst might not be receptive to an angry militant."

Through the curriculum, some students gained a greater understanding of white privilege and of racial inequalities. For Justin, a lower-income white student, white privilege was, he said, "something I'm aware of just because I've taken some classes in anthro or sociology." From her classes, Brianna, the black student from Houston, came to see that white students were raised unaware of their privilege, and as a result, she had come "not to *accuse* them of it but rather to get toward working with them in getting to *acknowledge* it." As one of the two white students who were black studies majors, Lauren, the affluent white student from Manhattan, found her coursework instrumental in "opening [her] eyes to all the racial inequalities." She felt she had gained a greater understanding of the importance of overcoming racial stereotypes. "Everyone has unconscious, subconscious assumptions. No matter how tolerant you may think you are, everyone has those implicit thoughts and stereotypes. Learning about other cultures is so important because it will destroy those stereotypes."

At times, a compelling classroom discussion would continue after class. As Lauren, often "the 'token white girl' in the black studies classes," noted, "We'll go to Val for lunch and keep talking about it." During the fall 2008 presidential election, Marc and all seven of the other students in his mixed-race group of close friends took the same class, "Race and Politics." "We were looking at the Obama stuff, and so a lot of the conversations this past semester were about race and looking at how the media is portraying Barack Obama." Their discussions would "tie into academic realms, talking about civil rights, the movement of blacks through history, and thinking about how the position has changed from a slavery-based society to what we have now and considering how far out we have actually come." "I think," Marc continued, "asking really engaging questions about race and things like that has opened their eyes and my eyes, too, to the ways you *can* talk about race and have it be okay and the ways you can talk . . . and really take something away from it."

Classroom discussions of racial issues could pose difficulties for black students beyond the pressure to represent their race. For Brianna, talking about racial issues in class could be disturbing. "People here take everything—especially if you haven't lived it—take readings and approach everything as theory. And it's offensive, because for me, it's not theory." For students like her, the material could be deeply personal, and some white students came to understand how the material might affect their black classmates. Sarah, an affluent white student, remembered taking a class in which students read "this really, really violent book that was about this African American woman that was in all these abusive relationships." She recounted, "[A black student] started crying in class and talking about how this was related to her, and I all of a sudden had this realization that for other people, maybe this wasn't just literature. But for me, it had felt removed."

Some black students chose not to share personal experiences and perspectives on race in the classroom because they found it too frustrating. Whitney, an affluent black student, felt she "*could* set people straight, in a way, in terms of providing a perspective with a racial filter," but at times she chose not to. "Sometimes I'm like, 'What's the point? Do I really feel like arguing with people?' People are going to go and still treat people the same way they did before they entered the class. But other times, I'll just say something." Other black study participants also spoke of pulls they felt to hold back at times in the classroom. To Brandon, discussing a race-related issue in a class with a white professor would make you "a lot less willing to completely open up and bring your personal experience into the discussion because you wouldn't feel that the white professor would be able to relate as well." He went on to say, though:

> Usually, I feel it's my responsibility to step up and enlighten people who may not otherwise find this information out or may not otherwise be able to hear a black person's perspective. Sometimes [I feel] it's a little uncomfortable. But then some other times I just roll with it. It's just one of the reasons why I'm here, and it's one of the reasons that I do take courses like this with other people so that I can bring my opinion and my experience into the discussion.

The sharing did not fall on deaf ears. Half the students, both black and white, reported that they had learned from the personal sharing of students of different races in courses that they took.[20] For Robert, the lower-income white student from a small town way out West, that entailed being made aware by black classmates of how much harder it was for them to blend into the world at Amherst. Relative to black students, he never really struggled to fit in. He came to see that he could go "buy a twenty-dollar polo and . . . look the part" of the affluent white majority, something black classmates could not do. Amy, the lower-income white student from Orlando, saw a film in class about Jack and Jill, an elite, by-invitation-only social group for affluent black youth. The material became real for her when a black student in the class said she belonged to Jack and Jill. "I didn't even know that [group] existed," Amy explained, "and so it was so interesting just hearing that did exist and that she was set up with all these boys, and there are these yearbooks that come out, and you pick out who you knew and where they're going to school and what you think they're going to become—and these family networks intersecting." Emily mentioned black students pointing out to their white classmates that white students "don't know what it feels like to be profiled in a store." That gave her pause. So, too, did a black student's comment that a particular reading was racist, a perspective that Emily had entirely missed.

A number of black students reported learning about race from personal comments made by other black students. Some affluent black students had not experienced much racial discrimination or any privation and benefited from hearing from other black students who had very different experiences. Talia, the affluent black student who grew up in a mixed-race neighborhood in Brooklyn, spoke of a class in which another black female classmate spoke about "racist things that had happened to her and her friends." She continued, "It caused me to see [racism] differently because I had never experienced that kind of racism. I get the 'Oh, you're so educated for a black.' She got something completely different." According to Monica, an affluent black student from Maine, hearing students talk about their backgrounds helped shed light on "how racism has affected some people [although] it hadn't affected me, or how stereotyping has affected them, [something] that I hadn't experienced. I think it's important to know that these things are going on, 'cause I'm sheltered."

Discussion

Many educators and researchers have advocated the importance of having a racially mixed student body.[21] Over a decade ago, William Bowen and Derek Bok, former presidents of Princeton University and Harvard University, respectively, wrote, "Both the growing diversity of American society and the increasing interaction with other cultures worldwide make it evident that going to school with 'the likes of oneself' will be increasingly anachronistic. The advantages of being able to understand how others think and function, to cope across racial divides, and to lead groups composed of diverse individuals are certain to increase."[22] Indeed, cross-racial interaction has been found to facilitate a wide range of educational outcomes.[23] As educational researcher Mitchell Chang puts it, "Students' interpersonal interactions with peers are one of the most powerful educational resources in higher education."[24]

Racial mixing *did* occur at Amherst. Over their four years at the college, almost all of the students in the study reported having gotten to know well two or more classmates of the other race. Through personal connections, shared experiences, and disclosures, many felt they better understood and appreciated those whose life experiences had been unlike their own. But did interacting with and getting to know students of a different race translate into feelings that *learning* about race had taken place? Not necessarily. At the end of their freshman year, a third of the students reported feeling that they had learned from the racial diversity at Amherst. This figure had increased to just over half in the spring of their senior year. While the potential for learning was great, much of that potential was not realized.

Some of the learning about race came from taking courses that addressed race as a primary topic or subtopic. Students who took such courses developed historical perspectives and analytical frameworks for understanding race and racism, and many benefited from the personal perspectives shared in classroom discussions. A great deal of the reported learning occurred through cross-group relationships.

Psychologist Thomas Pettigrew identifies four interrelated processes that help facilitate attitude change and reduce prejudice in intergroup contact situations: learning about members of another group, changing behavior, generating affective ties, and reappraising one's own group.[25] Students in our study showed evidence of all of these processes. Changes occurred in many students' understandings of and beliefs about members of another group. Some students gained a greater understanding of the variability that exists among members of a racial group. They became familiar with the perspectives on race of classmates of a different race and were made more aware of commonalities across race. Some white students showed increased awareness and appreciation of the extent and impact of racial discrimination on black people and of how much race matters. For some, the learning entailed greater insight into the inaccuracies of their racial stereotypes.

Regarding behavioral change and the development of affective ties, half of the white students became more comfortable interacting with black classmates. Students forming cross-race friendships or romantic relationships for the first time were embarking on new behaviors and developing affective connections. The formation of cross-race relationships opened the door to the development of more positive feelings for and deeper attachments to members of another race. Finally, in terms of reappraisal of one's own group, cross-group contact provided some white students with insight into themselves—into how little consciousness they had had of themselves in racial terms[26] and of their racial privilege. Some black students gained more awareness of the variability among members of their own race, as discussed in detail in Chapter 5.

The group that reported the least learning was the affluent white group, which made up the majority of students on campus. This finding has important consequences. In our larger society, people who are affluent and white wield power and influence, as will many affluent white graduates of Amherst. For those alumni to leave Amherst with little awareness of race and how it affects others and themselves is an invaluable opportunity lost, as is departing with little understanding of racial stereotyping, prejudice, and discrimination. If working toward racial understanding and equality is a desired outcome, these missed opportunities have ramifications. Without such learning and awareness, those wealthy white alumni may have little motivation to address these issues in the larger world and make changes.

Many black students graduating from Amherst will also have entrée to positions of power and influence. To assume that they will work to advance racial understanding and be involved in issues of social justice may be a mistaken expectation. Researchers have found that the values and beliefs of ethnic minorities who have risen to the top are not markedly different from their affluent white male counterparts.[27] Thus, it is important for all students, black and white, to learn to understand the experiences of those different from themselves and to develop knowledge about the inequalities that exist in our society. Steps that can be taken to increase students' learning are discussed in Chapter 9. We move now to an examination of what students learned from the class-based diversity at the college.

7

Haves and Have-Nots

Seeing Class Anew

Historically, elite colleges such as Amherst have assumed the role of educating a largely white student body drawn from our society's wealthiest backgrounds. Over the past quarter century, though, Amherst's view of its mission has changed, with concerns about promoting equity, social justice, and social mobility coming to the fore. At first, those concerns centered on racial diversity. More recently they have expanded to include admitting students from across the class spectrum, with strong efforts to recruit more lower-income white students.

The changes in admissions policy reflect more than a desire to open up educational opportunities to students from a wide range of class backgrounds. Having students on campus from different social classes is believed to have educational benefits. Like cross-race interactions, cross-class interactions can provide important opportunities for students to increase their understanding of those different from them and to challenge and possibly change previous class assumptions and prejudices. This belief is not well grounded in research. Numerous researchers have made the case for the educational benefits of *racial* diversity, but little data exist to demonstrate the educational benefits of class diversity. We explain here what our study found in this regard. To what extent did students learn from the socioeconomic diversity in the student body, and what was the nature of that learning?

Cross-Class Relationships

It is useful to begin by looking at whether students formed meaningful cross-class relationships. Most students *did*, in fact. Ninety-six percent of the students in the study (all but one affluent white student and one affluent black student) reported having made a close cross-class relationship. In addition, after four years at the college, almost every affluent student (93 percent) reported getting to know well two or more students from much poorer families than their own, and the same percentage of lower-income students reported that they had gotten to know well two or more students from much wealthier families than their own.[1]

At the end of four years at Amherst, students reported that close to half of their friends came from the same class that they did, whether the students reporting were lower income or affluent.[2] Those proportions had not changed significantly from the end of freshman year.[3] It is interesting to note that while the percentage of friends from the same class was about the same for lower-income and affluent students, only the lower-income students spoke of how important the ties of class were to them and how much they valued closeness with others from similar backgrounds. As Brandon, the lower-income black student from Newark, put it, it is "definitely comforting" to have friends of the same social class. "People with the same social class, they usually come from a similar background and have a similar upbringing. So there's a lot of similarities and common things that are going on in our lives and things to talk about and things that have gone on and things like that." For Marie, the lower-income white student from West Virginia, being of the same social class served as an important bond: "It's nice to have somebody who's doing the same thing, even just really small things like filling out the financial aid forms and complaining together about having to mail things back and forth six times to get parents' signatures on everything. It helps to have friends who are the same social class so that you don't ever have issues of somebody wants to go to Puerto Rico for spring break, and somebody wants to do something less expensive."

When it came to dating, 59 percent of the students reported having dated someone from a very different class background than their own. This pattern held true for two-thirds of the students in the two affluent groups and the same large fraction among the lower-income white group. The one group that experienced markedly less dating out of class was the lower-income black group, with only 39 percent reporting having dated someone wealthier.[4]

On the basis of these numbers on friendships and dating, it is quite clear that close contact between students of different social classes was a reality for the majority of students on campus. Did that contact result in learning? Not necessarily. When, after four years, students were asked whether living in a diverse community had changed their view of people of other classes or their own, 56 percent said yes.[5] The percentage was comparable to that reported at the end of freshman year,[6] although the learning may have deepened over the four years.

Stereotypes, Prejudice, and Change

Close to half of the students in the study (45 percent) reported that they had heard incorrect assumptions made about them on the basis of their social class, and all of the assumptions were negative.[7] The remarks surfaced in face-to-face encounters and in classroom discussions. Strikingly, 80 percent of all the students in the study heard negative assumptions made about wealthy students,[8] while only 30 percent heard them made about poor students.[9] It is impossible to know whether that was because students held less prejudicial beliefs about lower-income students or because it was less socially acceptable to express negative stereotypes about them than about their wealthy classmates.

Stereotypes of the Wealthy

Wealthy students were subject to being characterized by both lower-income and other affluent students as "arrogant," "very snobby," "stuck up," "haughty," "very materialistic," and "sheltered and pretentious and obnoxious." They were seen to have "off-putting personalities," to "act very spoiled," to "show off their wealth," to "take everything for granted," to "live in a world of their own," and to "only hang out with kids who are extremely wealthy." Affluent girls in particular were viewed as "snotty"—as people who "go shopping all the time" and "would exclude people based on class issues" or be "all about keeping people out." Wealthy students "never clean up their stuff" and "expect others to clean up after them." Because of their wealth, it was presumed that they "don't take their education as seriously" and "don't really care about school" because "their parents will hook them up with a job." "Their futures were assured," "they'll be taken care of," or "they'll just inherit money."

Joking was one way that students expressed their resentment toward wealthy students. Just over two-thirds of students reported hearing the rich ridiculed,[10] hearing "sarcastic comments about the trust fund kids," and hearing about students whose "parents pay for everything." The young man who kept a "stock of expensive liquor" and the young woman whose parents had a helicopter were subject to derisive comments. When an issue about expenses came up, it was suggested "humorously" of a wealthy student, "Oh, why doesn't *he* pay for all this?" Joking at the expense of the poor, on the other hand, was heard by only 31 percent of the students.[11]

Joking aside, some lower-income students looked disparagingly on their wealthy classmates. Dana, the lower-income black student from a largely Caribbean neighborhood in Queens, spoke of a student whose mother, an interior designer, had "just completely decked out her room. She has a thirty-inch plasma screen TV on her wall, and her mom painted it because they can afford to pay the dorm-damage fines. She has all this elaborate furniture. Someone was walking by the room talking about how ridiculous it is, how all these rich people have so much money to waste." Martin, a lower-income black student from Oakland, recalled with disdain a wealthy girl from New York who lived on his floor freshman year: "She had a maid at home. She just couldn't just take care of her stuff when she was here. Her room was in just disarray; the floor was covered with things. She would leave her stuff everywhere. She'd leave her two-thousand-dollar laptop just sitting in the common room for days at a time. We would joke about how she couldn't get along without her maid. It wasn't meant to be hurtful, but it was just ridiculous."

Pejorative stereotypes of wealthy students were given voice anonymously on the Confessional, the student online forum where students were "calling people [out] on their wealth." One extremely wealthy student was targeted with criticism, becoming "the reference for the stereotypical 'really, really rich quadruple legacy person who is not actually very smart but is here because his parents give twenty million dollars to the school' kind of person." Wealthy athletes were a subset of the affluent subjected to verbal attack. Dana had read on the Confessional "tons of comments disparaging wealthy jocks. People have this stereotype of the jocks that come to Amherst, that they have money and they're not that great at sports, but their parents have the money so they can come to Amherst and play sports and not do well in classes." The lacrosse players were for some students "the epicenter of this group of wealth," displaying that wealth "proudly, mostly through choice of clothes and what alcohol they drink—the prep-school, old-money category." Hanging out with them were the "richer girls" and "the rich kids who don't play lacrosse."

Reduction in Stereotypes of the Wealthy

Over the course of college, as they got to know students from wealthy families, many lower-income students came to see the variability in the character and values of their affluent classmates. Speaking of the learning she experienced by interacting with wealthy students at Amherst and the effects that learning had on her, Tanya, the lower-income white student from Brighton Beach, reflected:

> I'm almost certainly less likely to make any broad generalization about people from that class, especially since I know [a wealthy friend] so well. And I know other people who are of that class that are not at all anything that you would assume, any of those kinds of generalizations that I've heard made. . . . I hope that I am less likely to jump to conclusions about people when I find out what their

social class is, [less likely to assume] that they don't really have to work for things as hard, [that] things sort of just fall into their laps.

Tanya was not alone. The following statements are some examples of the takeaway messages about class assumptions that lower-income students voiced: "You can't make a lot of generalizations based on people's lives or privilege. . . . I resist [stereotyping] because I've learned so much about different people that you could say were from similar [wealthy] backgrounds but have been affected in very different ways from those similar backgrounds"; "If anything, it's maybe broken down some of those stereotypes from when I first got here"; "People are individuals. Their socioeconomic classification does say something about them, but it doesn't say everything about them. So I think maybe that's changed. . . . I realize that generalizations are just that—general—and that there are individuals"; "I feel like I'm more tolerant, or I try not to pass judgment as easily, or I don't assume anything because all of my assumptions tend to be wrong"; "[I've gained] a little bit more sympathy" for people from other socioeconomic backgrounds and an ability to "empathize a lot more" with them.

Amber, a lower-income white student from Pittsfield, Massachusetts, came to Amherst believing that rich kids felt that "they have all the money in the world. They can do whatever they want. They have no limitations. They have no restrictions." In getting to know some wealthy students, she discovered that her stereotype was "not necessarily true." She explained, "Now I know that it really depends on the person and the parents and their upbringing." Marie, the lower-income white student from West Virginia, had arrived on campus thinking that "all wealthy students have parents who give them as much spending money as they need. In reality there are some wealthy students who have a lot more than everybody else, but . . . there's not a huge amount of disparity in disposable income." Emily's assumption about her wealthy classmates centered on the notion that with money came a problem-free life. But "making friends with people who are of those [wealthy] classes, you see a lot of the problems."

A number of lower-income students reported change in their notion that the rich invariably display their wealth. Trina had gone to an elite private high school in New York City attended largely by "very, *very* wealthy students," many of whom were "all about showing off . . . wealth." Getting to know wealthy students at Amherst and "hearing somebody who's honestly wealthy not being caught up in proving it all the time . . . was very eye-opening" to her. Robert, the lower-income white student from a small town out West, told of an edifying visit to a friend's home. It turned out that his friend's family was extremely wealthy, something Robert had been unaware of. The discovery led to greater respect for this friend, "who could afford polo shirts and could drive a BMW and all this stuff, but he chooses not to. . . . He doesn't really need to show off his money." Marie developed a relationship with a wealthy male friend that "probably lessened some stereotypes" she had about wealthier people, "just because he's pretty down-to-earth, and he doesn't really spend more money, even though he has more. People from different amounts of money don't necessarily live all that differently."

Another characterization of affluent students, that they were all "so elitist, such snobs" or "stuck up," could not be sustained over four years at Amherst, as lower-income students discovered that many of their wealthy classmates were "just regular people." "I've lost the stereotype or the stigma that every rich person I meet is going to be a jerk," noted Cory, a lower-income black student. Robert brought with him the stereotype of the rich as "snobby." He explained, "And some people I've met have reinforced that, and some people I've met have made me realize that it's not where they're from or how much money they have but who they *are*. I wouldn't categorize them all together, but then there are the few kids that give the whole group a bad name."

Some lower-income students, assuming that they themselves would be judged negatively on the basis of their social class, worried about the kinds of prejudices that wealthy students might hold toward them. Tanya, the lower-income white student from Brighton Beach, had harbored those concerns but soon learned that a person's social class "doesn't really matter to them. . . . They are not going to judge you based on that. They are going to judge you as a person." Brandi, a lower-income black student, had a similar experience:

> I was going to come to Amherst, and I was going to meet a whole bunch of jerks who were like, "You're poor, and you're lesser than me." And then you get here, and actually, people don't invest that much time to judge you on your income. . . . I definitely feel like a lot of preconceived notions people have get dispelled, or confirmed, depending on your *friends*. The people I'm friends with were never the type to make you feel uncomfortable.

One more notion held by some lower-income students that could not be sustained in the face of experience was the belief that they could not have relationships with their wealthy classmates. Marc came to see that he could "have a completely normal, completely healthy, and great relationship" with students outside his social class, in part because he realized the wealthy "are not just all about themselves and money." The message Dana received growing up in her family was "Try not to hang out with the kids who are too rich because they'll make you feel badly about yourself." Her church gave her a similar message:

> "Try to stay away from the really wealthy families, because their families are stuck-up, and they'll treat you really badly." . . . I was

among a group of people who assumed all rich people were arrogant, entitled. Being at Amherst, I see both ends. Maybe there are people who act like that without realizing it, but in general, it's not fair to make that assumption about anybody. Most of the people who are upper class are just regular people.

Stereotypes about the Poor

Stereotypes about the poor were less frequently voiced on campus than were stereotypes about the wealthy, but it is interesting to note that lower-income students were three times more likely to report having heard assumptions about the poor than were their affluent classmates (48 percent versus 15 percent).[12] Perhaps lower-income students were more attuned, more sensitive, than affluent students to assumptions made about the poor and to slights directed at the less privileged. In any event, the stereotypes voiced about the poor were quite similar to the stereotypes of black people, which is perhaps not surprising given the strong association in our larger society between race and class.

The following are some of the characterizations of poor people that students in the study had either heard on campus or read on the Confessional. The poor were assumed to "come from broken homes" and to be "exposed to more crime and violence." They "don't have anything," their communities were like "a third world country," and they might well have lived in "a dark apartment, bunch of kids running around, parents never there." As for the fit between Amherst and the poor, they "don't belong," were "not qualified," and "don't deserve to be here." They were "not as smart," "can't be educated," and "can't be intelligent." The consequences of admitting more low-income students to the college would be that "we'd have to slow down things for them," and that "we'[d] have to add remedial classes for all the poor kids." The poor were described on occasion as "white trash," "redneck," "hick," "hillbilly," "inferior," and "cheap." These class-based put-downs could be directed at the staff as well as at fellow students. Robert, the lower-income white student, noted that he had never heard someone "from a working-class background make a comment about the staff at Val or the custodial staff the way that [he had] seen some people from wealthier, privileged families make comments."

Hearing pejorative remarks about the poor could arouse considerable anger among some lower-income students. Trina often found herself "on the offensive" when she heard what she felt were demeaning remarks based on class. She recalled a time when she overheard someone in her hall talking with his friend, reporting that he owned two hundred T-shirts: "He's like, 'I was going to give some away, but what would poor people do with an Armani Exchange?' I said, 'Are you kidding me? . . . You obviously live a very privileged life, and your conscience or your social guilt is probably telling you to give some of this away. But you're worried what the poor people are going to do? Like their body can't wear an Armani Exchange shirt because they're poor?' I almost killed him."

Brianna spoke of a conversation in which students were joking and laughing about homeless people "like it's just the funniest thing in the world." One student said, "I don't like homeless people. They're dirty." Brianna found the comments extremely offensive and set out to inform these classmates:

> I didn't yell at them. I was just, "Firstly, you're talking about a person, not a dog on the street. Secondly, I'm sure if they had the choice, they would want to be clean, but it's not always an option." And they're like, "No, they can be clean. Why don't they go to a shelter and shower? Why don't they just move in with their family? My family would never let me be homeless." And yadda, yadda, yadda. I said, "Firstly, shelters are very dangerous places. And on top of that, you're talking about people with dignity. They don't want to be treated like children. They don't want to have a curfew, 'cause you're talking about adults here. In a lot of cases, they don't have family [to live with]." I think a lot of people have this view of homeless people—like drunk, alcoholic men. *I* used to be homeless, when I was four and I was leaving an abusive relationship with my dad. And [my mother] had nowhere to go and couldn't support two children on her own. And is that her fault? Ya know, no. So it was just really making me mad, and I'm trying to explain this to them.

Brianna felt an "obligation to be the voice of the unheard" as "one of very few people" from her socioeconomic background who attended "one of these elite colleges."

What impact, if any, exchanges such as those that Trina and Brianna described had on the other students is, unfortunately, an unknown. What we do know is that hardly any students in the study spoke explicitly of stereotypes about the poor being disproved. Alexander, an affluent white student was an exception. "I guess going to Amherst, where everyone is very smart, you can see that you've got smart people from every social class," he said. Alexander had entered college assuming "that people who were poor were not as smart. . . . Now I might still expect that, but maybe not quite as much. I wouldn't be surprised at all to find anyone [smart] from any social class."

Unreliability of Class Markers

"Looks can be deceiving in terms of social class," observed a student, providing another example of learning. While all students in the study could point to markers of social class, almost half (43 percent) became aware that those "markers" could be inaccurate—that class could be difficult to discern from them.[13] Remarks such as these were common: "The vast majority of people do a good job of not being 'showy' with how much money they have or how little money they have"; "Don't judge a book by its cover. Every now and then you're surprised."

An obvious, visible indicator of class was dress. Or was it? One student observed that wealthy students "might wear a lot of stuff from thrift stores." Marc had a friend from an affluent family who "never really flaunted his social class at all. He dressed very plainly. . . . If you were to talk to him or see him, you would think he was just a regular kid, not superrich or super-*anything*." Rebecca, a lower-income white student from a big city, had wealthy friends who "just dress very casual. They don't have to have brand name stuff and necessarily show everybody. So if you just looked at them, it would be hard to tell what their social class is." She herself loved shopping, used her earnings on dress, and was mistaken by wealthy friends as being wealthier than she was because, as she put it, "I wear not expensive but *nice* clothes." Robert reported that his own wardrobe had changed since he had come to Amherst. He had purchased polo shirts in order to "fit in" on campus. Polo shirts suggested affluence, in contrast to T-shirts, which signaled lower income. "It's tough for people to tell what class I'm from. Some days I'll wear the polo. Maybe people make assumptions. Another day I'll wear my T-shirt, and maybe they're making a different assumption."

Class assumptions based on travel could also be deceptive. Some lower-income students whose parents were immigrants had traveled abroad to see relatives. A lower-income black student was totally taken aback to discover that a brilliant classmate who spoke four or five different languages and had traveled was not, in fact, wealthy. "You'd never guess that he lived in a trailer in Texas somewhere" and that without his scholarships he would not have had the means to travel.

How much or how little spending a student did on campus could be another misleading indicator. One student reported discovering that "the friend whose parents probably earn the most was the one who seemed [to have] the least money to spend." As for any direct correlation between having a job on campus and class, another student noted, "Some of the wealthiest kids I know have campus jobs." That perception was correct. No class differences existed in the hours students reported working at a job per week.[14]

Class Awareness

Learning about social class took forms other than a reduction in stereotypes. For many students, interactions with classmates from across the class spectrum heightened their awareness of social class and increased their understanding of the impact of class in shaping people's lives. Many affluent students came to Amherst having given little previous thought to class. "I just didn't really notice," William, an affluent black student, stated. He went on to note that he had become "more aware of social classes in general, what people have and what people don't have." Another affluent student spoke of coming to recognize how social class "affects people's lives" and the "different opportunities people have because of social class." For Alexander, a wealthy white student, conversations with a lower-income friend who had faced a very different reality from his expanded his "recognition of there being other people out there." Over the course of college, Anthony, a lower-income black student from upstate New York, came to believe that social class played a larger role than race in the treatment of black people and that racism was more about black people being poor than about their being black. "While I think that racism still exists in some forms, I think that nowadays it's much more about social class. And maybe that is because Amherst is very open and nonjudgmental about race, in my opinion. . . . Therefore, the judging is done based on your class instead. When I was younger, I used to think that race had more to do with people's similarities and differences, and now I feel that it is 95 percent about your social class, upbringing, background, etc., and has very little to do with race."

For some affluent students, getting to know classmates who had to worry about money was eye-opening. These wealthy students were confronted with their own privilege, something they may well have taken for granted, and with the realities that those with so much less means had to struggle with. Learning about low-income classmates' experiences helped one affluent student "understand how dire their situations can be sometimes." It was something the student "didn't really have a grasp of . . . before." For another student, a connection with a person who lived with financial hardship was, she said, "one of those moments where I [had] never really had to look outside of my situation, and that forced me to, and see someone else's experience." David, the affluent white student from Washington, D.C., had gotten "a better sense of what it's like to really have to worry about money all the time, a better sense of what it's like to not be able to afford things like books." As a freshman, Matthew listened to the struggles his freshman roommate had been through, living on his own and supporting himself through his final two years of high school. Those struggles were, Matthew said, "something I've never had to think about really. And it does open your eyes to what's out there." As a senior, Matthew controlled the money for an extracurricular organization he belonged to, as well as for the apartment he lived in off campus.

> So every week I have very, very meaningful conversations with kids who are saying, "I want to be a part of this; I can't pay, so how can we work this out?" And it's really hard. The hardest thing I've done at Amherst by far is dealing with those issues. You don't really realize how much disposable income gap there is between the

median and the bottom. It's startling. I'll try to help them create payment plans, and I'll say, "Well, how about twenty dollars a week?" or something like that. And while for me, that's like, "Oh yeah, twenty dollars a week—I have a campus job; I make that easily. But for them, "I have my campus job, but that money goes toward tuition and eating and books." They literally cannot work another hour to make [a] five-dollars-a-week contribution. So you really understand the gap better from that seat.

Matthew and other wealthy students reported ways in which they gained new appreciation for how financial need affects questions about whether to attend college. Matthew had a lower-income friend who had taken time off from Amherst to help support his family. Matthew himself had never thought about the "cost of going to school for your family. It's not just the *tuition*." He noted, "For my family it's not a big deal that I'm not working and contributing to buying food. But for his family it's a big deal. It's the lost production." Another affluent student was struck to learn that some classmates were fulfilling the requirements for medical school because they needed to "make lots of money because their parents need their money. It puts it in a different light." The student said, "I just think a little more carefully about the reasons that people are doing things." Along similar lines, other affluent students reported becoming aware that some lower-income friends felt "an obligation" to major in something that would enable them to make enough money to support parents, felt "more of an urgency to be successful," and were not as free to take courses that were not "on point" or would not be useful in the job market. There was a sense for some affluent students that because some of their lower-income classmates' families struggled to help pay for their education, those classmates appreciated the opportunity more than they, the wealthy, did. In contrast, as one student from wealth put it, affluent students "seem to take their education for granted." The student continued, "I think it's definitely made me more aware that there are a lot of people out there with backgrounds different from my own."

From her perspective as a lower-income student, Emily was struck by how a wealthier friend's family did not take his education for granted and how concerned they were about his academic work. If her friend did not do well, Emily said, "his parents are like, 'What's going on?' and 'We need to talk about this. And you need to study.' And my parents could care less."

The effects of the 2008 stock market crash on an extremely affluent friend and his family were surprising to Corey, the lower-income black student from New Bedford, Massachusetts. He described his friend as "very, *very* wealthy":

His family comes from a lot of money. He was just talking to me about a conversation he had with his father. He's like, "My dad lost $180,000 today," some really big number. That was the first time I thought, "Oh, I'm not suffering from being in that tier of wealth, because my family isn't that wealthy." So we talked about [how] that's something he has to think about. From my perspective, I would never think if you have money, you have to worry about money. But his dad *is* worried, and that worries *him*. So that was a meaningful conversation. I didn't expect it at all.

As touched on previously, many affluent students gained a new perspective on *themselves* and their lifestyles through relationships with friends of another class. One affluent student stated, "Hearing about other people's obstacles over the past few years has definitely opened my eyes in a lot of ways. . . . It's just made me look at how my family spends money." A wealthy student shared an apartment over the summer with a lower-income friend who "didn't want to spend too much on food because he wanted to be able to go out, and things like that." She had never thought about food "as something [she] should skimp on at all." Another affluent student looked at the kind of activities his friend group did through the eyes of a lower-income friend and saw how much those activities involved spending money and the burden that placed on lower-income students. Talia, the affluent black student from Brooklyn, said, "[Lower-income friends] call me spoiled. They say I'm sheltered. They say I have no concept of money, things like that." Talia did not have a job on campus, and her parents did not want her to work. "They pretty much give me an allowance, and I like to splurge sometimes." She came to see that her friends' depiction of her "isn't completely far off," although she felt their judgment of her was "a little unfair."

Her friendship with a lower-income student led Marissa, the affluent black student from Chicago, to reexamine her own lifestyle, in terms of the money she was spending and the things she was taking for granted, because her friend, she said, "saves every receipt from everywhere and keeps them in an envelope. She's impeccably organized. She's the master of her own life in a way." Marissa continued, "All these things that I'm depending on other people to do for me, or to remind me about, or to help me with, she does on her own." The relationship changed the way Marissa saw herself. Aware of "the sheer difficulties" her friend contended with, Marissa was struck by the advantages that she, Marissa, lived with. For example, she said, "[I could just] call home and ask my mom to send me something I need, and it will be there in three or four days. I know how special that is, but I didn't *always* know it. Now I do. . . . I've seen the degree to which I am not independent."

Examples of affluent students gaining an awareness of their many unearned privileges in relation to lower-income peers are numerous and varied. These privileges included "being able to attend a private school," "being able to travel," having "a lovely house," not having "a mortgage on our house," being "tutored for the SATs," having "the computer in my room," and having educated parents. They spoke of "not having to work at all . . . in high school," of "the security of money," of taking money for granted, of not having to contribute financially to their education, of "coming out of school debt-free," of having a savings account, of having "insurance and doctors," of having money "poured" into them, and of having no worries about money for food.

Living with students who could not afford to go home for a weekend or holidays made some wealthy students very aware of their own economic privilege. And as graduation approached, and students faced a difficult job market because of the recession, affluent students realized that the cushion they could fall back on, financial support from their parents, was not an option for many of their classmates. Lower-income students, for the most part, had to become self-sufficient immediately after graduation. While wealthy students could "take unpaid internships because they can afford it," some wealthy students were aware that that was not an option for their less-privileged friends.

The following observations made by David, the affluent white student from Washington, D.C., serve as a good summation of the kind of learning about themselves that some affluent students experienced. He said, "[I came to see] how privileged I am to be able to do the things that I do or to be able to go on vacations and not think as much about money, as I know some people really do. We all think about money, but to be able to know that at the end of the day, even when I don't have a lot of money or you say, 'Oh, I'm really broke right now,' I'm not, comparatively. I'm fine. I can still afford to do things. I'm not in fear of going into massive debt." David realized that when he got his paycheck for his campus job, which he put toward his rent, he did not have to worry about how to divide it: "I didn't have to say, 'I know I need to pay rent, but I really need to pay credit card bills and debt and loans.'"

Perception of Class Identification

Some students learned that their perception of their economic status could be influenced by those around them. Attending private high schools with much wealthier classmates led some affluent students to enter Amherst thinking of themselves as not well-off. Once at the college, with its economic diversity, that perception changed. As one student noted, "The way you think about your class depends so much on the people you grow up around and wealth you're exposed to." Sarah, the affluent white student from Westchester County, had gone to high school with extremely wealthy students: "I felt in high school that I was on the lower spectrum, because my family didn't have as much money as most people I went to high school with. So I felt that I was very middle class. And then I got to Amherst, and I realized whereas I felt disadvantaged in my high school, here I feel I'm pretty advantaged. I learned that I was a lot more affluent than I thought I was." As Sarah was growing up, her parents talked a great deal about "how [they] didn't have enough money and how everything was so expensive": "I felt very excluded from things. . . . People would go for shopping sprees and spend two thousand dollars on their mother's credit card. When I came here, it took me a little while to figure out that that was no longer the dynamic and that my family, while we weren't superrich, we were probably upper middle class." Sarah came to view her wealthy community as "a real bubble, and it's really hard to see outside the bubble." Katherine, an affluent white student from Montclair, New Jersey, came to recognize at college that her family was from a higher social class than she had thought. She knew her family was "well-off" but said, "We're not a family that flaunts it a lot, so I always used to think we were just middle class because that's what everyone says they are. And then I started having to fill forms [asking,] 'What's your yearly income?'And I'd have to go to the top one. I was like, 'What?'"

Katelyn, the affluent white student from Phoenix, had an unusual perspective on her social class before she entered Amherst. The students in her middle school were from very different class backgrounds from those in her high school. Katelyn had been one of the lowest-income students in "a very, very wealthy middle school." But her view of her economic status shifted when she entered a very low-income high school. "I was very upper class there. Coming to Amherst reinforced that I'm not actually lower class compared to most people. I have someone paying for my tuition. I have someone I could ask for money." At Amherst, Katelyn's sense of her social-class position varied depending on the class of the friends with whom she was interacting. While she knew that she was not from a lower socioeconomic class, she sometimes lost sight of that when she was surrounded by extremely wealthy students. Talking to her lower-income friends brought back an awareness of her affluence.

Some lower-income students gained an appreciation of the relative privilege *they* had when they compared themselves to classmates whose economic circumstances were worse. Amy had a friend who came from a family with less money than hers. She explained, "I don't go out all the time. I don't have a house on the Cape. But I also am not really, really struggling. I'm working so that if I want to go out or do something, I have some spending money. But *she* was working because she had to pay for housing and room and board and tuition here. And so when I would complain, I would think twice before I would say something. So I definitely learned."

For students like Emily, who grew up in a rural community with little class variability, lack of contact with people of wealth meant her basis for comparison was to people of similar means. As a consequence, she observed, "I definitely thought I was middle class, [an] average person, when I came here." But at Amherst, Emily got to know students with considerable wealth, and when comparing her family to families of wealthy classmates, her perception of her own social class shifted: "It's definitely been an eye-opening thing to slide down the ladder and to realize where you fit in it all, [to realize] maybe you aren't where you thought you were."

Acquiring Exposure and Cultural Capital

Getting to know classmates from wealthy backgrounds not only made some lower-income students aware of their own relative lack of financial resources but also gave them direct exposure to a world of wealth and privilege that they might otherwise have known only through the media. When she arrived at Amherst, Emily realized, "I knew nothing about the outside world. I grew up very isolated, among people who were only of my class, and they only did the things that were available in my town." She learned a great deal from wealthy classmates "who have gone to different parts of the world and who have done so much more and just have different experiences." She gained an appreciation of private schools. People in Emily's home community could not afford private school and could not imagine why anyone would even consider that option. In getting to know students who had gone to prep schools and private day schools Emily came to see that those students "really did have a lot of opportunities and a lot of advantages" that she had not had access to.

Over time, lower-income students acquired new forms of cultural capital, including knowledge, credentials, skills, and connections that would enable them to become part of the world of the affluent. They learned how to "interact with people from different groups" and "how to be around people with money." They learned the rules—"what you need to do or what people have done to get where they want to go." Lower-income students talked of learning new cultural references, such as "the Upper East Side" of New York or "the Hamptons," and of gaining knowledge about different prep schools, a cappella singing groups, designer labels, sailing yachts off Cape Cod—the way the world worked for those with wealth. In thinking about "folks with a lot of money," Marc now felt he had a sense of "how their life is structured." Some lower-income students spoke of gaining an appreciation for what getting a degree from Amherst meant to the larger world they were about to enter, commenting that "if they weren't at a school like Amherst, they might not have access to the same jobs."

For some lower-income students, the Career Center also played an important role in their acculturation. Robert had attended an "etiquette dinner" given by the center. He explained, "A professional etiquette coach came in to go over some of the basics of fine dining and how to carry yourself and writing thank-you notes for interviews." But he was quick to add, "At the same time, I can go back home and eat macaroni and cheese," a remark that harks back to the issues of living in two worlds. Students talked of learning how to dress for interviews, getting practice being interviewed, getting help writing resumes, and learning that "this is how to act;

this is how to do everything." Alisa, the lower-income black student from Mississippi, had attended workshops on interviewing. "I still need to work on those skills, but it's been helpful," she commented. She had learned "the proper handshake—how [it's] the grip that matters. And then the small talk before or during or right after, just to get people to like you. And then definitely making sure you ask questions because it makes you seem interested. And just tips—like drink coffee, be really energetic right before, and stuff like that." These approaches and behaviors were utterly new to her.

The importance of connections to future success was a revelation to many lower-income students.[15] They observed their affluent classmates use parents, other family members, family friends, and Amherst alumni to help them get interviews that led to excellent preprofessional summer jobs and internships and to postgraduation job offers. Through the college Career Center, some lower-income students learned that their professors and the Amherst alumni could provide them with connections to job opportunities. The Career Center provided listings of all alumni and the professions they were in and hosted meetings with alumni coming to campus to talk about their professions. Alicia, a lower-income black student, met on campus with the founder of a company. She was offered a stipend to go to New York for three weeks to work for that alumna, which, in turn, led to Alicia being asked to go to Africa over the summer. She explained, "The alumni connections that we're encouraged to make are generally with alumni who have been successful. Their success is based on wealth. Those are generally the ones who are able to come back to the school and able to interact with us. And so those are the people we meet and who we aspire to be and who we get connections with—alumni who are CEOs, and even CEOs of NGOs, nongovernmental organizations."

Emily had had no understanding of the importance of connections when she got to Amherst, and she realized after four years how important they could be—and that she had not built them. In her senior-year search for jobs, Emily had gone to the Career Center to find out about possibilities. She remarked, "It's just hard because a lot of the times they tell you, 'Your classmates are some of the best opportunities that you have. Look to them and find out what their parents do, and a lot of times especially they'll have Amherst grad parents who are even more willing [to help].'" Emily's core friendships were with students from her social class. She had not networked and did not have any close relationships with professors. She did, however, have one valued connection: "I babysit for a woman who works in alumni affairs, and she's been really helpful getting me alumni names and people to contact."

Increased Self-Acceptance

A few students spoke of gaining greater acceptance of their class position. Matthew, affluent by the standards of this study, had attended high school at Deerfield Academy, where he was surrounded by *extremely* wealthy students. He said, "I looked up to those kids and wanted to be them so much [and felt] very much pushed to the side because of my social class." Arriving at Amherst, Matthew thought, "Now I can be them because nobody knows who I am or where I'm from. . . . I pretended almost to be wealthier than I was." Initially, he sought friendships with students who were wealthy. But his experiences with diversity at the college led Matthew to undergo a change in values and perspective on wealth and social class. He came to feel that social class "doesn't matter." He elaborated, "What people like about you has nothing to do with wealth. Certainly, it makes things easier in life, but people want to know who you really are, and that's what matters most. . . . My time at Amherst has really shown me that you've just got to act like who you are; trying to be something different for whatever reason is not good for you." He came to see, too, that he had idealized what it meant to be wealthy: "You always see it as the grass is greener up there . . . but there are things wrong up there, too."

Rebecca, a lower-income white student, came to similar realizations about her own social-class position and class more generally:

> I don't feel that I am any less for not being upper class. I don't think that that makes me any less important or any less valuable. I don't think that class defines who you are. And maybe when I was in high school, I was a little more naive about that. I would have been much more impressed about someone who was wealthy—and had a lot of things that I wanted and couldn't have. But now I'm not so impressed anymore. I have a few friends that are extremely wealthy, and I learned not to compare myself with people of a different class and say, "Oh, look what I don't have. Poor me. I feel bad for myself." I don't do that anymore, because in being friends with them, I learned that even though they can pretty much have whatever they want, they have a lot of upsets and disappointments, too, over things they can't control. So I don't think that how much money you have or your class, where you fall in the category of social class, defines you as a person.

Recognizing Commonalities across Class

"People aren't that different just based on social class. It doesn't have as much of an influence as sometimes you'd expect it to have," one student commented. With friends, another student observed, the difference in class background "doesn't really set us apart as much as I otherwise would have assumed." These two students' remarks, reporting their unanticipated sense of commonality across class, were echoed by a number of other students, both lower-income and wealthy. As noted previously, when Dana, a lower-income black student, came to Amherst, she "assumed all rich people were arrogant, entitled." She was wary of approaching someone from a different class background, worried about whether they would have anything in common. Over the course of her freshman year, she began to ask herself, "Are we really that different? I don't think we are." As a senior she had come to feel that "most of the people who are upper class are just regular people." Interestingly, Dana's recognition of commonalities among people regardless of class extended to at least one classmate, a close friend, who grew up in much *worse* circumstances than hers. That friend was from "a *very* lower-class background" and had grown up "without her parents, because her mom was in jail and her dad was in rehab most of the time." "It was just an interesting experience getting to know her and hearing about her experiences," she explained. "I remember freshman year she would tell me about things going on in her family, and it would sound like a really intense movie. Then I realized she's a regular person like me, just with a lot more obstacles."

The following are some other lower-income students' remarks about what they learned: "A lot of our families are the same. We just have a different amount of zeroes behind our checks"; "Some of the richest people can be accepting of people who aren't as rich. That's a good thing, to see that they're normal people." Echoing that insight, another student observed, "They're just normal people. . . . A lot of them are very similar to me; it's just they have more money." Nicole, the lower-income white student from rural Illinois, became friends with a wealthy white male classmate. While differences existed between them, which she saw as class based, she had come to this conclusion: "There aren't really that many *fundamental* differences. . . . While he may oppose unions for whatever reason based on his background, I'm for them for whatever reasons, based on mine."

Commonalities across class were noted by students on the other end of the class spectrum as well. Kevin, the affluent black student from Orange County, California, said, "I realized that no matter what social class you're in, people have ups and downs in life. Good things happen to rich people, and bad things happen to rich people, just as good things happen to poor people, and bad things happen to poor people in their lives." Some affluent students came to Amherst with the assumption that class would be easy to discern in a person—that there were particular characteristics attached to a particular class. Benjamin, the affluent white student from of Hastings, New York, was one of those students. His friendship with a lower-income female student disabused him of that notion, as he learned that "social class doesn't bear much on personality or taste." He concluded, "I couldn't distinguish her from the daughter of millionaires."

Classroom Learning

Beyond the learning that occurred through informal interactions with peers from different class backgrounds, students had the opportunity to learn about social class through the curriculum. The college offered a course titled "Social Class" in the Sociology Department. That course held little interest for affluent students—only one affluent white student and one affluent black student chose to take it. The course was more attractive to lower-income students but drew twice as many lower-income white students as lower-income black students (36 percent versus 17 percent).[16] Black students showed a greater interest in studying race than they did in studying issues of social class, as three-quarters of black students took courses specifically about black people or Africa.

In addition to the sociology course, courses existed in ten other departments, as well as in the freshman seminar program, that addressed class as a subtopic. Just over half the students in the study took one of these courses, but the distribution of students by class was not even. Three times as many lower-income students as affluent students (74 percent versus 26 percent) took one of these courses.[17] Even with half of the students getting *some* classroom exposure, at the end of four years, only 17 percent of students reported that they had learned about social class through the curriculum. Not surprisingly, almost twice as many lower-income students as affluent students reported this learning experience (21 percent versus 12 percent).[18] Overall, social class as a subtopic in a single course did not have much impact on students' assessments of their learning.

For some lower-income students, however, the courses they took that addressed social class provided some of the most important learning experiences they had at the college. Reflecting on his classroom exposure to issues of class, Robert offered this assessment:

> The most prominent thing in my mind that I've learned at Amherst or that I thought about the most would be social class. I don't know if it's important for everyone else to learn [about] it, but I think it's one of those things that everyone's aware of but nobody talks about, in American culture especially. And after reading all this material and going to all these classes, it boggles my mind that it's not a more salient issue in American society.

As an example of what he learned, Robert noted, "There are certain social forces that create barriers for some and opportunities for others." That was a new and important awareness for him.

Understanding the structure and function of class hierarchies and the reproduction of social class is not the type of learning that typically occurs through informal relationships. Courses on social class were important to lower-income students like Emily because through those courses they gained an analytical framework for understanding their families and society. "I have learned so much about how the country works," Emily reported, "and how wealth distribution works and things like that."

Another way that courses were able to inform students about social class was through the personal sharing that took place among the students in those classes. That sharing could be hard emotionally for some lower-income students. Marie, from West Virginia, said that in some classes she withheld details of her family's difficult circumstances. "If we're having a discussion about social class, then I might identify myself as lower income, but I probably wouldn't go into a whole lot of depth about parents searching for jobs." In contrast, Emily felt obliged to speak as a representative of her social class, "to represent a group of people that isn't necessarily talked about here." Nicole, the lower-income white student from rural Illinois, said, "Hopefully, in some of my classes I have also been able to contribute a different perspective and a different analysis of problems based on my experiences." She felt that other lower-income students, too, would bring in personal experiences "as a way to temper generalizations people were saying."

Brianna found sharing her personal class perspective very difficult at the start of college, but she became increasingly comfortable with and proficient at doing so over her years there. Early on, Brianna noted, "I wasn't able to say what I wanted to say, and I wasn't able to get the point across that I was thinking. . . . In my four years here, I've become more verbal and more expressive—and more adept at debating with people and expressing 'I disagree' with them and being able to continue a dialogue with them in a classroom."

What impact did the sharing of different class perspectives have on students' learning? In contrast to the low number of students who felt they learned about class through the curriculum, two in five students reported having learned something about social class from personal sharing in the classroom. They found it, for example, "interesting and enriching."[19] Hearing the personal experience of a lower-income classmate gave Julian, the affluent black student from Baltimore, a view into a world far from the one he grew up in and left a strong impression. The student, Julian said, "told his story. He was from the 'hood, and he's the first person in the family to go to college. And that was valuable because I don't know what that's like."

Talia, an affluent black student, spoke of a student in a sociology course who opened up a lot about her personal experience. The student was poor and Latino. Talia reported, "It was just another one those moments where I never really had to look outside of my situation, and that forced me to, and see someone else's experience." Corey described a student in a course who "would start whatever point he was going to make with 'I'm from a lower-class background. This is what I feel.' . . . I think it was beneficial for everybody."

Dana, the lower-income black student from a Caribbean-dominated neighborhood in New York, took a course called "Race and Educational Opportunity in America." She explained, "There were a good amount of affluent students in my class who were very interested in the welfare of underprivileged children growing up in America. At first I was like, 'These rich people with a complex want to save the poor people.' Slowly, I got to see that wasn't the case. They were genuinely interested and caring. It was really unfair of me to make any sort of assumptions."

Discussion

In the past decade concern has grown about the failure to provide low-income and first-generation students access to the benefits of an elite college education. While underrepresented minority students had been given an admission advantage at these schools through race-sensitive admissions policies, until recent years, lower-income and first-generation college students, and in particular white students, have had little access to the elite institutions and have received no real admission advantage.[20] Scholars have stressed the importance of equity and social mobility—of offering equal opportunity to all students regardless of their financial resources and of providing the access to the broader employment opportunities, better jobs, and increased income that comes with a college degree.[21] Access to an elite school, in particular, confers additional benefits—status as well as connections to "white male elites," who in turn provide "access to jobs, financial capital, and marriage partners of high social standing. The newcomers there become part of the ongoing institutional framework that defines and shapes the power elite in the United States, even though only a few of them are likely to reach the very top."[22]

When arguments are made in support of racial diversity, they are based on not only equity and social mobility but also the educational benefits that are presumed to ensue for students from living and learning in a racially diverse community. The potential educational benefits for students of living in a *socioeconomically* diverse community have received little consideration. William Bowen and his colleagues claim, "The quality ("excellence") of the campus learning environment is improved for everyone when students from a wide variety of socioeconomic backgrounds are present. Students need to learn how to put themselves in other people's shoes."[23] But little data exist to support that claim. The results of this study, however, point clearly to the positive impact a socioeconomically diverse student body can have on learning outcomes for students.

The majority of students in the study had meaningful contact with students from a class background very different from their own, and learning occurred for many students as they interacted with classmates from different class backgrounds and became aware of their class differences. Learning about class was facilitated because extremes of wealth on a campus made social class salient.[24] Lower-income students noticed their differences from affluent peers in economic, cultural, and social capital, and many affluent students became aware of their privilege relative to lower-income peers.

Many students came to see that the class stereotypes they held were inaccurate. Their understanding of the impact of class in shaping people's lives increased. Some students got past their differences to recognize their commonalties, which were greater than they had imagined. Many lower-income students reported a reduction of prejudice about the rich. They gained knowledge and learned skills that would enable them to become part of the world of the affluent. Many affluent students acquired a new perspective on *themselves*, their lifestyles, and their unearned privilege. Most of the learning about class reported by students occurred outside of the classroom. Only a small proportion of students took courses that addressed social class, and those students were mostly lower income. Some who did found that those courses provided some of the most important classroom learning experiences they had at the college. As with learning about race, the courses provided analytical frameworks for understanding class that do not come from cross-class interaction.

Class differences are on the minds of many students but are not easy to discuss because class inequalities engender discomfort—jealousy, resentment, shame, and guilt. Most students (87 percent) reported that they had had meaningful, honest conversations about social class.[25] But many commented that conversations about class could be "a little awkward," that people "become defensive of their own social class no matter where they fall on the spectrum," that conversation about class "just exacerbates our differences," and that "things get said, and things get heated." Many students perceived conversations about class as likely to occur only if "you know someone well" or are "among your closest friends." More active programming and a greater presence of class issues in the curriculum are needed to promote more learning.

Considerable resources are being devoted to enable low-income and first-generation students to attend Amherst, but few resources are being devoted to promoting learning from the socioeconomic diversity that has been created. This is a matter of values and priorities. How important is it for students to learn about class differences and inequalities? Affluent white students who graduate from elite colleges such as Amherst have entrée into positions of leadership in our country, the core of a powerful elite that has retained its "subjective sense of hard-earned and richly deserved class privilege."[26] Colleges such as Amherst have the potential to challenge these entrenched beliefs, and to not do so has implications for the perpetuation of class inequalities.

8

Where We Are

In this chapter we look at some additional aspects of how students fared on campus over their four years—their overall well-being, their social integration, and their academic performance. We also review their perspectives on what the college could have done to improve their experience and increase learning about race and class. Finally, we look at what advice the study's participants would pass on to future students of their race and class.

Social Adjustment

In addition to the face-to-face interviews, which are the primary focus of this book, students in the study completed three online surveys—in the fall and spring of freshman year and at the end of four years. In that senior-year spring survey, the students—be they black or white, affluent or lower income—gave *positive* reports in answering questions on a number of key aspects of their experience at Amherst. Specifically, race and class did not make a significant difference in their self-reported psychological well-being, their social lives, or their feelings of comfort and inclusion in relation to their peers. Nor were there significant differences between the groups on students' assessments of whether they had grown as a person, found a place at the college, or felt they were coping effectively with important changes in their lives.[1]

The surveys, however, did reveal race and class differences that were statistically significant, although not large in magnitude. After four years, white students reported that their race made social integration a little easier—that is, it made it easier for them to feel comfortable on campus, to find like-minded friends, to gain refuge when things were going badly, or to be included in informal activities with classmates. Black students felt that race made these situations a little harder for them.[2] These results were similar to the ratings done at the end of freshman year. As for social class, affluent students of both races found that their social class made social integration easier when compared to reports of lower-income students.[3] No class differences were found freshman year. It was the perceptions of the affluent students that had changed over the four years. As seniors, affluent students felt their class position made social integration easier than they did freshman year, indicating they had become more aware over time of their class advantage and of the ease with which they were able to fit in on campus and find like-minded friends.

Academics

The complicated area of academic achievement was not the focus of the current study. Considerable literature exists about issues of academic preparation, remediation, and retention for lower-income and minority students, but these issues go beyond the scope of this book. We do look briefly, however, at some academic measures that were collected to give a sense of students' academic achievement and at some of the issues that may have factored into their experience and performance in their classes.

Three measures of achievement were collected: grade point average (GPA), election to the national honors society Phi Beta Kappa, and graduating with Latin honors (i.e., cum laude, magna cum laude, and summa cum laude).[4] On all these measures, the academic achievement of students in the affluent white group exceeded that of students in the other groups.[5] Specifically, in terms of grades, affluent white students attained the highest GPA, graduating with a 3.77 average.[6] Students in the lower-income black group graduated with the lowest GPA, with a 3.23 average. White study participants graduated with a significantly higher GPA than black participants (3.65 versus 3.32); affluent students graduated with a significantly higher GPA than lower-income students (3.59 versus 3.39).[7] Affluent white participants were overrepresented in the top quarter of the class (46 percent made the top quarter). One lower-income black student and two lower-income white students in the study graduated in the top quarter of the class.[8]

On the other two measures of academic achievement, Latin honors and Phi Beta Kappa, students in the affluent white group again outperformed students in the other three groups. Over three-quarters of the affluent white students graduated with honors; lower-income black students (25 percent) were the least represented.[9] Half of the affluent black students and almost two-thirds (64 percent) of the lower-income white students received degrees with honors. Five students in the study were elected to Phi Beta Kappa.

Three were affluent white students, one was a lower-income black student, and one was a lower-income white student.[10]

It is not possible from our study to identify the many variables that might account for these measurable differences in achievement. We can, though, include some student observations that may shed light on what contributed to creating the differences. Many lower-income students, and particularly lower-income white participants, spoke of feeling less well prepared academically for the college than their affluent classmates, reporting that they had attended less-demanding high schools. Nicole, for example, the white student from rural Illinois, had gone to a community high school at which there were more agriculture courses offered "than science, math, and English combined." She said, "I felt like that's great if that's what you want, but I wanted to be challenged in a more academic way than the school provided." Other lower-income students touched on the inadequacies in their high school preparation: "I was always able to get good grades without that much work"; "I don't think I'd read a book in all of high school. I can't think of one book that I read from front cover to cover." By and large, lower-income students had done much less writing and received less writing instruction. Mechanics aside, many had less experience with being asked to think and write critically and analytically. As they got to know affluent classmates, lower-income students became increasingly aware that, as one student put it regarding academics, some students during their time at Amherst had "to work harder to get to the same place."

Some lower-income students spoke of their lack of the study skills—skills involving time management and planning ahead—that other students had acquired. "I take things as they come instead of just scheduling," said Emily. She explained, "[Better study skills] would make me more productive and make me happier. I see people who do that, and I want to be like them. And I'm trying. But in high school I just didn't do anything. I flew by the seat of my pants. And it still is how I do things now."

An additional disadvantage for some lower-income students was that they did not always own the books for courses. Although in theory their financial aid packages included money to cover books, in practice a third of the lower-income students reported that financial considerations had led them at times to not buy course books.[11] "How am I supposed to buy all these books if I don't have that money on hand?" mused a lower-income student. The student continued, "Or I do have that money, but I don't feel like spending it on books because I just spent the entire summer working really hard for it." Instead students like this tried to access books on reserve at the library or borrow them from friends.

Initially, the lower-income as well as the affluent black students were less likely than their affluent white classmates to take advantage of the academic resources available at the college—professors' office hours, help sessions, tutoring, review sessions, the Writing Center, and the Quantitative Skills Center. Some lower-income students regarded asking for help as a blow to their sense of independence, competence, and pride. Emily realized her tendency was to "take care of it" herself. She explained, "[Asking for help goes] against what my natural inclination is—to not ask for help. . . . I want to present myself as someone who knows what they're doing. And it's hard to go against that."

Over time, however, they sought more help.[12] By the end of four years, lower-income students were seeking academic help more than their affluent peers.[13] Lower-income students had become more comfortable approaching professors. Running into academic difficulties and hearing classmates talk about the benefits of seeking help had spurred some lower-income students to finally reach out. Robert started going to office hours because he had, he said, "guys chatting in my ear, like, 'Go talk to this professor; that'll help.'" By senior year, Robert reported, "I go to the Writing Center for every one of my papers. . . . I've become a better writer, just by . . . 'rewrite, rewrite.' Most of my professors were great and like, 'Yeah, I'll give you another chance.' And so I would rewrite, rewrite, rewrite."

More generally, though, in looking back over their four years, lower-income students reported more than affluent students did that their social-class position posed more difficulties to their academic integration—that is, being taken seriously by professors, forming relationships with professors, and earning good grades in coursework.[14] They also reported lower academic confidence than their affluent classmates.[15] Race was not perceived by black students to make academic integration easier or more difficult than white students perceived it, and race alone did not have an effect on academic confidence.

One last area that had an impact on academic performance was student involvement with issues and problems with their families back home, as discussed in Chapter 3. Students in the affluent white group had an easier time than students in the other three groups weathering family problems without compromising their academic work. In addition, they may well have had fewer crises at home that called for their involvement.

Overall Well-being

Although they were outnumbered by affluent white classmates on campus, lower-income black and white students as well as affluent black students in this study did *not* find themselves on the margins of the college's social life. Their increased numbers on campus meant that they could more easily form friendships with classmates like themselves than was the case in the past. Many diverse and overlapping friendship groups existed, and unlike the Amherst of old, no clear group made up a social "elite."

It is striking that although they spent four years surrounded by many wealthy, privileged classmates, the majority of lower-income students in the study left Amherst with positive feelings about their roots and what they had and did not wish they had been born into more affluent circumstances.[16]

In fact, the number of lower-income students who would have opted for such a change decreased over the four years, from 44 percent in the fall of freshman year to 33 percent. No doubt this level of satisfaction was a result of many factors, not the least of which was the fact that they had gotten to and through Amherst College. As Danny, a lower-income white student from New Jersey, noted, "What benefit would it really have been if my dad made a few hundred thousand dollars a year? Could I have a nicer car? Probably. Could I go on better vacations? Probably. But I don't really think in the long run that that's really affected [me] negatively in any way."

The families of many of the lower-income students in the study had experienced serious financial difficulties over the course of those students' lives. Some students spoke of parents losing jobs and benefits, of being homeless, of the family going on welfare, of struggles to pay medical bills, and of bankruptcies. But many students who had experienced this kind of severe hardship growing up saw value in the experience:[17] "I've gone through some hard times, but I feel like they've helped me"; "I like where I come from, and I like what I've experienced, even though it has been maybe more difficult than it could have been. I think it's been valuable to me."

Comparing themselves to their affluent classmates, many lower-income students felt they had an "overall awareness and appreciation for everything" because they knew "what it's like to not be able to have anything." That sense of appreciation included being at Amherst. The college was not "something to take for granted." To some lower-income students, it was clear that they had a better grasp of money—what things cost and how to budget—than many of their affluent classmates, and that, too, was a source of satisfaction.

That said, resentments over perceived class inequities surfaced in the interviews—over affluent students' access to top-notch schooling, tutoring, and SAT preparation courses; over students' ability to travel abroad for spring break simply by asking their parents for the money; and over students' families' ownership of multiple houses "when for some people it's just hard enough to own one." While some students without means wished that they had more opportunities to travel or to buy things, a frequent wish was to help out their parents so that, for example, their parents "could live a little bit more comfortably and not worry as much about making sure that [the students'] education is paid for," or "would have an easier time retiring."

The fact that the lower-income students were attending Amherst College may go a long way toward explaining how little class envy and resentment surfaced in the study. The American dream was alive for them; they were living it out, climbing the ladder of social mobility with their ambition, hard work, and ability. Reflecting on his social position, Justin, a lower-income white student, noted, "It's maybe easier to get angry at someone who has more or is more privileged than someone who has less privilege, but I don't really feel angry about it. It is what it is. One thing that is helpful to know is many people have moved up in the ranks in this country. It's not impossible. It's just you have to be aware of the challenges, and you have to find a way to navigate them." Lower-income students were well aware that the college had given them incredible opportunities. They would soon be graduating with almost no loans and an Amherst degree. They recognized that "Amherst has opened a lot of doors."

Many black students, both lower income and wealthy, expressed appreciation for getting to attend Amherst—for having gotten an opportunity that members of their race have "traditionally been denied"—and for what they had gained while there. Steven, an affluent black student, was aware and thankful that the college provided "students of color with a great opportunity. Having a degree from Amherst offers extremely beneficial opportunities." He noted that it was not that the college "is really going to do something for you. It equips you to go do it yourself."

For some black students, their years at Amherst left them feeling more effective in asserting themselves and their views. Devon, affluent like Steven, felt her Amherst experience had helped her become more articulate and find her voice. "For the most part, having graduated from here, people develop a way of speaking authoritatively, which is advantageous if you actually learned something and can actually defend the things you say." A number of lower-income black participants concurred. Brianna felt she had developed, she said, "the ability to express myself verbally . . . to defend my position and articulate articulately." She was now able to "debate and to challenge positions without breaking down, without becoming so disheartened that you can't even speak." Being at Amherst allowed Brandon to "grow as a person and really embrace race-related issues and talk about them in a confident manner."

Some black students were leaving Amherst with good feelings about the ways black and white classmates had mixed with one another. Corey, the lower-income black student from New Bedford, Massachusetts, remarked, "Thirty or forty years ago at the same college, I'm positive that the black and white students weren't interacting in a very friendly manner. Now, the fact that we can exist together, when we go out into the world we're going to be able to interact with white people because of the experience we've had here." He applauded the integrated community as a "step in terms of ending racism, because you get these people interacting."

Suggestions for Institutional Change

The college had invested considerable financial resources in creating structural diversity—that is, the inclusion of previously underrepresented groups in the student body. Recruiting lower-income and/or minority students, however, needs to be accompanied by programs and policies designed to help these students successfully deal with the challenges they face once they arrive and to help ensure that students, black or white, affluent or lower-income, reach outside their comfort zones and take advantage of the opportunities for learning from their differences. Students' reports on their experiences over four years at Amherst make it clear that more needs to be done to improve aspects of the campus climate, to facilitate students' integration into campus life, to help students meet the challenges they face, and to ensure that positive learning outcomes occur. Corey's positive view of interracial interaction at Amherst differed from the perspective of Marissa, the affluent black student from Chicago, who noted, "In a lot of ways Amherst has this image of being a very progressive and very liberal place, but the reality and where it is right now are very different. I think it's working towards the goal of becoming that place. But . . . as a community, there's a lot of work to do in terms of really being that place that is progressive and accepting."

In Chapter 9, we move beyond Amherst to address what institutions are doing across the country to meet the challenges of diversity. For now, we turn to the Amherst students' perspective on what the college might do to make the experience better with respect to race and class.

Dialogue about Class and Race

For a variety of reasons, many participants in the study found race and class difficult subjects to discuss. That does not mean that students did not want to do so, however. Many students felt that more conversations between students from different social classes were needed: "It always seems to be the thing that gets put on the back burner"; "We're living on the same campus, but we're not talking to each other." It was not clear to one student whether "the wealthy, upper-class students have really met the most poor, or even just some regular students." Reflecting back after four years, 44 percent of the students wished they had had more conversations with classmates about social class,[18] as those conversations "really help people understand each other better" and "enlighten people on the experiences of others." Such conversations can be "clarifying about other people's experience, which is always a good thing, and can help you understand your own experience and things you might not have realized." Katelyn, the affluent white student from Phoenix, said, "Knowledge is a good thing, and people in general have very little accurate knowledge about how other classes live. They have ideas about it, but since they've never lived those lives, they don't really know. And since we don't really talk about it, they don't really know."

Just over a third of the students wished more *structured* opportunities had existed in which cross-class dialogue could take place in a safe and productive manner.[19] Amy, the lower-income white student from Florida, had attended a dialogue on social class and race in which students expressed the feeling that these topics were "stifled on campus." As a result of that forum, she took the sociology course "Social Class."

For various reasons the remaining two-thirds of the students were not interested in more structured dialogue about class. Some felt that class was one of the many issues they had talked and learned about informally while on campus, and to their minds no more institutional support was needed. They had had "enough" talk about class, or "a healthy amount of it," and they did not like "fixating" on it. "There are a lot of forums on campus where, if people want to seek out information or talk to people, they can. I haven't really because it hasn't been a pressing issue for me."

Students saw race as a more crucial issue to confront than class. Two-thirds of the white students wished at the end of four years that they had had more conversations with their classmates about race.[20] Amy had many questions about race that she was "just too afraid to ask." She worried whether it was "politically correct" to bring up racial issues. "Am I, like, suddenly a racist because I want to talk about that? I feel that a lot of times here, you're not supposed to bring up those issues because we're all supposed to be experts in it already, and also not [supposed to] acknowledge that there are those differences." White students spoke in these terms: "You can always learn something and gain a new perspective"; "I feel like [race is] just lurking there, and it's another thing that should be talked about. And I would like to understand how different people see things or had different things affect them"; "I don't really know much about what it's like to be black or Hispanic or any ethnicity other than my own. I'd like to know."

Half of the lower-income black students said they wished they had had more conversations about race. Brianna noted, "By not actually discussing these different aspects of diversity, you're only diverse on paper, a statistic. 'Oh, we have this many people from these neighborhoods or this many from these races.' But as far as a living and breathing aspect of the culture, it hasn't gotten there yet." Only one affluent black student regretted not having more conversations about race.

Because conversations about race could be difficult to undertake, half the students wished the college had provided more opportunities for structured dialogue around race.[21] As Brianna put it, "Instead of expecting diversity to just happen, the institution needs to step up and actively start implementing some of these things. . . . The community as a whole is suffering because there's the underlying tensions that no one wants to talk about except in a classroom." Some students were not satisfied with the nature of the structured dialogues that *were* taking place on campus. David, the affluent white student from Washington, D.C., who had a great deal of pre-college experience with diversity, was disappointed in the way discussion about race had been handled on campus. David would have been happier "if there had been more critical discussions about diversity that weren't so intellectualized." He felt the college did not do "a good job of framing the conversation in a way that's productive." He continued, "I think we treat multiculturalism in a tokenish way and don't have the hard conversations. It's easy to avoid hard conversations here. And it's always going to be possible to avoid them anywhere you go. And the college can't force them. But for the people interested in having the conversations, they're sick of having the conversations because they're never the *right* conversation."

For the half of the students who had no desire for more structured conversations about race, again, the reasons were varied. For some white students, it was simple: "It makes me uncomfortable to tell you the truth." Others felt they had had their fill of conversations on the topic: "Things that needed to be said have been said"; "I did that phase and pretty much milked it"; "We covered it a lot in [the English course] 'Reading, Writing, Teaching'"; "I've had plenty. Pretty happy with the ones I've had." Some black classmates agreed: "I'm all race talked out. You deal with that a lot when you're younger"; "It's been fine. I've had a lot of conversations"; "We talk about it maybe not every day but every week"; "I'm worn [out] on it from being in class and talking about it all the time."

Some white students did not see race as a crucial issue that needed to be discussed. One student felt "indifferent towards race." Another stated, "I don't feel like race has as big issues as social class." For some black students, as well, talking about race was not a priority: "I think it's going out of fashion"; "There are other people on campus who want to get race issues out and do things. Isn't there a center here for diversity? There are students on campus who are vocal enough for me, who, if that's something they're passionate about, I'd rather sit back and take in what they have to say." When asked about the desirability of having more conversations about race, one student stated flatly, "I don't think it would've gone anywhere, honestly."

For those students who wanted to explore issues of race and/or class but were uncomfortable discussing them informally or who wanted to further their understanding, structured dialogues, facilitated by well-trained, experienced personnel, might have proved invaluable. We discuss structured dialogue further in Chapter 9. An important challenge that colleges face is how to engage the unmotivated, many of whom might well profit from participating in such dialogues.

Support Systems and Mentors

Looking back over their Amherst careers, some lower-income students and some wealthy black students expressed the wish that there had been more support systems in place at the college to help them manage difficulties that arose. Marissa, the affluent black student from Chicago, had created a small community for herself on campus that, she said, "protected me from discrimination I might've faced." But she knew black classmates who had had more difficult experiences on campus and did not have the same support she did. Brandon, the lower-income black student from Newark, considered himself "definitely more independent than most" and was satisfied with the support he received. But stepping back, he said that "there's definitely a lack of race-based support from the institution, definitely as far as people to talk to."

While all students were assigned an academic adviser, some students wished they could have engaged with someone more personally about issues beyond their academic programs, an adult who could "sit down with [them] for two hours and really talk about what [they] wanted: "Because I really didn't know what I wanted"; "It would have been comforting to feel like someone understands me not just as a student but also as a person." That person would have served, for one student, as "an outlet to talk about issues regarding race or class."

Some academic advisers did serve their advisees as mentors; many did not. Professors are trained to teach and do research in a discipline, not to mentor and counsel students regarding other areas of their lives. Many professors did not feel qualified, did not have the time required, or simply may not have been interested in serving as mentors. Students did have access to trained professionals through the Dean of Students office, the Counseling Center, and the Career Center. Some students who found mentors, usually one of the deans, stressed the importance of these "personal relationships"—of having someone who "looks out for [them]." They spoke glowingly of the crucial role those mentors had played in their success: "a lifesaver," someone who was able to "guide me through a lot of my problems," and in some cases an important intermediary in interactions with their parents.

It is striking that many more lower-income black students than lower-income white students (92 percent versus 20 percent) and more affluent black students than affluent white students (50 percent versus 33 percent) found adult mentors on campus outside the faculty.[22] This may be because of the presence of several outstanding black deans in the Dean of Students office. Lower-income white students might well have benefited from such mentoring. In many situations they were unlikely to be able to rely on their parents for advice, as their parents were unfamiliar with life at an elite liberal arts college and did not have the knowledge of the system and the strategies to make it work to their children's advantage.

When asked directly whether they might have found it helpful to have been *assigned* a mentor of their race and/or class, only one in three black and lower-income students said yes.[23] Those lower-income students who thought having a mentor of the same class would be helpful stressed the need "to get someone's perspective that has already been there . . . someone who lived through that," someone "who had been to a high school like [theirs] or come in with a similar academic preparation," or someone who would "show [them] the ropes." Some black students stressed the importance of forming a relationship with an adult of the same race who would know how race "plays out in the real world." "If you're looking at someone who looks like you, it's a little easier to talk to them about personal issues." Two of three lower-income and black students, however, were not in favor of being *assigned* to a mentor of the same race and class. Most felt that mentors should be *available* to and *chosen* by students or that, while having a mentor mattered, the race and class of a mentor did not.

Student Advice for Entering Students

Reflecting back on four years at the college, study participants had a variety of suggestions to offer incoming students to help them make the most of their college experience. Some advice was specific to people of their race and class, and other advice was applicable to all entering students.

Advice for Black Students

The guidance some black students had to offer began with the question of whether to apply. Attending an elite, predominantly white college could entail unanticipated issues, challenges, and conflicts. Brianna had gained a great deal from her experience at Amherst, but it had not been without strain. She had this advice for students like her who considered going to elite schools:

> Be very sure that you actually *want* to go to Harvard. People think of the credentials and the benefits of going to Harvard, and they never think of the costs. . . . Being that you're southern, black, female, low income, you're going to be engaged in a battlefield, an unspoken battle for your four years here at that college. You're going to be very aware of that underlying tension about class and race. I've seen people break down crying just because it's so disheartening. So just be careful of knowing the cost of going to [an elite] college.

Whitney, the affluent black student from Detroit, cautioned black applicants "to really evaluate what they want from a college experience. . . . A lot of blacks talk about the lack of social life here for them, and the parties that *are* thrown are not what they're used to." She continued, "So I would say, 'Is the education to the point where you don't mind not having a social life?' Because I don't think [black students] enjoy the social scene much."

Some lower-income black students addressed the pressures to assimilate into the largely white, upper-middle-class culture that awaited new students. Carl, who grew up outside Princeton Junction, had boarded at a Massachusetts prep school. He worried that incoming students would lose themselves at Amherst—that the culture at the school would disconnect them from their past. To him it was important that those students "have a good sense coming in [of] who they are" so that they would be able "to maintain that same sense of self leaving, because this school can change you." He also advised prospective black students to keep up their relationships from their home communities "because those matter. People start to look at you differently if all of a sudden, now that you're an Amherst College kid, you cut off ties."

Brandon advised black students to "really embrace the culture [at Amherst] while not forgetting your own." He was concerned about "the lack of visibility of black culture at Amherst," and he encouraged black students "to really enlighten people" about it.

Two affluent black students offered advice on how best to go about fitting into the largely white world of the college. Christopher noted, "One thing which I am learning more and more is you have to keep in mind that people see you as a black person, or biracial or whatever the case is, so keep that in mind. When you are in a circle of friends, it's nothing you have to be hyperconscious of, but it's safe to keep that in the back of your head. Things could be misinterpreted. It helps to be a little bit more polite, a little bit more accepting than everyone else." Jason advised black students "never" to respond to an offensive racial comment with anger and rarely to take on the burden of being the educator. He greatly valued fitting in and thus recommended, "If somebody says something offensive, always go with option two [hide your feelings]."

A number of black study participants, both affluent and lower-income, wanted to encourage incoming black students to move outside their comfort zones and open themselves up to those different from them. Three lower-income black participants who held this view were Corey, Angela, and Trina. Corey urged black students "not to separate themselves, to be open. . . . Don't bring stereotypes from your home, your outside life, here. The group of black students that like to hang out by themselves—that could hold you back, probably keep you from some interesting options." Angela commented, "I'd tell them to not feel like they only had to be friends with people of the same race or same class. . . . It limits your experience. Amherst is already a small place. You don't have to make it even smaller for yourself." Trina encouraged students to "pursue the friendships they make freshman year, because it's probably the most diverse group of students they'll encounter at one time."

Affluent black students offered similar kinds of counsel. Steven advised, "Put yourself in situations where you may not feel supercomfortable, and see if they get better. . . . I'd say take chances, and give people a little more trust than you normally would. I think if you do that, good things will happen." Kevin suggested, "Be open to meeting as many people as possible and trying as many things that seem even remotely interesting."

Advice for Lower-Income Students

Some lower-income students wanted to encourage those who followed to take the long view—in time they would likely find their place in the unfamiliar and possibly intimidating world of the college. Tanya, the child of

Russian immigrant parents, recounted, "From my first week, I was kind of in shock and not very happy. But then it got a lot better, and I've been a lot happier with it since then. It just seemed like I would have a lot of trouble fitting in at first. But then it got much, much easier." She wanted the newly arriving to know that Amherst was "not an exclusive environment." She went on, "People are very accepting, and it doesn't really matter to them what your social class and your race [are]. They are not going to judge you based on that. They are going to judge you as a person." Marie, the lower-income white student from West Virginia, advised, "Don't be scared. Yeah, just be confident; work hard. And if this is the place for you, you will find your way. Don't be intimidated to talk to professors. They will help you. They want to help you, for the most part. And just make the most of it."

"Make the most of it." For a number of lower-income white students that meant forming relationships across class and race lines. Rebecca advised students to "try to really diversify your group of friends because it can be a very stimulating and enlightening experience to get to know all the different points of views that people have." Emily believed that "making a list of priorities is important—what you want from this experience." She had, she said, "wanted to grow personally just as much as I wanted to grow academically." She saw the learning that could come from relationships with peers and believed that "it's not just about the academics, that you can gain so much more beyond that."[24]

Advice for Affluent Students

In a similar vein, many affluent white and black study participants wanted to encourage students to take chances, embrace difference, and allow for new perspectives. Andrea, an affluent black student, suggested, "Be open to anything." She advised students "not to get stuck in a 'clique.'" She continued, "I'm sure if you were in a clique, you'd make good friends, but just try to be as open to many things as you can, because you're constantly being surprised. And they're great surprises, and they're interesting surprises, [and that] makes your experience more enriching." Talia, another black student, counseled, "Just keep an open mind. Try to see people as people, not as a color, and just be patient until you find your niche, because it takes a while." Lauren, the affluent white student who majored in black studies, had this to say:

> Take black studies classes. Do as much as you possibly can on campus. Don't go the comfortable route. And study abroad. Studying abroad in South Africa changed my life. It's one of those things where I learned so much about myself. If you don't leave this campus and don't do something that really pushes you, I feel it's really a disservice to yourself. Even though it was the hardest experience of my life, I would do it again in a heartbeat.

Discussion

On the whole, students' reports on numerous aspects of their experience on campus were positive. For the most part, they were able to find a place for themselves and to establish satisfactory social lives. They had a sense of psychological well-being, felt comfortable among their classmates, and felt they were coping successfully with the important changes taking place in their lives. That success was attained at times with some difficulty and with needed outside support. While black students and lower-income students had not attained the degree of academic success of their affluent white classmates, they graduated with a B+ average in a challenging academic program. At the end of five years, all but two of the original students in the study (one lower-income white student and one lower-income black student) had graduated from the college.

To know what kinds of programming and support might be helpful in meeting students' needs, it is important to keep in mind the considerable variability that exists within groups. One of the prominent themes that emerges from students' recounting of and reflections on their experiences at Amherst is that one student's voice may not be representative of those of classmates of the same race and class. Putting one or two black students or two low-income students on a committee addressing diversity issues does not ensure that their experiences represent those of many peers of their race or class.[25] To understand what students are experiencing, the problems they confront, what they feel most contributes or might contribute to their adjustment, and what might promote greater learning, many students' voices need to be heard.

It is also insufficient to rely on students alone to point the way. Students lack a broad framework from which to understand their experiences. They do not know about other possibilities that exist to enhance those experiences and their learning. Colleges can benefit from looking outside their walls—at curricular and extracurricular initiatives aimed at increasing learning from and about diversity, at mentoring and advising programs, and at research that has been carried out on the effectiveness of diversity programming—to learn what other institutions across the country are doing. These topics are the focus of Chapter 9.

9

Where Do We Go from Here?

To this point, this book has focused on the fifty-eight Amherst students in the study, drawing heavily on their words to present a picture of the issues they dealt with and the challenges they faced on campus involving race and class. We have seen the complexities some students faced, be it encountering a culture at Amherst that was unfamiliar, getting to know people of a different race and class than their own for the first time, responding to race and class stereotypes, or handling the difficulties of bridging very different worlds of home and college. We have also looked at what students learned from their experiences. It is clear that many students derived great benefit from living in a diverse community. Many left the school with changed attitudes, beliefs, feelings, and understandings of those different from them. Their comfort interacting with students from a different race and/or class had increased. In some cases, they left with new perspectives on members of their own race and class. But the evidence is equally clear that many students, and in particular, many affluent white students, did not learn a great deal from their exposure to difference. The findings are not unique to this small liberal arts college. They are in keeping with larger research findings in the field.[1]

In this chapter we shift away from Amherst to examine what is going on in the larger world of academia. How are colleges and universities across the country addressing the challenges surrounding diversity that have been described at Amherst? What works? Unfortunately, programs and practices have often been put into place on college campuses

without formal follow-up assessments of their impact or with only anec-
dotal data to document what students gained from the programming. The
same pattern applies in many organizations. Diversity training initiatives
are conducted to increase positive and decrease negative intergroup behavior, yet almost none of these programs are evaluated.[2] The importance of
evaluating diversity training programs and practices is particularly important because some popular prejudice-reduction practices, when evaluated,
have been found to increase prejudice.[3]

Over the last two decades, a growing body of empirical data has been
collected on the outcomes for students of programs and practices whose
goals are to maximize learning from diversity or to help black and lower-
income students successfully meet the challenges they face on campus.
Many of these findings come from large-scale, self-report questionnaire
studies, often from national databases as opposed to small, qualitative
interview studies. Most examine questions of racial diversity and do not
address class-based diversity.

Before trying to summarize these data, it is important to note some
of the difficulties that exist in drawing conclusions from this research.[4]
Methodologies used in the data collection can make results difficult to in-
terpret. Some studies used no comparison groups, making it impossible to
determine whether students who did not participate in a particular course
or program would show similar gains simply through their experiences on
campus over time. In some studies that include control groups, students
were not randomly selected and randomly assigned to either participate or
not to participate in a particular diversity program, making it impossible
to know whether student characteristics (e.g., their backgrounds) produced
the outcomes rather than the program itself. The results of studies can be
difficult to compare because outcome measures are not standard. Some
studies do a combined assessment of many different types of programs,
making it difficult to know whether a particular practice or program had
more impact than another. Some studies combine data for different racial
groups, creating uncertainty as to whether outcomes of a program differ
from one racial group to another. Few studies look at the long-term effects
of diversity programming to determine the sustainability of the results.
However, despite the many differences in the samples studied, measures
and methodologies used, and limitations of those methodologies, consistent
findings do emerge.

We begin with two key findings consistently reported in the research
studies. The first is that students' precollege racial environments and experiences are a major predictor of their experiences with diversity on campus.[5]
Generally speaking, it is the students, both white and nonwhite, who come
to college from more racially diverse neighborhoods and high schools that
show the greatest interest in cross-group contact and who experience the
greatest learning from diversity. Those students have had more experience
studying with and interacting with diverse peers than their classmates and

bring a greater comfort with and openness to diversity issues. They tend to participate in activities that reinforce their inclinations—they engage in more cross-group interactions, have more positive interactions with diverse peers, take more diversity courses, and participate in more diversity activities. A related finding is that students who enter college with a higher level of motivation to reduce their own prejudice and promote social justice seek out more diversity courses and activities.[6]

Thus, having a diverse group of students live together does not automatically produce in the students a sense of knowing and understanding those different from them.[7] Having more diversity in the student body *is* associated with higher levels of cross-group interaction and cross-group friendships[8] and increases the likelihood white students will engage in positive interactions with diverse peers.[9] But a diverse student body is not in itself enough to ensure that learning occurs or that the cross-group interactions are *positive*.[10] Coming to college from segregated schools and neighborhoods may well weaken the quality and frequency of cross-race interaction for students and reduce the chance of learning from diversity. To improve the likelihood that positive learning occurs, institutions need to have programming and practices in place, embedded in institutional cultures in which learning from diversity is valued. Many such efforts are being made at various colleges and universities around the country. This chapter takes a look at these approaches with an eye to what is working.

The second key finding is that to succeed, students need a climate that is both welcoming and supportive. Offers of admission and financial support may be necessary to create a diverse student body on campus, but they are not sufficient to ensure that black and lower-income students will be able to *thrive* once they arrive. The perception of a hostile racial campus climate and experiences with discrimination have many adverse effects on minority students.[11] Living with these perceptions and experiences is related to lower feelings of belonging and to feelings of isolation. An awareness by minority students of being stereotyped as less academically capable, as well as being underrepresented, contributes to a sense of "belonging uncertainty"—to the hypothesis that "people like me do not belong here."[12] Such feelings in turn influence academic perseverance and achievement. In addition, a hostile racial climate leads students to feel less positive about cross-group interactions and to have more friends from within their group, impeding social integration. The effects of repeated instances of prejudice and discrimination can limit the potential positive effects of intergroup interactions.

Improving the social climate and promoting feelings of belonging on campus have numerous positive consequences for minority students. As the campus climate improves, so do academic and social self-concept, academic and social integration, social and intellectual development, degree completion/retention, and overall college satisfaction. In one particularly striking study, psychology professors Gregory Walton and Geoffrey Cohen developed a onetime, one-hour intervention aimed at increasing the sense of belonging in first-year black students. Over the next three years, that one intervention was found to have improved their academic performance, their self-reported physical health, and their well-being when compared to controls.[13] Taken together, these findings underscore the importance of colleges taking stock of their campus climate and, if need be, of taking steps to create a climate that is welcoming and accepting and promotes a sense of belonging.

We look now at diversity programming and practices across the country—at what seems to be needed, at what is being tried, and at how effective these efforts have been, both in terms of learning from diversity and meeting the challenges faced by black and lower-income students.[14] We begin with mission statements, why they matter, and what is needed to turn missions into action. We then turn to what is taking place on the ground—in the classroom, in interactions among diverse peers, and in diversity initiatives outside the classroom.

Why Mission Statements Matter

Some educators have argued that part of the mission of higher education should entail educating individuals to become productive citizens in a democratic multicultural society that strives for justice and equality.[15] By 2050, half of the U.S. population will be racial/ethnic minorities.[16] In that world students will need some understanding of the experiences of those who are very different from them, and they must have the skills to interact comfortably and effectively with them. Assuming the importance of these goals, how does an institution best go about attaining them?

Research informs us that students' learning from and about diversity at colleges and universities will be maximized if it is seen as an integral part of an institution's mission and purpose[17] and has the support of all constituencies—students, faculty, administrators, staff, and governing boards. Institutions that make that commitment to diversity in their educational missions help promote cross-group understanding and also facilitate students' academic and personal success.[18] When commitment to student learning about diversity is not pervasive in an institution, few efforts are put forth to ensure that learning from and about diversity occurs.[19]

The mission statements at many colleges include a commitment to *recruit* a diverse student body, faculty, and staff. For example, the University of Nebraska, Lincoln, "strives for a culturally diverse student body, faculty, and staff reflecting the multicultural nature of Nebraska and the nation."[20] Fewer schools, however, include learning about and from that diversity as goals, addressing the benefits of diversity, or fostering an appreciation of diversity.[21] An example of a school whose mission statement goes beyond just diversity in recruitment comes from Coe College in Iowa: "We believe that it is important for a liberal arts education to cultivate in students a desire to understand, a capacity for tolerance, and an ability to appreciate the ethnic and cultural diversity that make up humankind. It is the mission of the College to develop in students these abilities and attitudes."[22]

The goal of having a diverse faculty and staff as well as student body, as expressed in Nebraska's mission statement, is in keeping with a belief that minority students benefit from having adults of their race in positions of authority and from having role models and mentors whose backgrounds resemble their own. Additionally, the presence of accomplished scholars, teachers, and administrators who are not white and/or affluent helps challenge negative stereotypes based on race and class and likely brings new perspectives and alternative points of view to campus. Research has not assessed the effects of a well-integrated faculty and staff on minority students or on a college as a whole. However, research findings on related questions are suggestive. Encounters with successful members of one's own group increase beliefs in one's ability to succeed and enhance a sense of belonging.[23] Research on women students has found that women show a positive change in implicit beliefs about their leadership abilities and have more ambitious career goals when they are able to connect frequently and in a meaningful way with female professors.[24] Those results may be pertinent to racial minorities as well.

Leadership

While mission statements are important, it takes leadership to put those statements into action. The intensions and goals put forth in many mission statements go unrealized. Given the will, what actions are needed, and by whom? In decades past, the pursuit of a diversity agenda on campus often relied on leadership from the faculty, particularly faculty members of color, many of whom spent time working to bring about changes at a cost to their own careers, without appropriate support, compensation, or recognition.[25] This piecemeal approach is not the best. So argues Jeffrey Milem, professor of education policy studies and practice, and his colleagues, who did a comprehensive review of empirical evidence. They concluded that for educational benefits to accrue for students, diversity must be addressed in intentional ways.[26] Their review indicates that "ideally, the institution's commitment to diversity should permeate policy in all areas of institutional life. A first step in signaling an institution-wide commitment to diversity is for the top campus leadership to issue statements of support, purpose, and action."[27] Other researchers agree: Visible and sustained commitment is necessary from campus leadership, and the campus community needs to be aware that diversity is a priority.[28]

At the head of "the top campus leadership" are the presidents of our universities and colleges. These leaders play a vital role in determining how successful their institutions are in creating and adhering to a diversity agenda. They are needed to put forth the vision, help shape strategic plans of action, and empower a web of people—from the board to alumni, faculty, students, and staff—to support the diversity agenda and to ensure that the resources essential to institutionalizing a commitment to diversity are available.[29] A commitment to diversity requires leadership not only from the top but from every level of the institution.[30]

Statements of "support, purpose, and action" of the kind Milem and colleagues suggest, emanating from the leadership, can be used to hold institutional leaders accountable for diversity-related promises, and they communicate to students the institution's active commitment to diversity. Higher perceived levels of institutional commitment to diversity in turn are associated with a number of positive outcomes for students: a more positive racial climate, increases in personal goals to promote racial understanding, and lower levels of perceived hostility and discrimination.[31]

Work done at the University of Washington in Seattle provides an example of what is possible when an institution commits itself to change to meet the needs of a changing student body and follows that by visible action.[32] Funded originally by the Ford Foundation, the University of Washington became a major site for transformational change in diversity.[33] To provide coherence to diversity initiatives, the university formed a University Diversity Council in 2001 to oversee the change process, with representatives from all 150 of the university's academic and administrative units. These units were directed to assess the status of diversity on the campus and to identify ways diversity is and is not integrated into their academic mission. The focus of what they looked at was broad, including student access, development, and retention; diversity in the curriculum, faculty, staff, and administration; and campus climate. The assessment led to a deepened commitment on the part of the university's leaders to make diversity central to the academic mission of the institution and to the development of new strategies to achieve their aims. Among the initiatives were efforts to improve the university climate and the creation of a Center for Curriculum Transformation and a Diversity Research Institute. Diversity was made central to the institutional mission and to the planning process.

In line with the University of Washington's deep and wide commitment to best achieving its diversity goals, researchers have found that institutions need to examine *all* programs and practices and make change where needed to ensure that they are effective and inclusive.[34] Institutional customs and traditions need to be examined to see if they pose barriers to the success of some students. Attention must be paid to the implementation of diversity plans, to the assessment of the effectiveness of the resulting policies and programs, and to the difficult issue of funding.

Many colleges and universities have made commitments to diversity goals, have done self-assessments, and have developed new and often far-reaching initiatives. Fewer schools, however, have achieved their aims. Leadership must be held accountable for ensuring that funding is made available to translate ideas into practice, that plans are implemented, and that programs and practices are evaluated to see if diversity goals are being realized.

What are some of the benefits of having an institution commit to diversity? Individuals who perceive that diversity is valued express more interest in intergroup contact.[35] Thus, schools that are committed to diversity and are educating their students about the value of diversity are increasing the likelihood that students will take advantage of the learning potential. In addition, research indicates that those students who place greater value on diversity seek out more intergroup interaction.[36]

Creating a positive climate for diversity and encouraging cross-group interaction on a campus are positively related to intergroup engagement and to gains in understanding diversity.[37] Strikingly, merely attending a college at which students are more engaged with diversity (through knowledge acquisition or cross-race interaction) leads to increases in students' abilities to get along with people of different races or cultures, *irrespective of their own level of engagement.*[38]

On the Ground: What Is Needed in the Classroom

We shift now to achieving diversity goals as they are realized on the ground in three areas. We begin with classrooms, move on to experiences with diverse classmates outside the classroom, and lastly, examine extracurricular programming. The classroom can be a crucial site for growth and change. Most students come to college with little exposure to and knowledge about members of other groups, with stereotypes and prejudices that shape their thinking and behavior, and with little understanding of the ways racism and classism are entrenched in institutions and everyday life in our society. The classroom offers the opportunity to learn about diverse groups both through the curriculum and from diverse peers in the classroom setting.

Diversity Courses

Many institutions have made major strides in transforming their curriculum to promote learning about diversity. For example, at Wheaton College in Norton, Massachusetts, the faculty voted in 2001 to emphasize *across the curriculum* "race/ethnicity and its intersections with gender, sexuality, class, religion, and technology in both the U.S. and global contexts."[39] They created the Infusion Project. Academic departments formed "infusion" plans that involved changes in the curricular content of courses to include diversity issues. Such "infusion" plans have been implemented at many schools. Coordination is needed, however, across the curriculum to ensure that professors in different departments are not adding the same introductory readings on race, class, or gender to their syllabi.

To ensure that students learn about diverse groups, some colleges and universities have mandated that all students take a required course on diversity. No common definition exists, however, as to what constitutes a diversity course or what the content should be. Student learning depends on the characteristics of the particular course taken. Some courses provide a complex, interdisciplinary perspective on issues of identity, power, and privilege, with a focus on social justice. Issues addressed may include the intersections of race, gender, sexuality, and other dimensions of difference, illuminating the fact that people's identities have multiple dimensions and that while people may experience privilege in one dimension, they may experience oppression in another.[40] In other courses, the focus might be on involving students to make a difference in the civic life of communities by working with underserved populations, an approach discussed later in the chapter.

Requiring students to take a diversity course may not always achieve its aim. A diversity requirement may be perceived as yet another requirement to be gotten out of the way rather than an important opportunity for learning.[41] In some required courses, diversity content is treated merely as an add-on, a short section of a course that brings in material on race, class, sexuality, or other social identities. That said, without either instituting a requirement or infusing diversity issues throughout the curriculum, many students will get little exposure through the curriculum to these issues. Some will choose not to take multicultural or ethnic studies courses simply because they have little or no interest in the issues. Students who are raised "color-blind" (i.e., to overlook race) tend not to take multicultural or ethnic studies courses.[42] On the other hand, those who are already committed to taking social action are more likely to take diversity courses, which not surprisingly strengthens their commitment to take social action to work to end social injustices.[43]

Some diversity courses offer standard pedagogies—traditional lectures, readings, and discussions. These courses use a knowledge-based approach to learning. In contrast, some courses use active learning in the form of intergroup dialogues. This approach to learning about and from diversity was developed at the University of Michigan, where the Intergroup Relations Program (IGR) runs a variety of intergroup dialogue courses.[44] In these courses, ten to fourteen students from two different identity groups with a history of conflict (e.g., black people and white people, men and women, straight people and gay people) engage in dialogue with each other about the course content.[45] The courses are guided by two trained facilitators, one from each identity group, and meet weekly for two- to three-hour sessions over a semester. The goals of the dialogues include enabling students to "work through intergroup conflicts, build effective communication across differences to forge relationships between diverse peers, and confront the historical and structural inequalities that members of minority groups face in their everyday lives."[46] It is hoped that students will leave with an understanding of what they have in common with members of another group and the differences between and within groups.[47] A final goal is that students are motivated by what they have learned to work for social justice.[48]

Intergroup dialogue courses have been adopted at many large universities and a few small colleges.[49] It is important to note that courses using intergroup dialogue are more effective in producing learning outcomes than knowledge-based courses.[50] Further, studies that examine the amount of learning and how enduring that learning is make an impressive case for the intergroup dialogue approach. First-year students who took intergroup dialogue courses were compared to matched controls and followed over four years. After four years, students who participated in intergroup dialogues as freshmen showed greater motivation to take the perspective of others, greater learning about other racial/ethnic groups, and greater enjoyment learning about the experiences and perspectives of other groups. They had a stronger sense of the common values they shared with members of other racial groups and a greater belief that difference was not necessarily divisive.[51]

Other studies comparing students who took part in intergroup dialogue courses with students in control groups shed light on how powerful this approach to learning is. Outcomes for students in the intergroup dialogue courses include increased intergroup understanding; increased understanding of racial, gender, and income inequalities and of their structural causes; and increased empathy and motivation to bridge differences. Students who took the courses showed greater responsibility for educating themselves about their own biases, increased confidence and frequency in taking action, and greater commitment to redressing inequality postcollege by getting actively engaged in their communities.[52] The findings are not in yet, but a large-scale collaborative research study is under way across nine universities examining the educational effects of participation in intergroup dialogues.[53] More generally, beyond the specific intergroup dialogue model, "classrooms that offer more opportunities for dialogue and engagement across racially/ethnically diverse students tend to promote appropriate atmospheres for increased positive interactions in college."[54]

Some diversity courses are based on a service learning model.[55] Service learning courses entail students and faculty working to address the needs of a community partner (e.g., a school or a nonprofit organization). These courses provide students the opportunity to enhance and integrate knowledge they have gained in the classroom with the knowledge gained by working with people who are not part of the dominant culture. The service experiences are brought back to the classroom and critically reflected on. According to the research, participation in community service learning courses leads to increased sensitivity to other races and cultures, improved communication skills with those different from oneself, a reduction in racial bias, and increased learning about social inequalities.[56] The effectiveness of service learning courses depends on the quality of the placement, the nature of the interaction that takes place there, and the degree and quality of reflection on students' experiences. Compared to generic community service without the academic component, service learning courses have a more positive effect on critical thinking skills, on such values as commitment to activism and the promotion of racial understanding, and on plans to participate in service after college.[57]

An interesting example of service learning coursework comes from Dickinson College, in Carlisle, Pennsylvania. Faculty and administrators designed the Domestic Mosaic and the Global Mosaic programs, intensive semester-long research programs centering on fieldwork and immersion in either local or global communities.[58] An organization that has done an enormous amount to promote service learning is Campus Compact. Campus Compact is a higher education association that provides resources and training for faculty to help them forge community partnerships and integrate civic- and community-based learning into their courses.[59] Campus Compact has enabled over twenty million students to be involved in service learning.

Studies have compared outcomes for students who took diversity coursework in its various forms—knowledge-based courses, intergroup dialogues, and service learning courses—to those of control groups and have found favorable results.[60] Students who take diversity courses show increased positive interactions with diverse peers and greater comfort dealing with them. In studies involving both white and nonwhite students, diversity courses have been found to increase cultural awareness and sensitivity, increase understanding that racism is still a problem in our society, reduce racial bias and prejudice, promote racial understanding, and increase motivation to reduce one's own prejudices. Taking diversity courses has a positive impact on social action engagement—it increases students' interest and motivation to take social action to promote social justice and inclusion.[61] Strikingly, students who chose to take a course on prejudice and conflict showed a reduction in their *implicit* prejudice and stereotypes (i.e., automatic associations that are not available to introspection).[62] The importance of taking a course focused on diversity was also highlighted by a study that found that students who did not take such a course became less tolerant of African Americans and Latinos over the course of a semester when compared to those who did.[63] Despite the positive findings in regard to taking diversity coursework, more data are needed on the long-term effects of taking these courses and whether these gains hold over time.[64]

Models of Faculty Development: Two Case Studies

Some faculty members who teach students about diversity issues may not have sufficient knowledge and training to do so in an optimal manner. Faculty members have traditionally been trained in a discipline and thus do not have the broad interdisciplinary perspective needed to effectively create a syllabus. Many also do not have the training to handle the kinds of emotionally charged discussions that can occur when matters like race and class are under consideration, a fact that may well dissuade some faculty from ever considering teaching about diversity. Further, as noted in Chapter 4, professors often assume black students to be experts on race and call on them in discussions to give the "black perspective." For many black students, being regarded as representatives of their race, as experts on slavery or all things black, is offensive and alienating. Further, singling out black students in this way operates on the faulty premise and promotes the stereotype that a single "black perspective" exists. Professors need to be made aware that this teaching strategy, however well intentioned, does not achieve its desired effect. Assuming a school is committed to having its students learn about and from diversity in the classroom, it needs then to provide institutional support for faculty development that fosters the skills and knowledge entailed.

Two interesting examples of institutional support of faculty development come from opposite ends of the country. With the support of grant money, Bloomfield College in Bloomfield, New Jersey, invested in faculty, staff, and program development through semester-long seminars in which groups of faculty and staff worked on issues of diversity, globalization, and student-centered pedagogies, with the goal of transforming courses, pedagogies, and school programs.[65] Some faculty and staff members, for example, developed pedagogies involving storytelling—telling one's own story and learning from the stories of others—to help students discover and gain respect for differences. New courses were developed; older ones were revised. Courses for first-year students are now linked to diversity themes. More than half the faculty has been involved. Staff members put the results of the seminars' work to use in libraries, career services, and programming that occur outside of the formal curriculum.

The Difference, Power, and Discrimination (DPD) program developed at Oregon State University strives to create a more inclusive curriculum by providing opportunities for faculty to revise their course content and classroom practices to integrate issues of gender, race, social class, sexual identity, age, ability, and religion.[66] The DPD Program offers a three-week intensive summer faculty development seminar to help faculty acquire greater background knowledge and learn effective pedagogical strategies for teaching about difference, power, and discrimination. Students may now choose from forty or so DPD courses. To support and supplement classroom learning, the DPD program offers a film series, discussions, lectures, and teaching resources. Just as students who bring greater comfort with and openness to diversity issues self-select into diversity courses and activities, those faculty members who most value diversity and want to strengthen their teaching about diversity tend to self-select into such seminars. One challenge is how to reach a broad range of faculty for such training.

On the Ground: Experiences with Diverse Classmates

Students have opportunities to learn from diverse peers outside the classroom, either in informal interaction or in structured diversity activities.[67] In assessing the effects of diversity on students, it is difficult for researchers to separate out the particular effects of any *one* of these opportunities. For example, participation in diversity activities or courses may lead students to increased informal interaction with diverse peers over time and vice versa.[68]

Numerous studies document the benefits, for both white students and students of color, of experiences and activities with diverse peers. Some of the well-studied effects of informal interracial interaction (e.g., effects on the reduction in racial bias) have been summarized through meta-analysis, a statistical approach to reviewing research. In a meta-analysis, attention is paid to not only whether interaction with diverse peers had a statistically significant effect on students but also the magnitude or size of that effect.[69] The reviewer looks at the effect size found in the individual studies and aggregates effect sizes across studies to determine the overall magnitude of effect. Effect sizes are considered to be small, medium, or large. Many observed effects of college experiences would be classified as small. In the course of normal experience, small effects are not considered to be "large enough to be visible to the naked eye."[70] But small effects can be meaningful if they have important consequences. As small effects accumulate over time, as is the case with microaggressions, they can become large effects.[71]

Two main outcomes of interactions with diverse peers—cognitive development and the reduction of racial bias and prejudice—have been the subjects of meta-analysis.

Cognitive Development

For students who enter college lacking experience interacting with people unlike themselves, such interactions provide "novelty, instability, discontinuity and discrepancy"[72] with past experience. Students may encounter different viewpoints on a variety of social and political issues when they interact with students from different racial and ethnic groups (e.g., different perspectives on the death penalty, the prohibition of racist/sexist speech, the prevalence of discrimination).[73] They are exposed to a broader range of ideas and perspectives that may not fit with past worldviews. When new information is inconsistent with existing frameworks, people find themselves in a state of disequilibrium, which promotes effortful thinking. They will try to reconcile new experiences with existing views or will resolve the situation by changing their views to fit the new input, thus showing cognitive growth.[74]

Nicholas Bowman has synthesized the literature on the outcomes of a combination of classroom and cocurricular diversity experiences on cognitive development.[75] The studies Bowman reviewed look at the development of both cognitive skills and cognitive tendencies. Cognitive skills include skills at critical thinking, problem solving, and information processing. Cognitive tendencies reflect inclinations toward certain styles of thinking (e.g., a disposition toward critical thinking or a tendency to explain behavior as a product of complex influences). Bowman's meta-analysis reveals a positive relationship between diversity experiences and cognitive development, but the effects for cognitive tendencies were twice as large as for cognitive skills, and overall effect sizes for the impact of college diversity experiences on cognitive development were small. Bowman found that cross-race *interaction*s are more strongly related to cognitive development than are diversity courses and workshops. Simply enhancing knowledge is not as effective in promoting cognitive development as are interventions that offer both knowledge *and* intergroup contact. Thus, the training of faculty to effectively handle cross-race interactions in the classroom and address potentially offensive racial comments and emotionally charged reactions of students that can occur when matters like race are under consideration becomes particularly important.

Reduction in Racial Bias and Prejudice

A meta-analysis by Nida Denson, who studies the impact of diversity on student development, covers research on diversity courses and activities designed to reduce racial bias—be it prejudice, stereotypes, emotional reactions (e.g., negative affect, discomfort, anxiety), or discrimination. Denson found that diversity courses and activities do decrease racial bias. The effect size was moderate, a larger effect than was found for the impact of diversity experiences on cognitive development.[76] Because students may know little about members of another race, some courses and programs rely on promoting the acquisition of knowledge of other groups to reduce racial bias, while others rely on both a knowledge approach *and* cross-racial interaction. Similar to Bowman's findings regarding cognitive development, Denson's meta-analysis found that the effect of programming on reducing racial bias is greater if the pedagogical approach uses both knowledge *and* cross-racial interaction.[77] Both Bowman's and Denson's research findings that point to the importance of interpersonal interaction on learning are consistent with our observations about classroom learning, noted previously in this chapter. Another of Denson's findings is of note: White students derived greater benefits from diversity programs than did students of color.

Psychologists Thomas Pettigrew and Linda Tropp did a meta-analysis on a third area of research—the role of intergroup contact in the reduction of prejudice.[78] Their meta-analysis differs in a number of ways from Denson's. Unlike the research reviewed by Denson, the studies reviewed by Pettigrew and Tropp were not exclusively campus based but rather involved multiple settings, age-groups (from children to adults), and target groups (racial/ethnic groups, gay people, disabled people, mentally ill people, and elderly people). Thus their meta-analysis was not restricted to college students or to racial prejudice, as was Denson's, and it includes studies of racial prejudice or prejudice toward a variety of target groups. Pettigrew and Tropp's general findings about the relationship between intergroup contact and the reduction of prejudice are pertinent to our discussion, as we attempt to assess the value of such contacts in college, because their findings were similar across samples and settings.

As discussed in Chapter 6, Gordon Allport claims that intergroup contact can lead to the reduction of prejudice when members of majority and minority groups work together cooperatively on an equal-status basis in the pursuit of common goals and when the interaction is sanctioned by institutional support.[79] The meta-analysis by Pettigrew and Tropp reveals that contact under Allport's optimal conditions does reduce prejudice. In 94 percent of the samples studied, contact reduced prejudice. The overall effect size was small to medium. The effects of intergroup contact were largest when the optimal conditions described by Allport were present, but even when they were not present, contact led to reduced prejudice. Thus these optimal conditions must be seen as facilitating positive outcomes and may not be necessary for producing them. Pettigrew and Tropp found that "institutional support may be an especially important condition for facilitating positive contact effects,"[80] reinforcing the importance of a strong institutional commitment to diversity. Another interesting finding of their analysis is that studies using college students as participants found larger effects from intergroup contact than those based on contact between older adults. This suggests that college students have a greater openness to change than their seniors, underscoring the importance of diversity education at the college level.

It is important to note that the effects of intergroup contact generalized beyond the participants in the immediate interaction to other members of the out-group and even to out-groups not involved in the contact situation. And while intergroup contact effects were significant for members of both minority and majority groups, the effects of contact were stronger for majority than minority group members.[81] The latter result is consistent with Denson's finding that white students benefit more from diversity interventions than do students of color and Tropp's finding that interracial contact is more likely to produce feelings of closeness for white than for black Americans.[82]

Pettigrew and Tropp have also assessed the relative roles of knowledge, empathy, and intergroup threat and anxiety in reducing prejudice,[83] with empathy defined as either cognitive (taking the perspective of another person) or emotional (emotionally reacting to another person's situation or experiencing feelings similar to those of another person).[84] Of the three, decreasing the levels of threat and anxiety in intergroup interactions (e.g., fear of experiencing rejection or of offending others) plays the most important role in reducing prejudice. This is followed in importance by increasing emotional empathy and perspective taking. Enhancing knowledge about the out-group plays the least role, although Allport considers this to be the most important factor. Pettigrew and Tropp conclude that "anxiety must first be reduced with intergroup contact before increased empathy, perspective taking, and knowledge of the outgroup can effectively contribute to prejudice reduction."[85] These findings are important in structuring learning situations for students. The first task in such situations must be to reduce intergroup anxiety and create a safe space for students to talk to one another.

Other Outcomes of Informal Interaction

Beyond the benefits of intergroup interaction described by the three meta-analyses discussed above, intergroup interactions by students outside of the classroom produce a number of other important outcomes. What these outcomes are, however, depends on whether the interactions were positive or negative. Not surprisingly, negative interactions with diverse peers reinforce group differences rather than promote an exploration of commonalities.[86] Having more negative interactions with diverse classmates is associated with lower cultural awareness, lower concern for the public good, less support for race-based initiatives, stronger beliefs in fundamental value differences with classmates from other racial/ethnic groups, and increased identification with one's own racial group. On the other hand, students who have meaningful *positive* interactions with diverse peers show greater cultural awareness and interest in social issues, increased perspective-taking skills, greater interest in the public good, and more support for race-based initiatives.[87] These findings have important implications, underscoring the need for institutions to promote positive and reduce negative interactions among students of different races.

Frequent interracial interaction is associated with greater gains in knowledge about other races/cultures and in acceptance of them.[88] The gains in cultural knowledge from such interactions are greater than gains from attending a cultural awareness workshop.[89] The list of other positive outcomes associated with interracial friendship and interaction is impressive and extensive: increased ability to get along with people of other races/cultures; increased knowledge of and ability to accept different races/cultures; the promotion of racial understanding, positive ethnic attitudes, and a commitment to racial equity; increased critical thinking and problem-solving skills; a greater sense of belonging to one's school; increased college satisfaction; and higher educational aspirations, academic and social self-confidence, and college retention.[90] Students who have close cross-race friends tend to interact more frequently with students of another race who are outside that circle.[91] Students with a higher percentage of cross-race friends show less bias in favor of their ethnic group and, by the end of college, are less anxious around people of another ethnic group.[92] Cross-race interaction is particularly beneficial to the students who have racially homogeneous friendship circles, likely because such interaction takes them outside their comfort zones and presents more interpersonal, emotional, and intellectual challenges.[93]

Some research suggests that the positive effects of having relationships with diverse peers have important implications beyond the college years.

Retrospective reports from a sample of white alumni who attended highly selective colleges and universities show that having gotten to know well two or more black students during college was associated with having more extensive interactions across racial lines *after* college.[94] Similarly positive findings regarding the outcomes of diversity emerge in retrospective reports from University of Michigan alumni, class of 1994, nine years after graduation. Roughly 90 percent of alumni, black and white, reported diversity had had a positive impact on their lives since college, and their perception of that impact had increased since they were assessed in the study as seniors. When asked whether their experience with diversity was an influential aspect of their college years, over 80 percent of black and white alumni who agreed *also* reported that their education had a positive effect on their ability to get along with and work effectively with people of different races and cultures and that it had increased their ability to see the world from someone else's perspective. These percentages were more than double those of the black and white alumni who did not feel that diversity was an influential aspect in their college years. Further, in individual interviews and focus groups, Michigan alumni of all racial groups stressed the benefit of their college experience in preparing them for life and work in diverse settings and in increasing their comfort with diverse groups and perspectives. Finally, the vast majority of black and white alumni agreed that "enhancing a student's ability to live in a multicultural society is part of a university's mission."[95] These findings underscore the importance of colleges' and universities' commitment to diversity and all that it entails.

In the Dorm Room

What happens when students of different races are assigned to room together in a residence hall? Field studies (i.e., studies occurring outside the lab, in natural settings) have been conducted to examine the outcomes of living with a cross-race roommate.[96] In these studies, entering first-year students were randomly assigned to either a cross-race or same-race roommate, and roommates were followed over the course of a semester or an academic year. The findings of these studies are not consistent and paint a mixed picture of cross-race roommate experiences and learning. Many positive outcomes of living with a cross-race roommate have been reported—increased positive affect, attitudes, and comfort by white students toward various ethnic groups; a reduction in intergroup anxiety; increased interethnic competence; a reduction in racism; more personal contact with people from other racial/ethnic groups; more heterogeneous friendship groups; more out-group dating; and more positive attitudes toward affirmative action two to four years after college. One particularly interesting study by psychologists Natalie Shook and Russell Fazio found that living with a black roommate affects white students' implicit, automatically activated racial attitudes as well: White students randomly assigned to live with black roommates showed more positive implicit racial attitudes over time, while white classmates living with white roommates showed no such attitude change.[97]

Many negative outcomes, however, have also been documented in studies.[98] The negative findings should not be entirely surprising, given the prevalence of racial prejudice and stereotyping in our society, the lack of experience and skills most students have in bridging differences, and the fact that roommates interact with one another often under less-than-optimal conditions—when they are tired, stressed, and thus possibly less able to monitor and control their behavior. Researchers report that, compared with those in white-white roommate relationships, interracial roommates show less compatibility; tend to spend less time together inside and outside the room; engage in fewer joint activities; and find the relationships less satisfying, less socially involving, and less comfortable. White students show less intimacy-building behaviors with minority roommates over time, feel less intimate with them, and have fewer positive emotions toward them. Interracial roommates are less likely to stay together after a semester and are less likely to choose an interracial roommate again in the following years.

Research on interracial roommates has examined some of the factors that predict outcomes. One of the important obstacles to developing successful relationships is white students' implicit stereotypes of black people, which lie outside of conscious awareness and control but can be activated and have the potential to affect judgments.[99] Relationships dissolved earlier if white students had more negative, automatically activated racial attitudes that might unconsciously leak into the relationship and influence outcomes.[100] White students' motivation to control prejudiced attitudes made no difference. Those with negative implicit racial attitudes who were motivated to prevent those attitudes from influencing their actions were no more successful in developing enduring relationships with their black roommates than white students who were less motivated.

The attitudes of ethnic minority students (not exclusive to black students) also influence the quality of roommate interactions in the early weeks of school. The more negative the attitudes ethnic minorities held toward white people, the less close they felt to white roommates, the more they avoided them, and the more negative affect they expressed about them.[101] The more minorities expected to be the targets of prejudice, the more negative affect and the less authentic they felt in their interaction with white roommates.[102]

From these studies it is clear that positive outcomes do not necessarily result from being assigned to live with an interracial roommate. To achieve the potential for learning inherent in that living arrangement, the students involved need the skills in hand to communicate effectively, manage conflicts that arise, and deal with the effects of their own prejudices.[103] Undergraduate residence counselors are generally not adequately equipped to teach these skills and to optimally manage the problems that arise in such roommate situations. To produce positive outcomes, more professional staffing and programming are necessary.

On the Ground: What Cocurricular Initiatives Work?

For students, attending a few short diversity events over the course of their college years is not sufficient to achieve the outcomes desired by the institution or the attendees. To be truly effective, cocurricular diversity initiatives require structure and instruction and need to be pervasive and deep.[104] Most institutions offer some forms of programming related to diversity to complement the regular curriculum—for example, diversity workshops and retreats, intergroup dialogues, and peer-facilitated training (i.e., experientially based programs facilitated by students).[105] Consistent with the research on diversity courses, research has shown that diversity-related activities that have both a knowledge component *and* the experience of cross-group interaction have a larger effect on reducing racial bias than those that focus on knowledge alone.[106]

Studies have been done that assess effects of participation across a variety of types of cocurricular diversity programming. As was true for outcome research on cross-group interaction and friendship, the list of educational outcomes from these programs is extensive and positive, although the magnitude of these effects has not been assessed and remains unknown,[107] as are the long-term effects. Participating in more diversity activities is associated with reporting higher levels of positive interactions with diverse peers.[108] Such participation is also associated with greater multicultural competence, increased cultural awareness, and greater awareness and knowledge about the contribution other groups and one's own group have made to society. Participating was related to increased interest in social issues and increased concern for the public good. Beliefs, too, were subject to change, moving toward the ideas that social inequality is not acceptable, racial inequality is a problem, and making a civic contribution is important. Students also acquired an increased belief in their competence to produce social change. They reported greater support for institutional diversity and race-based initiatives. Finally, research that has addressed the outcomes of participation in *specific* diversity activities has found similarly positive outcomes.[109]

One finding that emerges from the research on cocurricular diversity initiatives is similar to findings cited previously from the research on the reduction of racial bias and prejudice. White students learn more than those who are nonwhite from all kinds of diversity programming.[110] Diversity programming increases perspective taking in white but not in nonwhite students; for white students, it increases a sense of commonality with students of color but does not have the same effect for students of color.[111] Thus, in designing diversity programming, it is important to consider ways to construct initiatives that will be of benefit to both white students and minority students.

Given the consistent finding that active learning produces the strongest outcomes, it is encouraging to note that some colleges have developed and/ or are using a variety of types of cocurricular programming that involve active engagement of students in their learning. Let us look at several examples. The IGR program at the University of Michigan, described previously, offers not only academic courses but also cocurricular programs and community activities with the goal of education for social justice.[112] Student organizations, groups, or residence halls can request workshops through the Common Ground Workshop Program on topics such as racism and classism. As is the case with the IGR's intergroup courses, the workshops engage students in dialogues to increase students' awareness and knowledge about issues of identity, power, privilege, and social justice. Research shows that participation in these intergroup dialogues increases students' ability to see the world through another person's perspective. Further, it helps develop a pluralistic orientation and a concern about poverty.[113]

At Columbia University, the ROOTEd (Respecting Ourselves and Others through Education) program facilitates discussions about diversity—about the differences in the social and political treatment accorded different groups in our society.[114] Peer facilitators are trained each year by the Office of Multicultural Affairs to run dialogues for residential students as well as student organizations. According to the program's web page, "ROOTEd teaches anti-bias strategies in conjunction with conflict resolution to help students create a community that is truly anti-oppressive."[115] ROOTEd attempts to provide students with skills and insights they will use beyond their college years.

A number of campuses are using interactive theatre techniques to enhance student and faculty sensitivity to and understanding of diversity issues. By performing sketches about controversial personal and social issues, interactive theater troupes enable students to see their experiences mirrored on stage. The University of Missouri, Columbia, for example, has an Interactive Theatre Troupe that was founded in 2003 when the university joined a multicampus program sponsored by the Carnegie Academy for the Advancement of Teaching and Learning and the American Association for Higher Education.[116] The troupe performs for classes and is also used for faculty development. Typically, the troupe does a ten-minute sketch in which students encounter a diversity issue they do not know how to handle. The scene freezes at a dramatic point in the action, and actors remain in character and dialogue with the audience. Students can ask actors what they were thinking and feeling. The company than asks students to come onstage and try out their own ideas to improve the situation. Students enter the scene and attempt to influence the conflict.

Many colleges and universities are actively trying to engage students in local and global communities through cocurricular service learning, described earlier in this chapter. Service learning programs have been found to increase knowledge and understanding of different racial groups and the ability to relate to diverse others, to reduce negative stereotypes, and to increase students' concern for the public good and their belief in the importance of making a civic contribution.[117]

Living-Learning Communities

What happens when students who live together also take one or more courses together and attend workshops together focused on multicultural issues? Such communities, called living-learning communities, have been found to produce positive learning outcomes. Compared to living in traditional residence halls, students in living-learning communities have more interaction with one another and have more positive perceptions of the climates of their residence halls and their campuses regarding racial/ethnic diversity. Peer interaction in living-learning communities is related to a greater openness to diversity, greater appreciation of differences, and the ability to get along with people different from oneself.[118]

The Phelps Scholars Program at Hope College in Holland, Michigan, serves as an example of the living-learning approach,[119] this one designed for first-year students with a strong interest in learning about issues of race and culture. Phelps scholars include African American, Asian American, European American, Hispanic American, Native American, and international students. They live together in a dormitory, enroll in one of three fall seminars on a diversity-related topic together, and in the spring take "Encounter with Cultures," a class that examines selected racial, ethnic, religious, and cultural groups in the United States. The students participate in workshops, discussions, and other activities related to race and culture throughout the year. The program provides participants with the opportunity to put curricular and cocurricular learning into practice in building meaningful cross-group relationships with their dorm mates. The faculty members who teach in the program also serve as academic advisers to the students. Phelps Scholars report an easier transition to college than other first-year students. They form a larger number of meaningful relationships with students, faculty, and staff and are more involved in cocurricular activities. Their four-year graduation rate exceeds the campus average.[120]

Racial/Ethnic Cultural Centers: Upsides and Downsides

In response to the increased ethnic diversity on campus, many colleges and universities have created racial/ethnic community centers and/or residence halls. Along with student cultural organizations, these offer ethnic minority students a "home away from home," providing academic, social, and emotional support, as well as mentoring. They serve as a "safe space" to which minority students can retreat from perceived hostility on predominantly white campuses. They are places in which students can explore their ethnic heritage and discuss issues of identity and difference in many forms. They provide support to minority students to promote their cultures on campus while celebrating and affirming their collective identity.[121]

On many campuses, staff members are associated with black cultural centers (BCCs). An interview study of black members of a BCC at a predominantly white college found staff members "often act as surrogate family members in helping students to overcome academic and personal challenges. Black students often call on BCC staff members to provide support, encouragement, advice, and critiquing, when necessary."[122] The study speaks both to the importance of student affairs professionals to BCCs and to the fact that staff members often go beyond the call of duty to meet the needs of the students.

The decision of minority students to join race-based student organizations, become involved in race-based community centers, and/or live in residence halls with others largely of their own race/ethnicity is related to many factors, ranging from the degree of centrality of ethnicity to self-definition to the perceived racial climate on campus. Perhaps unsurprisingly, participation in ethnic organizations leads to increases in ethnic identity, in ethnic activism, and in the desire to support their group politically, as well as an increased sense that they and their ethnic group have been targets of discrimination.[123] It also leads to increased agreement that "more good jobs for other groups come at the expense of fewer good jobs for members of my group."[124]

Some educators have raised concern that these "safe space" initiatives promote racial segregation and intergroup tension.[125] Students who belong to ethnic organizations or who live in racially focused or theme housing have less frequent cross-race interactions.[126] In addition, over time members of ethnic organizations are more likely to perceive that ethnic groups are locked in a zero-sum conflict with one another than minority students who choose not to join.[127]

In response to concerns that ethnic organizations promote racial segregation, some campuses are striving to find ways to create interaction between members of different cocurricular groups. Stanford University has four ethnic community centers—the Asian American Activities Center, the Black Community Services Center, El Centro Chicano, and the Native American Cultural Center. The centers collaborate to offer Leading through Education, Activism, and Diversity, a joint leadership development program to facilitate students' ability to work together for social change.[128] Six students from each of the four centers take part in a two-quarter program that culminates in a social change project. At Columbia, the Office of Multicultural Affairs Diversity Initiative Grant can be used by student organizations to support events that fulfill at least two of three criteria: foster diversity education, promote multicultural awareness, and/or create avenues for cross-cultural dialogue.[129] Additionally, the grant supports intergroup communication and collaboration among student organizations. Emory University in Atlanta has a Multicultural Council to foster collaboration and interaction between diverse student organizations on campus.

Advising, Mentoring, and Support Groups

Institutions have a responsibility to provide the support necessary to help ensure the success of all students they bring to campus. Many lower-income and minority students need that support to adjust to unfamiliar situations; to learn the often unspoken rules and competencies important to success at college; and to cope with academic, social, and personal difficulties.[130] These students often benefit from a deeper, more personal relationship with faculty members or other professionals on campus than is usually offered by academic advisers[131] or from support groups composed of students like themselves.

Mentors, be they concerned faculty or student affairs professionals, can provide support and guidance to students in adjusting to college, help them forge relationships with faculty and peers, and connect them to needed campus resources. Mentors can encourage students to take advantage of opportunities that would prepare them for the future but might go unrecognized: internships or jobs that offer meaningful work experience for professional development, study abroad for personal and academic development, participation in extracurricular activities for building new competencies and leadership skills, making connections with students and faculty that may be useful in finding future jobs.[132] Mentors can provide the encouragement, support, and motivation needed to persist in the face of obstacles. Research suggests that faculty and peer mentoring programs help promote retention and success.[133] Many faculty members, however, lack the knowledge, skills, experience, or interest to be effective mentors to minority and low-income students, and some may see minority groups as defective or substandard.[134] To be skilled mentors, faculty will need additional training, as noted previously in our discussion of curricular change.

Many colleges offer peer and/or faculty mentors to lower-income, first-generation, and underrepresented minority students. For example, the University of Virginia has a peer advising program for African American first-year and entering transfer students to provide personalized support in getting through the difficulties of adjustment. The program begins once the student is admitted to the college. A peer adviser contacts the mentee over the summer, serving as "a knowledgeable resource, an encourager, a friend and role model."[135] The program's motto is "Lending a Helping Hand: Academically, Psychologically and Socially."[136] At Davidson College in North Carolina, academic, cultural, and social support is offered to first-year ethnic minority students through STRIDE, a peer mentoring program that helps facilitate adjustment to the college.[137] Peer mentors serve as resources for first-year students; they meet with them initially at an enrichment program before college starts. During the academic year, STRIDE runs monthly activities for participants and brings them together for a retreat at the beginning of the second semester to evaluate their first semester.[138]

A number of institutions have mentoring programs specifically for low-income students. At the University of North Carolina at Chapel Hill, first-year low-income students who meet the financial criteria to be "Covenant Scholars" are assigned to faculty/professional staff mentors as well as to peer mentors to help with their adjustment to campus life. The students are encouraged to take part in academic, social, and cultural enrichment programs. Workshops provide them with some of the cultural capital they may lack. Topics covered include study skills, time management, note taking, test taking, financial literacy, public speaking, and dinner etiquette. Classes are offered to help these students explore possible careers.[139] At North Carolina State University, the neediest students have access to Pack Promise. In addition to financial assistance, these students receive the benefit of an upperclassman mentor throughout their first year to help them solve problems. They also have a faculty or staff member who serves as an academic coach. Much like the Covenant Scholar program in Chapel Hill, Pack Promise offers its students workshops on topics such as time management, academic strategies, and how to organize finances.[140]

Some universities have developed summer research mentoring programs through which students develop a better understanding of research and learn some of the skills needed to do it. In addition to this hands-on learning, the students ideally develop relationships with faculty members who can later provide references and connect them to future research opportunities.[141] In reality, unfortunately, faculty members have often left their undergraduates to work independently and have not invested sufficient time and effort in the mentoring relationship to realize its intended effect.

As noted in the section on racial/ethnic cultural centers, support groups made up of students like themselves have proved helpful to lower-income and minority students. The Posse Foundation makes such groups an integral part of its efforts to support minority students at the colleges and universities who have partnered with it. The Posse Foundation helps recruit, train, and bring talented inner-city high school students with academic and leadership potential to individual partnered campuses in groups of ten, with full-tuition scholarships. These groups, or "posses," are central to carrying out the mission of the program, as their members serve as a support system for one another. In addition, Posse Foundation students are given special mentors to help them adjust to college life.[142]

Many colleges have organized support groups for students of color or subsets of these students (e.g., women of color, men of color, Latinos) to address the unique needs and experiences of these students. The University of Michigan, for example, runs the Nourish Program, a lunch series for all women of color, including undergraduates, graduate students, faculty, and staff. In "an open, spirited atmosphere," the Nourish Program "seeks to empower women of color around issues of identity, intercultural competency, and health and wellness that affect them. . . . It offers a space for self-expression, reflection, and open dialogue."[143]

Other Class-Based Initiatives

One last example of how an institution can be of help to its increasingly diverse students is one directed at a very practical concern—how to fit in with limited economic resources. Harvard University created the Harvard Financial Aid Initiative, which, in turn, led to the publication of *Shoestring Strategies for Life @ Harvard: A Guide for Students on a Budget.*[144] The publication includes advice on buying furniture and textbooks, information on subsidized music lessons and tutoring, and the procedures for getting free tickets from the Student Events Fund. *Shoestring Strategies* also offers inexpensive date ideas and information about the Beneficiary Aid fund, which provides assistance for emergency expenses. Students can use the publication to learn how to find job openings on campus or affordable summer housing in Cambridge/Boston, how to get summer internships, or how to handle graduation expenses. Harvard also has a Winter Coat Fund, which provides first-year low-income students from warm climates with the money for winter coats, boots, gloves, and other items needed to help them get through winter, as well as information about where to purchase them.

Conclusion

Diversity is "clearly our present and our future," writes Daryl Smith, a professor of education and psychology,[145] and higher education can play an important role in educating students to become citizens of our increasingly diverse society. Creating a diverse student body is a necessary step, but it is not sufficient to ensure that students will be able to thrive on campus or that positive cross-group interactions and learning from differences will occur.

To attain those outcomes, colleges and universities must take an active role, beginning with recognition of the importance of what is at stake and a willingness to address the issues with sustained institutional commitment. Institutions need to ensure a positive climate and promote a sense of belonging for all students. To enhance the chances that positive learning from diversity takes place, institutions need to provide coursework and programming that are experiential and knowledge based and led by well-trained faculty and facilitators.[146] Along with diversity courses, diversity issues need to be incorporated where appropriate across the curriculum. Cocurricular activities and mentoring need to be in place. With a clear mission statement, dedicated leadership, and a diverse faculty and staff committed to making diversity work, colleges and universities can serve as models of well-functioning, diverse communities—models that students will carry with them as they move out into the larger world.

Appendix A: Online Survey Measures

ACADEMIC CONFIDENCE

Students were asked to indicate the following on a 7-point scale (1 = not at all confident, 7 = very confident): "how confident you feel about" your academic preparation, your writing skills, your general academic knowledge, your intelligence, your ability to express your ideas, and your meriting being at Amherst College. Scores on these six items were averaged to form a measure of Academic Confidence (Chronbach's alpha = 0.80).

FEELINGS OF COMFORT AND INCLUSION IN RELATION TO PEERS

Students were given a list of thirteen bipolar adjectives and asked to indicate the following: the point on the 7-point continuum between the two poles that "best described your feeling in the past week." The list of adjectives included comfortable/uncomfortable, included/excluded, insider/outsider, adequate/inadequate, optimistic/pessimistic, not intimidated/intimidated, capable/not capable, distant/close, valued/not valued, knowledgeable/ignorant, listened to/unheard, superior/inferior, and appreciated/unappreciated. Scores on these thirteen items were averaged to form a measure of Feelings in Relation to Peers (Chronbach's alpha = 0.88).

OVERALL WELL-BEING, GROWTH, AND ADJUSTMENT

Students were asked to rate their psychological health and social life on a 7-point scale (1 = poor, 4 = good, 7 = excellent). Students were asked to indicate the following on a 7-point scale (1 = not at all, 4 = somewhat, 7 = a lot): "up to this point in your college career, how much you feel you have" grown as a person, changed in order to fit in at Amherst College, and found a place at the college. The items were derived from those developed by N. E. Cantor and D. A. Prentice (1996).

Students were asked to indicate the following on a 7-point scale (1 = never, 7 = very often): "In the past month, how often have you felt" that you were unable to control the important things in your life, that you were coping effectively with important changes in your life, that you were confident about your ability to handle your personal problems, and that difficulties were piling up so high that you could not overcome them? Scores on these four items were averaged to form a measure of Coping Effectively with Important Changes (Chronbach's alpha = 0.78).

ACADEMICS

Students were asked whether they were willing to release their grades on file at the college. They were asked to list their major(s). Students were asked to indicate the following on a 4-point scale (1 = for most assignments, 2 = for some assignments, 3 = rarely, 4 = never): "Approximately how often do you go to the Writing Center, Quantitative Center, professors' office hours, review sessions, and problem-solving sessions?" Scores on these five items were averaged to form a measure of seeking academic help (Chronbach's alpha = 0.70).

DIFFICULTIES POSED BY SOCIAL CLASS AND RACE

Students were asked to rate twelve items on a 7-point scale (1 = much easier, 4 = neither easier nor more difficult, 7 = much more difficult), indicating whether being a member of their social class made each item easier or more difficult. They were then asked to rate the twelve items again, indicating whether being a member of their race made each one easier or more difficult. The items were based on those developed by Cantor and Prentice (1996). Three items were highly intercorrelated: being taken seriously by professors, forming relationships with professors, and earning good grades in coursework. They were averaged to form a measure of Academic Integration (Chronbach's alphas regarding social class and race were 0.77 and 0.66, respectively). Four items were highly intercorrelated: feeling comfortable on campus, finding like-minded friends, finding refuge on campus when things are going badly, and being included in informal activities with classmates. Scores on these four items were averaged to form a measure of Social Integration and Comfort (Chronbach's alphas regarding social class and race were 0.80 and 0.60, respectively). The remaining five items did not highly intercorrelate and were retained as single items: making friends of different races/social classes, making contacts for the future, getting invited to social events, going home for family visits/occasions, and having parents or family members visit the students at Amherst.

FRIENDSHIPS ACROSS RACE AND CLASS

Students were asked: "Have you gotten to *know well two or more* students who are white? Have you gotten to *know well two or more* students who are black? Have you gotten to *know well two or more* students who are from much wealthier families than your own? Have you gotten to *know well two or more* students who are from much poorer families than your own? How many close friends do you have at Amherst College? How many of those close friends are members of your social class? How many of those close friends are members of your race? Have you had a roommate or student in your room group of a different race than your own freshman year, sophomore year, junior year, senior year (specify race[s])?"

SALIENCE OF RACE AND CLASS

Students were asked: "Over the past month, how much thought have you given to your social class? Over the past month, how much thought have you given to your race? Approximately how often do you: Discuss racial issues with other students? Discuss issues of social class with other students?" Response categories included the following: daily, two or three times per week, once a week, a few times a month, a few times per semester, and never.

PARTICIPATION IN EXTRACURRICULAR ACTIVITIES AND WORK

Students were asked to do the following: "List the extracurricular groups that you belong to (e.g., athletic teams, religious groups, performance groups, community outreach, ethnic/cultural groups)." They were also asked if they had a job on or off campus and how many hours they worked.

LIFE ON CAMPUS

Students were instructed, "Indicate how many *hours in a typical week* (including the weekend) you spend" in class/lab, studying/working on class assignments, and working at a job.

Appendix B: Interview Questions

Questions preceded by an asterisk (*) were asked again, substituting "race" for "social class."

If students answered "yes" to a question, they were asked follow-up questions (e.g., Can you give me an example? Could you describe the incident?).

Questions preceded by a superscript "b" ([b]) were asked to black students only.

Questions preceded by a superscript "w" ([w]) were asked to white students only.

SOCIAL CLASS AND RACE IN DAY-TO-DAY LIFE ON CAMPUS

- Do you feel you can discern what social class students are by their clothes, possessions, personalities, or lifestyles?
- Do you ever think about differences in wealth between students on campus? How often do you think about class differences between students?
- Have you ever felt uncomfortable around peers about your family's resources, or what you or your family have or do not have? Have you ever felt the desire to hide your class origins?
- Have you ever felt excluded based on your social class—for example, from trips, activities on campus or off campus, summer plans, or conversations?
- Have you ever spent money to be part of an activity you really could not afford so as not to stand out?
- Have students ever offered to pay for you in order to include you or changed plans to include you in some activity? Have you or you and a group of friends ever made allowances to include someone who could not pay?
- Have you heard students make assumptions about wealthy students or about poor students?

- Have you ever read any offensive comments about people who are wealthy or who are lower-income on online forums like the Daily Jolt or the Amherst Confessional, or in a student publication?
- Have you ever heard joking about people who are very wealthy or who are poor?
- Have you developed a close relationship with a student who comes from a very different class background than you do?
- Was it important for you to have friends of the same social class?
- Was it important for you to have friends of a different social class?
- *Do you feel your experience at Amherst living and interacting with people from different class backgrounds has changed the way you see people of other social classes or your own social class?
- Suppose that it were possible for you and all of your family to be born all over again. Would you want to be born into the same social class or a different social class? Why?
- *Are there times when you have felt being a member of your social class opened up social opportunities for you or allowed you to be included—for example, in conversations, activities, or social gatherings?
- *Has there ever been an incident here on campus when you felt your class position caused you to be put down or dismissed?
- *Have you had meaningful, honest conversations with students about issues of social class? [If yes:] Did these conversations cause you to see something differently?
- *Do you wish you had more honest conversations about social class and class issues?
- *Do you feel there are cliques of students based on social class from which you feel excluded, or are there cliques of students based on social class you have avoided because you would not want to be part of them?
- *Have people made other assumptions about you because of your class background that you feel are incorrect?
- *Do you ever feel that you are regarded as a representative of your social class? [If yes:] How have you experienced that—for example, as a burden? As an opportunity? Do you feel this in the classroom or with peers outside the classroom?
- *Have you dated someone from a different social class while at Amherst? [If yes:] What, if any, issues came up in negotiating this relationship that you would ascribe to social class differences?
- Have you found it easier to become friends on campus with someone of the same race than someone of a different race?
- Do you feel people on campus make assumptions about black students? About white students?
- Have you ever heard students make offensive racial comments about black students or students of other races?
- Have you ever heard racial comments made as jokes? [If yes:] Have you found racial joking to be humorous? Offensive?
- Do you ever joke about race?
- Have you perceived incidents of racism, large or small, on campus? How frequently have you witnessed or experienced this?
- Have you ever read any offensive comments about people of your race or other races in online forums like the Daily Jolt or the Amherst Confessional, or in a student publication?

- What were your attitudes toward interracial dating when you arrived at Amherst?
- How do you feel about black students dating white students?
- Do you feel your attitudes about interracial dating have changed over your four years here?
- [b]How salient is your race for you on a day-to-day basis?
- [b]Do you ever feel students assume you got accepted to Amherst College because you were black?
- [b]How comfortable do you feel interacting with students who are white? Is this a change from how you felt when you first arrived?
- [b]Have you developed a close relationship with a student who is white? [If yes:] Do you talk about race or racial issues?
- [b]Have you felt pressures to hang out with students of your race?
- [b]Has your "blackness" ever been questioned, or have you ever been accused of "acting white"?
- [b]Do you eat at the tables of black students in the dining hall? How do you view those tables?
- [b]Have you gotten close to another black student from a very different class background than your own?
- [b]Black students talked freshman year about three ways of handling offensive racial comments made by white students: (1) getting angry, (2) hiding their feelings at the time but venting them to black friends later, or (3) educating the white person. Do you feel there are other options? How do you respond to offensive racial comments you might hear? Has your response changed over time?
- [b]Have you ever heard derogatory comments, even if framed in a joking manner, from other black students on campus about skin tone—about being light or dark skinned? [If yes:] How did you feel and respond?
- [b]Have you heard derogatory comments about white students made by black students?
- [b]Do you feel there are different challenges for black women than for black men on campus?
- [b]If you look back on your four years, are there any negative experiences you have had here that you attribute to being a black student?
- [b]If you look back on your four years here, what strengths do you think Amherst offers for black students?
- [w]How comfortable do you feel interacting with students who are black? Is this a change from how you felt when you first arrived?
- [w]Have you developed a close relationship with a student who is black? [If yes:] Do you talk about race or racial issues?
- [w]Do you feel that black students self-segregate?
- [w]What are your thoughts, if any, about the tables of black students eating together in the dining hall?
- [w]If a group of black students is hanging out together, do you feel comfort[?] joining that group?

ACADEMICS AND CLASSROOM ISSUES

- Do you feel you were underprepared academically when you arrived at Amhers[?]
- Were you able to acquire the skills you needed to get up to speed with othe[?] students? How did you do that?

- Have financial constraints ever kept you from buying books for your courses or buying other course-related materials?
- Do you feel you have had trouble asking for help? Did that change over time? [If yes:] What led to that change?
- If you cannot turn in an assignment on time, how do you handle that?
- Do you speak up in classroom discussions? [If no:] What keeps you from sharing your views?
- Are there burdens you carry from your family that have pulled you away from your coursework or that you feel have kept you from doing your best academically?
- Are there professors, deans, or other adults who you feel really know you well and who you turned to for help and who helped you be successful at Amherst?
- *Do you feel there were academic obstacles you faced at Amherst because of your social class?
- *Do you feel there were academic advantages you had at Amherst because of your social class?
- *Did you take any courses that addressed class issues?
- *Have you ever felt put on the spot in a course to speak for your social class when class issues were under discussion?
- *Have you ever heard negative class-based stereotypes or offensive class-based comments in class from students or professors?
- *Has personal sharing occurred by students of different social classes in any of the courses you took at Amherst that caused you to change the way you understand social class or your class position?
- ᵇDo you feel professors ever viewed or treated you differently because of your race?

RELATIONSHIPS WITH FAMILY, FRIENDS, AND HOME COMMUNITY

- Over your years at college, are you aware of having changed in any ways to "fit in" at Amherst—for example, buying different clothes or adopting different ways of thinking, speaking, or interacting?
- Have the changes you have made while at Amherst brought you closer or made you more distant from family? [If more distant:] Do you feel you have developed ways to help bridge differences?
- Are there aspects of your life and experiences at Amherst that you cannot share with family members at home?
- Do you ever help pay family expenses when you are home?
- Do you ever send money home to your family?
- In what ways, if any, do you view your friends from home differently now that you have been at Amherst? Do they view you differently?
- Have the changes you have made at Amherst brought you closer or made you more distant from friends at home? [If more distant:] Do you feel you have developed ways to help bridge discontinuities?
- Are there aspects of your life and experiences at Amherst that you cannot share with friends from home?
- Do you view your home community differently now from the way you did before you got to Amherst—people's values, outlooks, or attitudes?
- Have you ever felt you were juggling two worlds or cultures, one at Amherst and one at home, where you must change how you speak or dress or act as you move back and forth between them?

- Are there people at home—family or friends—who you feel are vicariously living through you, or who want you to live out things they did not?
- Have you sought advice from family members about academic or social problems that have arisen on campus?
- Have your parents or family members visited you here on campus? How many visits did they make? What were those visits like?
- What advice, if any, have your parents given you about what you should do after college?
- What were your summer jobs or internships over the last three summers? Did any of these summer experiences influence or help further your career aspirations?
- How important do you feel it is to have connections in order to become a success—that is, connections through family, students at Amherst and their families, or Amherst faculty and alumni?
- After you finish your schooling, do you see yourself helping to support your family or as getting support from your family? [If helping to support family:] Has that had an influence on your major or your career plans?

SUPPORT FOR DIVERSITY

- Could you tell me some of the ways you think Amherst has been a good place for you as a member as your race and social class—for example, what strengths does Amherst offer?
- What could Amherst College have done, if anything, to have made this a better place for you as a person of your race and social class?
- As a person of your race and social class, given what you hoped for when you chose Amherst, how has the reality matched what you imagined?
- Do you feel it might have been valuable to have been assigned a mentor of your race or of your social class?
- What advice would you offer to someone of your race and class coming in as a first-year student, based on your experience?
- *Would you like to see more structured dialogue about social class between students led by trained professionals?
- [b]Do you feel there has been adequate institutional support for you as a member of a minority group? What kind of support would you have found helpful?

BACKGROUND QUESTIONS (FOR STUDENTS WHO RELINQUISHED CONFIDENTIALITY)

- Where are you from? Could you tell me a little about the community you grew up in?
- Could you tell me a little about your high school? What is its size, its resources, and the quality of preparation it provided you? How much exposure to and interaction with people of different races and classes did you have in high school?
- Could you tell me a little about your family? Who lives in your household? What do your parents/guardians do? How many siblings do you have? How old are your siblings? What do your siblings do? Have your parents or siblings gone to college? To a residential college like Amherst?
- What would you say are the unearned privileges, if any, you have had in your life?
- What would you say were the disadvantages, if any, you have faced in your life?

Notes

CHAPTER 1

1. Skrentny 2002; Zweigenhaft and Domhoff 2006. For a more thorough discussion of affirmative action and diversity, see also Skrentny 2001; and Zweigenhaft and Domhoff 2011.

2. Perez and Hirschman 2009.

3. Rudenstine 2001, 116.

4. Students were not surveyed at the end of the second and third years of college for practical reasons. Given the small sample size, and the variability within groups, it would have been extremely difficult to detect year-to-year changes by group. Further, the collection and analysis of qualitative data is extremely time-consuming, and it was not feasible to collect and analyze that quantity of data.

5. For more detail on the backgrounds of students in these groups, see Aries 2008. See also Davis 2010 for a discussion of the distinction between first-generation college students and low-income students.

6. See U.S. Census Bureau 2012.

7. Aries 2008. See Appendix A for the survey questions asked in the final wave of data collection; see Appendix B for the interview questions.

8. Waiving confidentiality was not offered as an option in the study of the first year. In the final wave of data collection, two lower-income students, one white and one black, and one affluent white student declined to be interviewed. The two white students were on campus; the black student was taking the semester off and planned to return the following semester. Only one of the original fifty-eight students, a lower-income white student, had left the college, but she was considering returning and agreed to a phone interview.

9. Orfield, Frankenberg, and Lee 2002/2003.

10. Sidanius et al. 2008, 321.

CHAPTER 2

1. For lower-income black students ($N = 13$), 23 percent had thought about their social class "little to not at all" over the past month, 46 percent "some," and 31 percent "a lot." For affluent black students ($N = 14$), 36 percent had thought about their social class "little to not at all" over the past month, 43 percent "some," and 21 percent "a lot." A χ^2 test could not be calculated because four cells had expected values less than five.

2. For lower-income black students ($N = 13$), 15 percent had thought about race "little to not at all" over the past month, 46 percent "some," and 39 percent "a lot." For affluent black students ($N = 14$), 14 percent had thought about their race "little to not at all" over the past month, 43 percent "some," and 43 percent "a lot." A χ^2 test could not be calculated because two cells had expected values less than five.

3. Thirty-three percent of lower-income white students ($N = 15$), 46 percent of lower-income black students ($N = 13$), 33 percent of affluent white students ($N = 12$), and 50 percent of affluent black students ($N = 12$) said they had spent money to join an activity they could not afford. A χ^2 test could not be calculated because two cells had expected values less than five.

4. Seventy-five percent of lower-income white students ($N = 12$), 77 percent of lower-income black students ($N = 13$), 75 percent of affluent white students ($N = 12$), and 69 percent of affluent black students ($N = 13$) said they had changed their plans in order to include others who could not pay. A χ^2 test could not be calculated because four cells had expected values less than five.

5. Fifty-three percent of lower-income white students ($N = 15$) and 92 percent of lower-income black students ($N = 13$) said students had offered to pay for them, or changed plans to include them. For lower-income students race made a significant difference in students' reports that classmates had offered to pay for them, Fisher's exact test, $p = 0.038$. A χ^2 test could not be calculated because two cells had expected values less than five.

6. Eighty percent of lower-income white students ($N = 15$) and 46 percent of lower-income black students ($N = 13$) said they felt excluded from activities on the basis of their social class. For lower-income students race did not make a significant difference in students reporting feeling excluded on the basis of social class, Fisher's exact test, $p = 0.113$. A χ^2 test could not be calculated because one cell had an expected value less than five.

7. Sixty-seven percent of lower-income white students ($N = 15$), 39 percent of lower-income black students ($N = 13$), 67 percent of affluent white students ($N = 12$), and 64 percent of affluent black students ($N = 14$) said they had dated someone from a very different social class. A χ^2 test could not be calculated because one cell had an expected value less than five.

8. Fifty-seven percent of lower-income white students ($N = 14$), 75 percent of lower-income black students ($N = 12$), 83 percent of affluent white students ($N = 12$), and 54 percent of affluent black students ($N = 13$) took summer jobs that furthered career aspirations over two or three summers during college (versus zero to one summer). A χ^2 test could not be calculated because four cells had expected values less than five.

9. Forty-seven percent of lower-income white students ($N = 15$), 39 percent of lower-income black students ($N = 13$), 75 percent of affluent white students ($N = 12$), and 71 percent of affluent black students ($N = 14$) said they expected to receive

support from parents after they graduated. Group membership was not related to the expectation of receiving support from parents after graduation, χ^2 (3, $N = 54$) = 5.26, $p > 0.05$.

10. Twenty-seven percent of lower-income white students ($N = 15$), 15 percent of lower-income black students ($N = 13$), 50 percent of affluent white students ($N = 12$), and 14 percent of affluent black students ($N = 14$) said they had felt the desire to hide their class origins. A χ^2 test could not be calculated because four cells had expected values less than five.

11. Seven percent of lower-income white students ($N = 15$), 15 percent of lower-income black students ($N = 13$), 25 percent of affluent white students ($N = 12$), and 0 percent of affluent black students ($N = 14$) said they felt their social class caused them to be put down or dismissed. A χ^2 test could not be calculated because four cells had expected values less than five.

12. D. Smith 2009, 27.

13. See also Davis 2010; and Stuber 2011a.

14. Bourdieu 1977; Bourdieu and Passeron (1964) 1979.

15. See also Hoyt 1999; Lareau and Weininger 2003; and Reay, David, and Ball 2005.

16. Aries and Seider 2005.

17. Marcoux 2009.

18. Cole and Omari 2003; Cookson and Persell 1991; Datnow and Cooper 1997; Horvat and Antonio 1999; Zweigenhaft and Domhoff 1991.

19. Both personal accounts written by working-class academics and research studies document these challenges: Aries and Seider 2005; Baxter and Britton 2001; Bergerson 2007; Dews and Law 1995; Hoyt 1999; Hurst 2010; Lawler 1999; Lehmann 2009; Ostrove 2003; Pascarella et al. 2004; Ryan and Sackrey 1984; Stewart and Ostrove 1993; Stuber 2011a, 2011b; Tokarczyk and Fay 1993; Walpole 2003; Wentworth and Peterson 2001. See also Lubrano 2004.

20. See Aries and Seider 2005.

21. Forty percent of lower-income white students ($N = 15$), 39 percent of lower-income black students ($N = 13$), 58 percent of affluent white students ($N = 12$), and 36 percent of affluent black students ($N = 14$) said they had grown more aware of social class over time. Group membership was not related to becoming more aware of social class over time, χ^2 (3, $N = 54$) = 1.62, $p > 0.05$.

22. See Stuber 2011a.

CHAPTER 3

1. See Aries 2008.

2. At the end of four years 73 percent of lower-income white students ($N = 15$), 67 percent of lower-income black students ($N = 12$), 25 percent of affluent white students ($N = 12$), and 15 percent of affluent black students ($N = 13$) said they were juggling two worlds or cultures. Group membership was significantly related to students feeling that they were juggling two worlds, χ^2 (3, $N = 52$) = 13.61, $p < 0.003$. For affluent students the percentage of students who felt they were juggling two worlds increased from 4 percent at the end of freshman year to 20 percent at the end of senior year.

3. Whether class makes going home for family visit/occasions easier or more difficult: 1 = much easier, 4 = neither easier nor more difficult, 7 = much more difficult.

For lower-income white students, $N = 15$, $M = 4.33$, $SD = 1.63$; for lower-income black students, $N = 13$, $M = 4.54$, $SD = 1.81$; for affluent white students, $N = 13$, $M = 2.31$, $SD = 1.55$; and for affluent black students, $N = 14$, $M = 2.50$, $SD = 1.65$. There was a significant effect of social class, $F(1, 51) = 20.49$, $p < 0.001$, $\eta^2 = 0.29$. There was no significant effect for race, $F(1, 51) = 0.20$, $p > 0.05$, $\eta^2 = 0.004$ and no race by class interaction, $F(1, 51) = 0$, $p > 0.05$, $\eta^2 = 0$.

4. Whether class makes having parents or family members visit at Amherst easier or more difficult: for lower-income white students, $N = 15$, $M = 4.67$, $SD = 1.80$; for lower-income black students, $N = 13$, $M = 5.46$, $SD = 1.76$; for affluent white students, $N = 13$, $M = 2.31$, $SD = 1.65$; and for affluent black students, $N = 14$, $M = 2.50$, $SD = 1.65$. There was a significant effect of social class, $F(1, 51) = 32.79$, $p < 0.001$, $\eta^2 = 0.39$. There was no significant effect for race, $F(1, 51) = 1.13$, $p > 0.05$, $\eta^2 = 0.022$ and no race by class interaction, $F(1, 51) = 0.42$, $p > 0.05$, $\eta^2 = 0.008$.

5. Fifty-eight percent of affluent white students ($N = 12$) and 69 percent of affluent black students ($N = 13$) reported their parents had visited them on campus a few times a year or more. For affluent students, race was not related to parents visiting a few times a year or more versus once a year or less, χ^2 $(1, N = 25) = 0.32$, $p > 0.05$.

6. Forty percent of lower-income white students ($N = 15$), 46 percent of lower-income black students ($N = 13$), 8 percent of affluent white students ($N = 12$), and 14 percent of affluent black students ($N = 14$) said they could not share aspects of their experiences with family members. A χ^2 test could not be calculated because four cells have expected values less than five.

7. Twenty-one percent of the parents of lower-income black students and of affluent black students and 6 percent of the parents of lower-income white students had attended one of the nation's top fifty college or universities. See Aries 2008.

8. Sixty-seven percent of lower-income white students ($N = 15$), 62 percent of lower-income black students ($N = 13$), 25 percent of affluent white students ($N = 12$), and 39 percent of affluent black students ($N = 13$) reported they saw their home communities differently now. Group membership was not significantly related to perceiving home communities differently, χ^2 $(3, N = 53) = 6.04$, $p > 0.05$.

9. D. Reay, G. Crozier, and J. Clayton (2009) also describe working-class students at an elite university who growing up felt like fish out of water among their working-class peers because of their academic dispositions and focus.

10. Forty-seven percent of lower-income white students ($N = 15$), 23 percent of lower-income black students ($N = 13$), 25 percent of affluent white students ($N = 12$), and 23 percent of affluent black students ($N = 13$) said they could not share aspects of their experiences with friends at home. A χ^2 test could not be calculated because four cells have expected values less than five.

11. Seventy-one percent of lower-income white students ($N = 14$), 69 percent of lower-income black student students ($N = 13$), 33 percent of affluent white students ($N = 12$), and 50 percent of affluent black students ($N=12$) said people were vicariously living through them. Group membership was not significantly related to students' feelings that people were vicariously living though them, χ^2 $(3, N = 51) = 4.96$, $p > 0.05$.

12. Forty percent of lower-income white students ($N = 15$), 54 percent of lower-income black students ($N = 13$), 25 percent of affluent white students ($N = 12$), and 29 percent of affluent black students ($N = 14$) said they helped pay for family expenses when at home. A χ^2 test could not be calculated because two cells have expected values less than five.

13. Forty-seven percent of lower-income white students (N = 15), 39 percent of lower-income black students (N = 13), 9 percent of affluent white students (N = 11), and 43 percent of affluent black students (N = 14) said they carried burdens from their families that interfered with their coursework. A χ^2 test was not calculated because two cells have expected values less than five.

14. Seventy-three percent (N = 15) of lower-income white students, 62 percent (N = 13) of lower-income black students, 8 percent (N = 12) of affluent white students, and 14 percent (N=14) of affluent black students said they expected to or would like to support their parents down the road. Group membership was significantly related to the expectation/desire to support parents down the road, χ^2 (3, N = 54) = 18.21, p < 0.001.

15. Forty-seven percent (N = 15) of lower-income white students, 39 percent (N = 13) of lower-income black students, 75 percent (N = 12) of affluent white students, and 71 percent (N = 14) of affluent black students said they expected to receive some support from their parents after graduation. Group membership was not significantly related to the expectation to receive support from parents, χ^2 (3, N = 54) = 5.26, p > 0.05.

16. For example, see Baxter and Britton 2001.

17. See, for example, Bergerson 2007; Hoyt 1999; Ostrove 2003; Stewart and Ostrove 1993; Stuber 2011b; and Wentworth and Peterson 2001.

18. Baxter and Britton 2001, 93. See also Aries and Seider 2005; Granfield 1991; and Stuber 2011b.

19. Reay, David, and Ball 2005.

20. Hurst 2010.

21. In their study of working-class students in higher education in the United Kingdom, D. Reay, M. E. David, and S. J. Ball (2005) found student responses similar to those of Hurst's renegades and loyalists. Reay, Crozier, and Clayton (2009) found working-class students similar to Hurst's double agents.

22. Stuber 2011b.

23. See also Cole and Omari 2003.

CHAPTER 4

1. Letter dated December 12, 2006, in the author's possession.

2. Sixty percent of lower-income white students (N = 15), 92 percent of lower-income black students (N = 13), 50 percent of affluent white students (N = 12), and 64 percent of affluent black students (N = 14) perceived racism on campus. A χ^2 test was not calculated because three cells have expected values less than five.

3. See Harper and Hurtado 2007; and Hurtado et al. 2008.

4. Forty-six percent of lower-income black students (N = 13) and 57 percent of affluent black students (N = 14) said race caused them to be left out, put down, or dismissed. For black students being affluent or lower income was not significantly related to feeling race caused them to be left out, put down, or dismissed, χ^2 (1, N = 27) = 0.33, p > 0.05.

5. Thirty-three percent of lower-income black students (N = 12) and 46 percent of affluent black students (N = 13) said they had heard racially offensive comments made in the classroom. For black students being affluent or lower income was not significantly related to hearing racially offensive comments made in the classroom, χ^2 (1, N = 26) = 0.65, p > 0.05.

6. Sue 2010; Sue, Bucceri, et al. 2007; Sue, Capodilupo, and Holder 2008; Sue, Capodilupo, et al. 2007.

7. Microaggressions pertaining to gender and sexual orientation are prevalent as well (Sue 2010).

8. See Solórzano, Ceja, and Yosso 2000; and Sue 2010.

9. Dovidio and Gaertner 1998.

10. Eighty-five percent of lower-income black students (N = 13) and 71 percent of affluent black students (N = 14) said students made assumptions about them on the basis of race that were incorrect. For black students being affluent or lower income was not significantly related to hearing students make incorrect assumptions about them on the basis of race, Fisher's exact test p = 0.68. A χ^2 test could not be calculated because two cells have expected values less than five.

11. In the current study, all but five students were willing to release their SAT scores, and two had taken the ACT rather than the SAT. Based on fifty-one of the fifty-eight students, the numbers show that black students had an average SAT score of 1284, while white students had an average score of 1488. Espenshade and Radford (2009) report that all else being equal, black applicants receive a boost in admission of 310 SAT points out of 1600 at private institutions.

12. Eighty-five percent of lower-income black students (N = 13) and 69 percent of affluent black students (N = 13) said they were seen as representatives of their race. For black students, being affluent or lower income was not significantly related to being seen as a representative of their race, Fisher's exact test, p = 0.65. A χ^2 test was not calculated because two cells have expected values less than five.

13. Fifty-four percent of lower-income black students (N = 13) and 50 percent of affluent black students (N = 14) felt they were regarded as a representative of their race in the classroom. For black students being affluent or lower income was not significantly related to being regarded as a representative of their race in the classroom, χ^2 (1, N = 27) = 0.04, p > 0.05.

14. Sixty-seven percent of lower-income white students (N = 15), 100 percent of lower-income black students (N = 13), 60 percent of affluent white students (N = 10), and 93 percent of affluent black students (N = 14) said they engaged in joking about race. A χ^2 test was not calculated because four cells have expected values less than five.

15. Eighty percent of lower-income white students (N = 15), 85 percent of lower-income black students (N = 13), 75 percent of affluent white students (N = 12), and 79 percent of affluent black students (N = 14) found the racial joking on campus to be humorous and affectionate. A χ^2 test was not calculated because four cells have expected values less than five.

16. Seventy-three percent of lower-income white students (N = 15), 85 percent of lower-income black students (N = 13), 91 percent of affluent white students (N = 11), and 93 percent of affluent black students (N = 14) heard racist comments framed as jokes. A χ^2 test was not calculated because four cells have expected values less than five.

17. Eighty-three percent of lower-income black students (N = 12) and 64 percent of affluent black students (N = 14) had read offensive racial posts on the online forums. For black students being affluent or lower income was not related to reading offensive racial posts on the online forums, Fisher's exact test p = 0.39. A χ^2 test was not calculated because two cells have expected values less than five.

18. Thirty-one percent of lower-income black students (N = 13), and 14 percent affluent black students (N = 14) responded to racial offenses by getting angry.

For black students, being affluent or lower income was not related to responding to racial offenses by getting angry, Fisher's exact test $p = 0.39$. A χ^2 test was not calculated because two cells have expected values less than five.

19. Fifty-four percent of lower-income black students ($N = 13$) and 57 percent of affluent black students ($N = 14$) said they handled racial offenses by hiding their feelings. For black students, being affluent or lower income was not significantly related to handling racial offenses by hiding feelings, χ^2 ($1, N = 22$) $= 0.03, p > 0.05$.

20. Forty-six percent of lower-income black students ($N = 13$) and 50 percent of affluent black students ($N = 14$) handled racial offenses by educating the white person. For black students, social class was not significantly related to handling racial offenses by educating the white person, χ^2 ($1, N = 27$) $= 0.04, p > 0.05$.

21. See Hurtado, Arellano, et al. 2009; Hurtado, Griffin, et al. 2008; Pike and Kuh 2006; and Rothman, Lipset, and Nevitte 2003.

22. For example, see Feagin, Vera, and Imani 1996; Strayhorn and Terrell 2010; and Watson et al. 2002.

23. Feagin, Vera, and Imani 1996.

24. Ibid.

25. Dovidio and Gaertner 1998. Contemporary forms of racism have also been identified as symbolic racism (Sears and Henry 2003), modern racism (McConahay 1986), and implicit racism (Banaji, Hardin, and Rothman 1993).

26. Sue 2010. Sue argues that microaggressions can be verbal, nonverbal, or environmental. Environmental microaggressions refer to "the numerous demeaning and threatening social, educational, political, or economic cues that are communicated individually, institutionally, or societally to marginalized groups" (25). For example, looking around and not seeing people of color in the upper levels of the administration is an environmental microaggression that sends messages to students about how welcome they are, how comfortable they will feel, and how far they can advance.

27. Thomas 2008, 274.

28. Sue 2010.

29. Tatum 1997.

30. See Harper and Hurtado 2007; and Hurtado et al. 2008. The differential perception of racial discrimination is prevalent beyond the college gates as well. Black Americans perceive more racial discrimination against black people than white Americans do (T. Smith 2000; Tropp 2006). People who are black are more likely than those who are white to believe that black and white people are not treated the same and that race relations will always be a problem in this country. See "Black-White Relations" 2001.

31. Tatum 1997.

32. Ibid., 77.

CHAPTER 5

1. Harper 2006.

2. Tatum 1997, 70.

3. Sixty-two percent of lower-income black students ($N = 13$) and 57 percent of affluent black students ($N = 14$) felt their blackness had been questioned or had been accused of acting white on campus. For black students, being affluent or lower income was not significantly related to feeling blackness was questioned or accusations of acting white, χ^2 ($1, N = 27$) $= 0.05, p > 0.05$.

4. Fifty-five percent of lower-income black students ($N = 11$) and 43 percent of affluent black students ($N = 14$) felt pressure to hang out with other black students senior year. For black students, being affluent or lower income was not significantly related to feeling pressure to hang out with other black students, χ^2 (1, $N = 25$) = 0.34, $p > 0.05$.

5. Tatum 1997, 71.

6. Thirty-one percent of lower-income black students ($N = 13$) and 50 percent of affluent black students ($N = 14$) said they never ate at the black tables in the dining hall. Sixty-two percent of lower-income black students and 43 percent of affluent black students said they ate at the black tables in the dining hall on occasion. Eight percent of lower-income black students and 7 percent of lower-income black students said they frequently ate at the black tables in the dining hall. A χ^2 test could not be calculated because two cells have expected values less than five.

7. Smith and Moore 2000.

8. Eighty-five percent of lower-income black students ($N = 13$) and 71 percent of affluent black students ($N = 14$) had heard derogatory comments about skin tone. For black students, being affluent or lower income was not significantly related to hearing derogatory comments about skin tone; Fisher's exact test $p = 0.65$. A χ^2 test was not calculated because two cells have expected values less than five.

9. Fifty-seven percent of lower-income black women ($N = 7$) and 75 percent of affluent black women ($N = 8$) had dated nonblack students. For black women, being affluent or lower income was not significantly related to dating someone of another race; Fisher's exact test $p = 0.61$. A χ^2 test was not calculated because three cells have expected values less than five.

10. One hundred percent of lower-income black students ($N = 13$) and 93 percent of affluent black students ($N = 14$) had joked about race. A χ^2 test was not calculated because two cells have expected values less than five.

11. See Brewer and Brown 1998; and Fiske 1998.

12. Smith and Moore 2000.

13. See Cole and Omari 2003; and Crenshaw 1991.

14. A. Celious and D. Oyserman (2001) have proposed a heterogeneous racial group perspective that recognizes the differences between members of a racial group.

15. Quoted in Billingslea-Brown and Gonzalez de Allen 2009, 39.

16. Wade-Golden and Matlock 2007.

17. Harper and Nichols 2008.

18. Ibid., 199.

19. Graham 1999, 4.

20. Hunter 2005.

21. Klonoff and Landrine 2000.

22. Hughes and Hertel 1990.

23. Keith and Herring 1991.

24. Zweigenhaft and Domhoff 2006.

25. Tatum 1997; Waters 1999.

26. Tatum 1997.

27. See ibid.; and Winkle-Wagner 2009.

28. Tatum 1997.

29. Billingslea-Brown and Gonzalez de Allen 2009, 39.

30. Ibid.

31. Harper and Nichols 2008.

CHAPTER 6

1. Allport 1954.
2. Ibid., 267.
3. Pettigrew and Tropp 2006; Pettigrew et al. 2011.
4. Pettigrew and Tropp 2006.
5. Senior year, 87 percent of lower-income white students (N = 15) and 77 percent of affluent white students (N = 13) reported getting to know well two or more black students. For white students, being affluent or lower income was not significantly related to getting to know well two or more black classmates; Fisher's exact test, p = 0.64. A χ^2 test was not calculated because two cells have expected values less than five.
6. Senior year, 93 percent of lower-income black students (N = 13) and 100 percent of affluent black students (N = 13) reported getting to know well two or more white students. For black students, being affluent or lower income was not significantly related to getting to know well two or more white classmates; Fisher's exact test, p = 0.48. A χ^2 test was not calculated because two cells have expected values less than five.
7. Seventy-one percent of lower-income white students (N = 14), 70 percent of lower-income black students (N = 10), 77 percent of affluent white students (N = 13), and 60 percent of affluent black students (N = 10) reported having a roommate or suitemate of another race senior year. A χ^2 test was not calculated because four cells have expected values less than five.
8. Forty percent of lower-income white students (N = 15), 62 percent of lower-income black students (N = 13), 50 percent of affluent white students (N = 12), and 79 percent of affluent black students (N = 14) had dated someone of another race. Group membership was not significantly related to dating someone of another race, χ^2 (3, N = 54) = 4.78, p > 0.05.
9. At the end of four years, students reported the following percentages of same-race friends in their close friendship circles: for lower-income white students, N = 15, M = 0.64, SD = 0.25; for lower-income black students, N = 12, M = 0.53, SD = 0.24; for affluent white students, N = 13, M = 0.69, SD = 0.27; and for affluent black students, N = 143, M = 0.28, SD = 0.34. There was no significant effect of social class, F (3, 50) = 1.85, p > 0.05, η^2 = 0.036. There was a significant effect of race, F (3, 50) = 13.39, p = 0.001, η^2 = 0.21 and a significant race by class interaction, F (3, 50) = 4.10, p 0.048, η^2 = 0.076. Affluent black students had significantly less same-race friends than students in the other groups. Similar findings are reported by T. J. Espenshade and A. W. Radford (2009) and by J. R. Feagin, H. Vera, and N. Imani (1996).
10. At the end of freshman year, 47 percent of lower-income white students (N = 15), 39 percent of lower-income black students (N = 13), 21 percent of affluent white students (N = 14), and 31 percent of affluent black students (N = 13) said their interactions changed their views of people of other races or their own race.
11. At the end of four years, 53 percent of lower-income white students (N = 15), 62 percent of lower-income black students (N = 13), 33 percent of affluent white students (N = 12), and 57 percent of affluent black students (N = 14) said their interactions changed their views of people of their own race or other races. Group membership was not significantly related to students' interactions having changed their views of people of other races or their own race, χ^2 (3, N = 54) = 2.31, p > 0.05.

12. Forty-seven percent of lower-income white students ($N = 15$), 85 percent of lower-income black students ($N = 13$), 33 percent of affluent white students ($N = 12$), and 71 percent of affluent black students ($N = 14$) reported that students made assumptions about them on the basis of race that were inaccurate. A χ^2 test was not calculated because one cell had an expected value less than five. Seventy-three percent of lower-income white students ($N = 15$), 92 percent of lower-income black students ($N = 13$), 75 percent of affluent white students ($N = 12$), and 86 percent of affluent black students ($N = 14$) reported hearing students make assumptions about black students that were inaccurate. A χ^2 test was not calculated because four cells have expected values less than five.

13. Sixty percent of lower-income white students ($N = 15$), 64 percent of lower-income black students ($N = 11$), 46 percent of affluent white students ($N = 11$), and 77 percent of affluent black students ($N = 13$) reported hearing students make assumptions about white classmates that were inaccurate. A χ^2 test was not calculated because three cells have expected values less than five.

14. Banks and Eberhardt 1998.

15. Ninety-three percent of lower-income white students ($N = 15$), 85 percent of lower-income black students ($N = 13$), 83 percent of affluent white students ($N = 12$), and 79 percent of affluent black students ($N = 14$) reported they had positive attitudes toward interracial dating when they arrived at the college. A χ^2 test was not calculated because four cells have expected values less than five.

16. Sixty-two percent of lower-income white students ($N = 13$) and 25 percent of affluent white students ($N = 12$) reported increased comfort interacting with black students since they arrived on campus. For white students, being affluent or lower income was not significantly related to reporting increased comfort interacting with black students but approached significance, χ^2 $(1, N = 25) = 3.38$, $p = 0.066$.

17. Sixty-seven percent of lower-income white students ($N = 15$), 92 percent of lower-income black students ($N = 13$), 92 percent of affluent white students ($N = 12$), and 93 percent of affluent black students ($N = 14$) took a course that addressed race as the main topic or a subtopic. A χ^2 test was not calculated because four cells have expected values less than five.

18. Fifty percent of lower-income white students ($N = 14$), 82 percent of lower-income black students ($N = 11$), 46 percent of affluent white students ($N = 13$), and 67 percent of affluent black students ($N = 12$) had taken at least one course on black people or Africa. A χ^2 test was not calculated because two cells have expected values less than five.

19. Zero percent of lower-income white students ($N = 15$), 31 percent of lower-income black students ($N = 13$), 15 percent of affluent white students ($N = 13$), and 21 percent of affluent black students ($N = 14$) majored in black studies. A χ^2 test was not calculated because four cells have expected values less than five.

20. Sixty percent of lower-income white students ($N = 15$), 58 percent of lower-income black students ($N = 12$), 42 percent of affluent white students ($N = 12$), and 43 percent of affluent black students ($N = 14$) reported that they had learned about race from personal sharing about race in the classroom. Group membership was not significantly related to learning about race from personal sharing in the classroom, χ^2 $(3, N = 53) = 1.53$, $p > 0.05$.

21. See, for example, Gurin 2004; and Gurin, Lehman, et al. 2004.

22. Bowen and Bok 1998, 279.

23. See, for example, Antonio 2001b; Bowman 2010; Chang 1999; Denson 2009; Gurin with Dey et al. 2004; Gurin et al. 2002; Gurin, Nagda, and Lopez 2004; Hurtado 2005; and Hurtado et al. 2008.

24. Chang 2007, 28.

25. Pettigrew 1998.

26. See Carter 1997.

27. Zweigenhaft and Domhoff 2006.

CHAPTER 7

1. One hundred percent of lower-income white students (N = 15), 85 percent of lower-income black students (N = 13), 100 percent of affluent white students (N = 13), and 64 percent of affluent black students (N =14) said they had gotten to know well two or more students from a much wealthier family than their own. A χ^2 test was not calculated because four cells have expected counts less than five. Seventy-three percent of lower-income white students (N = 15), 77 percent of lower-income black students (N = 13), 100 percent of affluent white students (N = 13), and 86 percent of affluent black students (N =14) said they had gotten to know well two or more students from a much poorer family than their own. A χ^2 test was not calculated because four cells have expected values less than five.

2. Friends of the same social class: lower-income white students, N = 14, M = 0.39, SD = 0.26; lower-income black students, N = 13, M = 0.49, SD = 0.26; affluent white students, N = 13, M = 0.56, SD = 0.21; affluent black students, N = 14, M = 0.46, SD = 0.26. There was no significant effect of race, F (1, 50) = 0, p > 0.05, η^2 = 0, no significant effect of class, F (1, 50) = 0.31, p > 0.05, η^2 = 0.021, and no significant race by class interaction, F (1, 50) = 0.13, p > 0.05, η^2 = 0.045. There was no significant change over time from the end of freshman to the end of senior year.

3. Fifty-one percent of lower-income students' friends were the same social class, and 58 percent of affluent students' friends were the same social class freshman year.

4. Sixty-seven percent of lower-income white students (N = 15), 39 percent of lower-income black students (N = 13), 67 percent of affluent white students (N = 12), and 64 percent of affluent black students (N = 14) had dated someone from a different class background than their own. A χ^2 test was not calculated because one cell had an expected value of less than five.

5. At the end of four years, 67 percent of lower-income white students (N = 15), 54 percent of lower-income black students (N = 13), 58 percent of affluent white students (N = 12), and 43 percent of affluent black students (N = 14) reported that living in a diverse community had changed their views on people of their own class or other social classes. Group membership was not related to whether living in diverse community changed students' views on social class, χ^2 (3, N = 54) = 1.72 p > 0.05.

6. At the end of freshman year, 59 percent of students reported that living in diverse community had changed their views on people of their own class or othe social classes, with no significant group differences.

7. Forty-three percent of lower-income white students (N = 14), 39 percent o lower-income black students (N = 13), 58 percent of affluent white students (N 12), and 43 percent of affluent black students (N = 14) reported people had mad incorrect assumptions about them on the basis of social class. Group membershi

was not significantly related to students hearing incorrect assumptions about them based on social class, χ^2 (3, N = 53) = 1.14, $p > 0.05$.

8. Eighty-seven percent of lower-income white students (N = 15), 77 percent of lower-income black students (N = 13), 75 percent of affluent white students (N = 12), and 79 percent of affluent black students (N=14) said they had heard stereotypes about wealthy students. A χ^2 test was not calculated because four cells have expected values less than five.

9. Forty-seven percent of lower-income white students (N = 15), 39 percent of lower-income black students (N = 13), 25 percent of affluent white students (N = 12), and 7 percent of affluent black students (N = 14) said they had heard stereotypes about poor students. A χ^2 test was not calculated because four cells have expected values less than five.

10. Seventy-seven percent of lower-income white students (N = 13), 62 percent of lower-income black students (N = 13), 75 percent of affluent white students (N = 12), and 62 percent of affluent black students (N = 13) said they had heard joking about the rich. A χ^2 test was not calculated because four cells have expected values less than five.

11. Forty-two percent of lower-income white students (N = 12), 40 percent of lower-income black students (N = 10), 30 percent of affluent white students (N = 10), and 15 percent of affluent black students (N = 13) said they had heard joking about the poor. A χ^2 test was not calculated because four cells have expected values less than five.

12. See note 9.

13. Thirty-three percent of lower-income white students (N = 15), 39 percent of lower-income black students (N = 13), 42 percent of affluent white students (N = 12), and 57 percent of affluent black students (N = 14) reported class can be difficult to discern. Group membership was not significantly related to the perception that class can be difficult to discern, χ^2 (3, N = 54) = 1.83, $p > 0.05$.

14. Hours per week working at a job: overall, N = 50, M = 4.84, SD = 5.43. There was no significant effect of class, F (1, 46) = 0, $p > 0.05$, $\eta^2 = 0$, no significant effect of race, F (1, 46) = 0.032, $p > 0.05$, $\eta^2 = .001$, and no significant race by class interaction, F (1, 46) = 0.44, $p > 0.05$, $\eta^2 = 0.01$.

15. As seniors, 82 percent of lower-income students saw the importance of connections and talked about connections as "extremely important, the most important thing." Eighty-seven percent of lower-income white students (N = 15), 77 percent of lower-income black students (N = 13), 83 percent of affluent white students (N = 12), and 69 percent of affluent black students (N = 13) said connections were "very important" to success. Nine percent of students said connections were "important but not necessary," and 11 percent said their importance depended on the field. A χ^2 test was not calculated because eight cells have expected values less than five.

16. Thirty-six percent of lower-income white students (N = 14), 17 percent of lower-income black students (N = 12), 8 percent of affluent white students (N = 13), and 8 percent of affluent black students (N = 12) reported taking the sociology course titled "Social Class." A χ^2 test was not calculated because four cells have expected values less than five.

17. Seventy-one percent of lower-income white students (N = 14), 77 percent of lower-income black students (N = 13), 33 percent of affluent white students (N = 12), and 18 percent of affluent black students (N = 11) reported taking a course in which social class was a topic or subarea in the course. Group membership was

significantly related to taking a course in which class was a topic or subarea, χ^2 (3, $N = 50$) = 12.07, $p = 0.007$.

18. Twenty percent of lower-income white students ($N = 15$), 23 percent of lower-income black students ($N = 13$), 8 percent of affluent white students ($N = 12$), and 14 percent of affluent black students ($N = 14$) reported they had learned something about social class through courses that addressed social class. A χ^2 test was not calculated because four cells have an expected value less than five.

19. Forty-seven percent of lower-income white students ($N = 15$), 39 percent of lower-income black students ($N = 13$), 33 percent of affluent white students ($N = 12$), and 43 percent of affluent black students ($N = 14$) reported they had learned something about social class from personal sharing in courses by students of different class backgrounds. A χ^2 test was not calculated because one cell has an expected value less than five.

20. Bowen, Kurzweil, and Tobin 2005.

21. See ibid.

22. Zweigenhaft and Domhoff 2006, 232.

23. Bowen, Kurzweil, and Tobin 2005, 162.

24. Aries and Seider 2005.

25. Ninety-three percent of lower-income white students ($N = 15$), 85 percent of lower-income black students ($N = 13$), 92 percent of affluent white students ($N = 12$), and 79 percent of affluent black students ($N = 14$) said they had meaningful, honest conversations about social class. A χ^2 test was not calculated because four cells have expected counts less than five. This represented a 17 percent increase over freshman year. On average, these conversations took place a few times a month, but for 40 percent of students, such conversations occurred at least once a week. Means and standard deviations for frequency of conversations about race (6 = never, 5 = a few times a semester, 4 = few times a month, 3 = once a week, 2 = two or three times a week, 1 = daily): lower-income white students, $N = 15$, $M = 4$, $SD = 1.13$; lower-income black students, $N = 13$, $M = 3.31$, $SD = 1.65$; affluent white students, $N = 13$, $M = 4$, $SD = 1.58$; affluent black students, $N = 14$, $M = 3.86$, $SD = 1.17$. There was no significant effect of race, F (1, 51) = 1.24, $p > 0.05$, $\eta^2 = 0.01$, no significant effect of class, F (1, 51) = 0.54, $p > 0.05$, $\eta^2 = 0.024$, and no race by class interaction, F (1, 51) = 0.54, $p > 0.05$, $\eta^2 = 0.01$.

26. Zweigenhaft and Domhoff 2006, 7.

CHAPTER 8

1. No significant effects of race or class were found for the following variables: for psychological health overall ($N = 55$, $M = 5.09$, $SD = 1.49$), for social life overall ($N = 55$, $M = 5.20$, $SD = 1.60$), for feelings of comfort and inclusion in relation to peers overall ($N = 51$, $M = 5.16$, $SD = 0.89$), for grown as a person overall ($N = 55$, $M = 6.31$, $SD = 0.86$), for found a place at the college overall ($N = 55$, $M = 5.24$, $SD = 1.43$), and for coping effectively with important changes in their lives ($N = 51$, $M = 4.30$, $SD = 1.29$). These variables were measured on a 7-point scale.

2. Whether race makes social integration easier or more difficult: for lower-income white students, $N = 15$, $M = 3.67$, $SD = 0.61$; for lower-income black students, $N = 13$, $M = 4.21$, $SD = 0.58$; for affluent white students, $N = 13$, $M = 3.63$, $SD = 0.78$; for affluent black students, $N = 14$, $M = 4.11$, $SD = 0.66$. There was a significant effect of race, $F(1, 51) = 9.53$, $p = 0.003$, $\eta^2 = 0.16$. There was no

significant effect for class, $F(1, 51) = 0.17, p > 0.05, \eta^2 = 0.003$, and no race by class interaction, $F(1, 51) = 0.05, p > 0.05, \eta^2 = 0.001$.

3. Whether class makes social integration easier or more difficult: for lower-income white students, $N = 15, M = 3.75, SD = 0.58$; for lower-income black students, $N = 13, M = 4.21, SD = 1.11$; for affluent white students, $N = 13, M = 3.35$, $SD = 1.12$; for affluent black students, $N = 14, M = 3, SD = 0.78$. There was a significant effect of social class, $F(1, 51) = 10.71, p = 0.002, \eta^2 = 0.17$. There was no significant effects for race, $F(1, 51) = 0.06, p > 0.05, \eta^2 = 0.001$, and no race by class interaction, $F(1, 51) = 2.68, p > 0.05, \eta^2 = 0.05$. In a meta-analysis of social class differences in social integration, M. Rubin (2012) found working-class students to feel less integrated socially than middle-class students. The effect size was small.

4. Students who write senior theses have the opportunity to graduate with Latin honors—summa cum laude, magna cum laude, or cum laude. If the thesis is not judged of honors' quality, the thesis writer will not graduate with Latin honors.

5. Black and white participants did not enter the college with equivalent SAT scores. Black students' SAT scores, though in the top percentiles of black test takers nationally, were, on average, two hundred points below those of white students (Aries 2008). The gap in SAT scores between the affluent and lower-income students in the study was not statistically significant. Nationally, lower-income students score lower on the SAT than affluent students, but a highly selective institution like Amherst College with excellent financial aid can attract the top test takers nationally.

6. The data set for GPA was not complete because some students did not give permission to release their grades. Means and standard deviations for final GPA were as follows: for lower-income white students, $N = 13, M = 3.53, SD = 0.30$; for lower-income black students, $N = 11, M = 3.23, SD = 0.41$; for affluent white students, $N = 13, M = 3.77, SD = 0.20$; and for affluent black students, $N = 12$, $M = 3.41, SD = 0.34$. There was a significant effect of social class, $F(1, 49) = 5.34$, $p = 0.025, \eta^2 = 0.11$. There was a significant effect for race, $F(1, 49) = 13.16, p = 0.001, \eta^2 = 0.23$, and no race by class interaction, $F(1, 49) = 0.11, p > 0.05, \eta^2 = 0.002$.

7. F. E. Vars and W. G. Bowen (1998) report that white students attain higher GPAs than black students at highly selective colleges and universities. W. G. Bowen, M. A. Kurzweil, and E. M. Tobin (2005) and M. Walpole (2003) report lower-socioeconomic-status college students have lower GPAs than affluent college students.

8. The differences in the GPAs attained by the students could not be explained by differences in the amount of time they spent in class or studying.

9. Sixty-four percent of lower-income white students ($N = 14$), 25 percent of lower-income black students ($N = 12$), 77 percent of affluent white students ($N = 13$), and 50 percent of affluent black students ($N = 14$) graduated with Latin honors. Group membership was significantly related to graduating with Latin honors, χ^2 $(3, 53) = 7.51, p = 0.057$.

10. Eight percent of lower-income white students ($N = 12$), 10 percent of lower-income black students ($N = 10$), 23 percent of affluent white students ($N = 13$), and 0 percent of affluent black students ($N = 13$) were elected to Phi Beta Kappa. A χ^2 test was not calculated because four cells have expected values less than five.

11. Forty percent of lower-income white students ($N = 15$) and 23 percent of lower-income black students ($N = 13$) said financial constraints had kept them from buying books. For lower-income students, race was not significantly related to financial constraints keeping them from buying books, Fisher's exact test, $p = 0.44$. A χ^2 test was not calculated because two cells have expected values less than five.

12. Forty percent of lower-income white students ($N = 15$), 31 percent of lower-income black students ($N = 13$), 8 percent of affluent white students ($N = 12$), and 29 percent of affluent black students ($N = 14$) said they sought more academic help over time. A χ^2 test was not calculated because four cells have expected values less than five.

13. Seeking academic help (1 = for most assignments, 2 = for some assignments, 3 = rarely, 4 = never): for lower-income white students, $N = 15$, $M = 2.65$, $SD = 0.72$; for lower-income black students, $N = 13$, $M = 2.77$, $SD = 0.51$; for affluent white students, $N = 13$, $M = 3.12$, $SD = 0.55$; and for affluent black students, $N = 14$, $M = 3$, $SD = 0.48$. There was a significant effect of social class, $F(1, 51) = 4.96$, $p = 0.03$, $\eta^2 = 0.089$. There was no significant effect for race, $F(1, 51) = 0$, $p > 0.05$, $\eta^2 = 0$, and no race by class interaction, $F(1, 51) = 0.55$, $p > 0.05$, $\eta^2 = 0.011$.

14. Whether class makes academic integration easier or more difficult: for lower-income white students, $N = 15$, $M = 3.87$, $SD = 0.53$; for lower-income black students, $N = 13$, $M = 3.92$, $SD = 0.67$; for affluent white students, $N = 13$, $M = 3.23$, $SD = 0.93$; and for affluent black students, $N = 14$, $M = 3.21$, $SD = 1.03$. There was a significant effect of social class, $F(1, 51) = 9.48$, $p = 0.003$, $\eta^2 = 0.157$. There was no significant effect for race, $F(1, 51) = 0.008$, $p > 0.05$, $\eta^2 = 0$, and no race by class interaction, $F(1, 51) = 0.028$, $p > 0.05$, $\eta^2 = 0.001$.

15. Academic confidence: for lower-income white students, $N = 15$, $M = 5.50$, $SD = 0.88$; for lower-income black students, $N = 13$, $M = 5.62$, $SD = 0.70$; for affluent white students, $N = 13$, $M = 5.98$, $SD = 0.69$; and for affluent black students, $N = 14$, $M = 5.94$, $SD = 0.57$. There was a significant effect of social class, $F(1, 51) = 4.33$, $p = 0.042$, $\eta^2 = 0.078$. There was no significant effect for race, $F(1, 51) = 0.031$, $p > 0.05$, $\eta^2 = 0.001$, and no race by class interaction, $F(1, 51) = 0.17$, $p > 0.05$, $\eta^2 = 0.003$.

16. Senior year, 20 percent of lower-income white students ($N = 15$), 50 percent of lower-income black students ($N = 12$), 8 percent of affluent white students ($N=12$), and 8 percent of affluent black students ($N = 13$) said, if they could be born again, they would want to be born into a higher social class. Group membership was significantly related to wanting to be born into a higher social class, χ^2 (3, 52) = 8.59, $p = 0.035$.

17. See Lehmann 2009.

18. Forty-seven percent of lower-income white students ($N = 15$), 46 percent of lower-income black students ($N = 13$), 58 percent of affluent white students ($N = 12$), and 29 percent of affluent black students ($N = 14$) wished they had had more honest conversations about social class. Group membership was not significantly related to wanting more honest conversations about social class, χ^2 (3, 54) = 2.41, $p > 0.05$.

19. Thirty-three percent of lower-income white students ($N = 15$), 46 percent of lower-income black students ($N = 13$), 33 percent of affluent white students ($N = 12$), and 36 percent of affluent black students ($N = 14$) would have liked more structured dialogue about social class. A χ^2 test was not calculated because two cells have expected values less than five.

20. Seventy-seven percent of lower-income white students ($N = 13$), 46 percent of lower-income black students ($N = 13$), 50 percent of affluent white students ($N = 12$), and 7 percent of affluent black students ($N = 14$) wished they had had more honest conversations about race. Group membership was significantly related to wanting more honest conversations about race, χ^2 (3, 52) = 13.62, $p = 0.003$.

21. Fifty-three percent of lower-income white students ($N = 15$), 46 percent of lower-income black students ($N = 13$), 58 percent of affluent white students ($N = 12$), and 39 percent of affluent black students ($N = 13$) would have liked more structured dialogue about race. Group membership was not significantly related to wanting more structured dialogue about race, χ^2 $(3, 53) = 1.15$, $p > 0.05$.

22. Twenty percent of lower-income white students ($N = 15$), 92 percent of lower-income black students ($N = 13$), 33 percent of affluent white students ($N = 12$), and 50 percent of affluent black students ($N = 14$) spoke of deans or other adults who knew them well and had helped them be successful. A χ^2 test was not calculated because four cells have expected counts less than five.

23. Twenty-nine percent of lower-income white students ($N = 14$), 31 percent of lower-income black students ($N = 13$), 27 percent of affluent white students ($N = 11$), and 39 percent of affluent black students ($N = 13$) would have found a mentor of their race or class valuable. A χ^2 test was not calculated because four cells have expected values less than five.

24. Some of the suggestions lower-income students had to offer pertained to the academic realm, as many lower-income students discovered upon arriving at Amherst that they did not have the academic preparation of many of their affluent classmates. They advised new students "to not be intimidated" and to "try your best, and definitely try to do well, but don't get disappointed if you're not a straight A student anymore" because "you're in one of the best schools in the country, and you're with the cream of the crop."

25. Clayton-Pedersen et al. 2007.

CHAPTER 9

1. See, for example, Aries and Seider 2005; Espenshade and Radford 2009; Feagin, Vera, and Imani 1996; Harper and Hurtado 2007; Harper and Nichols 2008; Hurst 2010; Hurtado et al. 2008; Sidanius et al. 2008; Stuber 2011a; and Winkle-Wagner 2009.

2. Pendry, Driscoll, and Field 2007.

3. Legault, Gutsell, and Inzlicht 2011.

4. See Engberg 2004; and Paluck and Green 2009.

5. For example, see Fischer 2008; Locks et al. 2008; Sáenz, Ngai, and Hurtado 2007; Schofield et al. 2010; and Zúñiga, Williams, and Berger 2005.

6. Zúñiga, Williams, and Berger 2005.

7. Nagda 2006.

8. Espenshade and Radford 2009; Gurin, with Dey et al. 2004; Pike and Kuh 2006.

9. Sáenz, Ngai, and Hurtado 2007.

10. Nagda 2006; Tropp 2006.

11. For research on the costs to students of a hostile racial climate and benefits of improving campus climate, see Hurtado, Arellano, et al. 2009; Hurtado, Griffin, et al. 2008; Levin, van Laar, and Sidanius 2003; Locks et al. 2008; Mallett et al. 2011; and Tropp 2006.

12. Walton and Cohen 2007.

13. Walton and Cohen 2011. G. M. Walton and G. L. Cohen (2007) similarly found that an intervention designed to normalize black students' doubts about social belonging in college by portraying them as common to all racial groups raised the GPAs of black students.

14. See Paluck and Green 2009 for a general review of interventions for reducing prejudice. The authors examine research conducted in the laboratory, as well as in educational and workplace settings, and address programs targeted to reduce prejudice in regard to race, sexual orientation, age, weight, ethnicity, religion, and nationality.

15. For example, see Betances 2004; Checkoway 2001; Hurtado 2007; Kirwan 2004; Pike and Kuh 2006; Rudenstine 2004; D. Smith 2009; and Wade-Golden and Matlock 2007.

16. U.S. Census projections, released 2008 (based on Census 2000), available at http://www.census.gov/population/www/projections/summarytables.html (accessed December 27, 2011). See also Perez and Hirshman 2009.

17. Clayton-Pedersen et al. 2007; Hurtado 2007.

18. Association of American Colleges and Universities 2008.

19. See Harper and Hurtado 2007.

20. See http://nebraska.edu/history-and-mission/mission-statements.html (accessed December 22, 2011).

21. Meacham and Barrett 2003.

22. See http://www.coe.edu/aboutcoe/mission (accessed December 22, 2011).

23. Dasgupta 2011.

24. Asgari, Dasgupta, and Cote 2010.

25. McLaughlin et al. 2009.

26. Milem, Chang, and Antonio 2005.

27. Ibid., 23.

28. Wade-Golden and Matlock 2007.

29. See Kezar et al. 2008.

30. Clayton-Pedersen et al. 2007.

31. See Milem, Chang, and Antonio 2005.

32. See Bauman et al. 2005; Harper and Hurtado 2007; Kezar et al. 2008; and McLaughlin et al. 2009.

33. Association of American Colleges and Universities 2008.

34. Wade-Golden and Matlock 2007.

35. Tropp and Bianchi 2006.

36. Ibid.

37. Umbach and Kuh 2006.

38. Denson and Chang 2009.

39. Association of American Colleges and Universities 2008, 31.

40. McLaughlin et al. 2009; D. Smith 2009.

41. Milem, Chang, and Antonio 2005.

42. Reason and Evans 2007.

43. Zúñiga, Williams, and Berger 2005.

44. See http://www.igr.umich.edu/about/introduction (accessed December 22, 2011). See Gurin, Nagda, and Lopez 2004 for a description of outcome research based on courses run by the Intergroup Relations Program. See Nagda 2006 for research on the interrelated communication processes that take place in these dialogues that explain their effectiveness.

45. While the dialogues are focused on a single identity, students bring multiple identities to the table, and the course provides a framework for exploring the intersection of identities.

46. Sorensen et al. 2009, 12. See also Nagda and Gurin 2007; and Zúñiga, Williams, and Berger 2005.

47. Gurin and Nagda 2006.

48. See http://www.igr.umich.edu/about/introduction (accessed December 22, 2011).

49. Occidental College, Los Angeles, California, for example, offers an intergroup dialogue program.

50. Nagda et al. 2009; Sorensen et al. 2009.

51. Gurin, with Dey et al. 2004; Gurin, Nagda, and Lopez 2004.

52. Nagda et al. 2009; Sorenson et al. 2009.

53. Multi-university intergroup dialogue research project guidebook 2011. Researchers developed a uniform curriculum and common facilitator-training procedures across campuses. Students were randomly assigned to participate in an intergroup dialogue (on race or class) or a control group (a social science course on race or gender). The study also examines the processes entailed in the intergroup dialogues that explain their effectiveness. See also Nagda and Zúñiga 2003 for an analysis of the types of interaction processes that produce desired outcomes in intergroup dialogues.

54. Sáenz, Ngai, and Hurtado 2007, 29.

55. See Association of American Colleges and Universities 2008.

56. See Engberg 2004; Myers-Lipton 1996; and Rice and Brown 1998.

57. Astin et al. 2000.

58. See http://www.dickinson.edu/academics/distinctive-opportunities/commu nity-studies-center/content/Community-Studies-Center-Global-Mosaics/ (accessed December 22, 2011).

59. See http://www.compact.org/about/history-mission-vision/ (accessed December 22, 2011).

60. See Aberson 2007; Chang 2002; Engberg 2004; Gurin, with Dey et al. 2004; Hurtado 2005; Kernahan and Davis 2010; Laird, Engberg, and Hurtado 2005; Milem, Chang, and Antonio 2005; Rudman, Ashmore, and Gary 2001; Sorensen et al. 2009; and Zúñiga, Williams, and Berger 2005.

61. C. L. Aberson (2007) examined participation in diversity experiences, which included some combination of courses, readings, lectures, and discussions, as well as activities devoted to understanding other groups. These experiences were positively associated with changes in beliefs that affirmative action does not hurt academic quality and led to increased support for the use of different admissions criteria for different ethnic groups.

62. Rudman, Ashmore, and Gary 2001.

63. Henderson-King and Kaleta 2000.

64. Hogan and Mallott 2005.

65. See http://www.diversityweb.org/diversity_innovations/institutional_lead ership/bloomfield_college.cfm (accessed December 22, 2011).

66. See http://oregonstate.edu/dept/dpd/home (accessed December 22, 2011); and Association of American Colleges and Universities 2008.

67. The term "informal interactional diversity" has been used to refer to the frequency and quality of interactions among diverse groups of students that take place outside the classroom setting.

68. Sáenz, Ngai, and Hurtado 2007.

69. A statistically significant finding from a study says nothing about the size of the effect. Some studies using large sample sizes yield statistically significant effects that are very small in magnitude.

70. Cohen 1988, 26.
71. Abelson 1985.
72. Gurin, with Dey et al. 2004, 106.
73. Chang 2003.
74. Piaget 1975.
75. Bowman 2010.
76. Denson 2009. Cohen's d = 0.48. More methodologically rigorous studies with more controls showed smaller reductions in racial bias.
77. Denson 2009.
78. Pettigrew and Tropp 2006. See also Pettigrew et al. 2011.
79. Allport 1954.
80. Pettigrew and Tropp 2006, 766. The overall effect size was r = −0.215
81. Tropp 2007; Tropp and Pettigrew 2005.
82. Denson 2009; Tropp 2007. For members of minority groups, exposure to prejudice against their group and awareness of the devaluation of their group may inhibit the potential for positive outcomes of intergroup interaction (Tropp and Pettigrew 2005).
83. Pettigrew and Tropp 2008.
84. Stephan and Finlay 1999.
85. Pettigrew and Tropp 2008, 929.
86. Hurtado 2005.
87. Ibid.
88. Chang et al. 2006; Misa et al. 2006.
89. Antonio 2001b.
90. See ibid.; Chang, Astin, and Kim 2004; Chang et al. 2006; Denson 2009; Locks et al. 2008; and Milem, Chang, and Antonio 2005.
91. Antonio 2001a.
92. Sidanius et al. 2008.
93. Antonio 2001b.
94. Bowen and Bok 1998.
95. University of Michigan, n.d., 21.
96. See Boisjoly et al. 2006; Duncan et al. 2003; Espenshade and Radford 2009; Phelps et al. 1998; Shook and Fazio 2008a, 2008b; Sidanius et al. 2008; Towles-Schwen and Fazio 2006; Trail, Shelton, and West 2009; and van Laar et al. 2005.
97. Shook and Fazio 2008a.
98. Shook and Fazio 2008b; Towles-Schwen and Fazio 2006; Trail, Shelton, and West 2009; van Laar et al. 2005.
99. See Gaertner and McLaughlin 1983.
100. Towles-Schwen and Fazio 2006.
101. Shelton and Richeson 2006.
102. Shelton, Richeson, and Salvatore 2005.
103. See Sorensen et al. 2009.
104. See Harper and Hurtado 2007; and Sorensen et al. 2009.
105. McCauley, Wright, and Harris 2000.
106. Denson 2009.
107. Aberson 2007; Cheng and Zhao 2006; Gurin, Nagda, and Lopez 2004; Hurtado 2005.
108. Sáenz, Ngai, and Hurtado 2007.

109. See Cheng and Zhao 2006; Engberg 2004; Sáenz, Ngai, and Hurtado 2007; and Zúñiga, Williams, and Berger 2005.

110. Engberg 2004.

111. Gurin, Nagda, and Lopez 2004.

112. See http://www.igr.umich.edu/ (accessed December 22, 2011); and Association of American Colleges and Universities 2008.

113. Hurtado 2005.

114. See http://www.studentaffairs.columbia.edu/multicultural/diversityed/rooted.php (accessed December 22, 2011).

115. Ibid.

116. Association of American Colleges and Universities 2008.

117. See Engberg 2004; and Hurtado 2005.

118. Engberg 2004; Inkelas et al. 2006; Longerbeam 2010.

119. Association of American Colleges and Universities 2008; see also http://www.hope.edu/phelps-scholars-program (accessed May 7, 2012).

120. Association of American Colleges and Universities 2008.

121. See Strayhorn et al. 2010.

122. Ibid., 132.

123. Harper and Quaye 2007; Sidanius, Levin, et al. 2008; Sidanius, van Laar, et al. 2004.

124. Sidanius et al. 2004, 100.

125. See Milem, Chang, and Antonio 2005. Similar concerns have been raised about fraternities and sororities.

126. Espenshade and Radford 2009.

127. Sidanius et al. 2008.

128. See http://a3cservices.stanford.edu/lead/ (accessed December 22, 2011).

129. See http://www.studentaffairs.columbia.edu/multicultural (accessed December 22, 2011).

130. Betances 2004.

131. See ibid.; and Davis 2010.

132. See Davis 2010; and Stuber 2011a.

133. Clayton-Pedersen et al. 2007.

134. Torres, Howard-Hamilton, and Cooper 2003.

135. Turner 2004, 116.

136. Ibid.

137. See http://www3.davidson.edu/cms/x4609.xml (accessed December 22, 2011).

138. See also the website for the Black Student Union Leadership and Mentoring Program (LAMP) at Princeton University, available at http://www.princeton.edu/~lamp/programs.htm (accessed December 22, 2011). Other examples include the assignment of a faculty mentor/buddy as well as a regular faculty adviser to all underrepresented minority students at Kalamazoo College and the faculty-student mentoring program for upper-class students of color at the University of Virginia.

139. See http://www.unc.edu/carolinacovenant/ (accessed December 22, 2011).

140. See http://www7.acs.ncsu.edu/financial_aid/packpromise.html (accessed December 22, 2011).

141. Saddler 2010.

142. See http://www.possefoundation.org/ (accessed December 22, 2011).

143. See http://mesa.umich.edu/programs-initiatives (accessed December 22, 2011). The program is a partnership of the Office of Multi-ethnic Student Affairs and the Office of Counseling and Psychological Services.

144. See Harvard Financial Aid Initiative 2011.

145. D. Smith 2009, 3.

146. See Harper and Patton 2008; Milem, Chang, and Antonio 2005; and Reason and Evans 2007.

References

Abelson, R. P. 1985. A variance explanation paradox: When a little is a lot. *Psychological Bulletin* 97 (1): 129–134.

Aberson, C. L. 2007. Diversity experiences predict changes in attitudes toward affirmative action. *Cultural Diversity and Ethnic Minority Psychology* 13:285–294.

Allport, G. W. 1954. *The nature of prejudice*. Garden City, NY: Doubleday.

Antonio, A. L. 2001a. Diversity and the influence of friendship groups in college. *Review of Higher Education* 25 (1): 63–89.

———. 2001b. The role of interracial interaction in the development of leadership skills and cultural knowledge and understanding. *Research in Higher Education* 42 (5): 593–617.

Aries, E. 2008. *Race and class matters at an elite college*. Philadelphia: Temple University Press.

Aries, E., and M. Seider. 2005. The interactive relationship between class identity and the college experience: The case of lower income students. *Qualitative Sociology* 28 (4): 419–443.

Asgari, S., N. Dasgupta, and N. G. Cote. 2010. When does contact with successful ingroup members change self-stereotypes? A longitudinal study comparing the effect of quantity vs. quality of contact with successful individuals. *Social Psychology* 41 (3): 203–211.

Association of American Colleges and Universities. 2008. *More reasons for hope: Diversity matters in higher education*. Washington, DC: AAC&U.

Astin, A. W., L. J. Vogelgesang, E. K. Ikeda, and J. A. Yee. 2000. How service learning affects students. Higher Education Research Institute, University of California, Los Angeles, January. Available at http://www.heri.ucla.edu/PDFs/HSLAS/HSLAS .PDF.

Banaji, M. R., C. Hardin, and A. J. Rothman. 1993. Implicit stereotyping in person judgment. *Journal of Personality and Social Psychology* 65 (2): 272–281.

Banks, R. R., and J. L. Eberhardt. 1998. Social psychological processes and the legal bases of racial categorization. In *Confronting racism: The problem and the response*, ed. J. L. Eberhardt and S. T. Fiske, 54–75. Thousand Oaks, CA: Sage.

Bauman, G. L., L. T. Bustillos, E. M. Bensimon, M. C. Brown II, and R. D. Bartee. 2005. *Achieving equitable educational outcomes with all students: The institution's roles and responsibilities.* Washington, DC: Association of American Colleges and Universities. Available at http://www.aacu.org/inclusive_excellence/documents/bauman_et_al.pdf.

Baxter, A., and C. Britton. 2001. Risk, identity and change: Becoming a mature student. *International Studies in Sociology of Education* 11:87–102.

Bergerson, A. A. 2007. Exploring the impact of social class on adjustment to college: Anna's story. *International Journal of Qualitative Studies in Education* 20 (1): 99–119.

Betances, S. 2004. How to become an outstanding educator of Hispanic and African American first-generation college students. In *What makes racial diversity work in higher education: Academic leaders present successful policies and strategies*, ed. F. W. Hale, 45–59. Sterling, VA: Stylus.

Billingslea-Brown, A. J., and G. J. Gonzalez de Allen. 2009. Discourses of diversity at Spelman College. In *Doing diversity in higher education: Faculty leaders share challenges and strategies*, ed. W. R. Brown-Glaude, 39–60. New Brunswick, NJ: Rutgers University Press.

"Black-White Relations in the United States 2001 Update." 2001. Gallup, July 10. Available at http://www.gallup.com/poll/9901/blackwhite-relations-united-states-2001-update.aspx.

Boisjoly, J., G. J. Duncan, M. Kremer, D. M. Levy, and J. Eccles. 2006. Empathy or antipathy? The impact of diversity. *American Economic Review* 96 (5): 1890–1905.

Bourdieu, P. 1977. Cultural reproduction and social reproduction. In *Power and ideology in education*, ed. J. Karabel and A. H. Halsey, 487–511. New York: Oxford University Press.

Bourdieu, P., and J. Passeron. (1964) 1979. *The inheritors: French students and their relation to culture.* Chicago: University of Chicago Press.

Bowen, W. G., and D. C. Bok. 1998. *The shape of the river: Long-term consequences of considering race in college and university admissions.* Princeton, NJ: Princeton University Press.

Bowen, W. G., M. A. Kurzweil, and E. M. Tobin. 2005. *Equity and excellence in American higher education.* Charlottesville: University of Virginia Press.

Bowman, N. A. 2010. College diversity experiences and cognitive development: A meta-analysis. *Review of Educational Research* 80 (1): 4–33.

Brewer, M. B., and R. J. Brown. 1998. Intergroup relations. In *The handbook of social psychology*, 4th ed., ed. D. T. Gilbert and S. T. Fiske, 554–594. New York: McGraw-Hill.

Cantor, N. E., and D. A. Prentice. 1996. The life of the modern-day student-athlete: Opportunities won and lost. Paper presented at the Princeton Conference on Higher Education, Princeton, NJ, March 21.

Carter, R. T. 1997. Is white a race? Expressions of white racial identity. In *Off white: Readings on race, power and society*, ed. M. Fine, L. Weis, L. C. Powell, and L. M. Wong, 198–209. New York: Routledge.

Celious, A., and D. Oyserman. 2001. Race from the inside: An emerging heterogeneous race model. *Journal of Social Issues* 57 (1): 149–165.

Chang, M. J. 1999. Does racial diversity matter? The educational impact of a racially diverse undergraduate population. *Journal of College Student Development* 40 (4): 377–395.

———. 2002. The impact of an undergraduate diversity course requirement on students' racial views and attitudes. *Journal of General Education* 51 (1): 21–42.

———. 2003. Racial differences in viewpoints about contemporary issues among entering college students: Fact or fiction? *NASPA Journal* 40 (4): 55–71.

———. 2007. Beyond artificial integration: Reimagining cross-racial interactions among undergraduates. In *Responding to the realities of race on campus: New directions for student services, No. 120*, ed. S. R. Harper and L. D. Patton, 25–37. San Francisco: Jossey-Bass.

Chang, M. J., A. W. Astin, and D. Kim. 2004. Cross-racial interaction among undergraduates: Some consequences, causes, and patterns. *Research in Higher Education* 45 (5): 529–553.

Chang, M. J., N. Denson, V. Sáenz, and K. Misa. 2006. The educational benefits of sustaining cross-racial interaction among undergraduates. *Journal of Higher Education* 77 (3): 430–455.

Checkoway, B. 2001. Renewing the civic mission of the American research university. *Journal of Higher Education* 72 (2): 125–147.

Cheng, D. X., and C. M. Zhao. 2006. Cultivating multicultural competence through active participation: Extracurricular activities and multicultural learning. *NASPA Journal* 43 (4): 13–38.

Clayton-Pedersen, A. R., S. Parker, D. G. Smith, J. F. Moreno, and D. H. Teraguchi. 2007. *Making a real difference with diversity: A guide to institutional change.* Washington, DC: Association of American Colleges and Universities.

Cohen, J. 1988. *Statistical power analysis for the behavioral sciences.* 2nd ed. New York: Academic Press.

Cole, E. R., and S. R. Omari. 2003. Race, class and the dilemmas of upward mobility for African Americans. *Journal of Social Issues* 59 (4): 785–802.

Cookson, P. W., and C. H. Persell. 1991. Race and class in America's elite preparatory boarding schools: African Americans as the "outsiders within." *Journal of Negro Education* 60 (2): 219–228.

Crenshaw, K. 1991. Mapping the margins: Intersectionality, identity politics, and violence against women of color. *Stanford Law Review* 43 (6): 1241–1299.

Dasgupta, N. 2011. Ingroup experts and peers as social vaccines who inoculate the self-concept: The stereotype inoculation model. *Psychological Inquiry* 22 (4): 231–246.

Datnow, A., and R. Cooper, 1997. Peer networks of African American students in independent schools: Affirming academic success and racial identity. *Journal of Negro Education* 66 (1): 56–72.

Davis, J. 2010. *The first generation student experience: Implications for campus practice, and strategies for improving persistence and success.* Sterling, VA: Stylus.

Denson, N. 2009. Do curricular and cocurricular diversity activities influence racial bias? A meta-analysis. *Review of Educational Research* 79 (2): 805–838.

Denson, N., and M. J. Chang. 2009. Racial diversity matters: The impact of diversity-related student engagement and institutional context. *American Educational Research Journal* 46 (2): 322–353.

Dews, C. L., and C. L. Law. 1995. *This fine place so far from home: Voices of academics from the working class*. Philadelphia: Temple University Press.

Dovidio, J. F., and S. Gaertner. 1998. On the nature of contemporary prejudice: The causes, consequences, and challenges of aversive racism. In *Confronting racism: The problem and the response*, ed. J. L. Eberhardt and S. T. Fiske, 3–32. Thousand Oaks, CA: Sage.

Duncan, G. J., J. Boisjoly, D. M. Levy, M. Kremer, and J. Eccles. 2003. Empathy or antipathy? The consequences of racially and socially diverse peers on attitudes and behaviors. Available at http://www.eric.ed.gov/ERICWebPortal/content delivery/servlet/ERICServlet?accno=ED472566.

Engberg, M. E. 2004. Improving intergroup relations in higher education: A critical examination of the influence of educational interventions on racial bias. *Review of Educational Research* 74 (4): 473–524.

Espenshade, T. J., and A. W. Radford. 2009. *No longer separate, not yet equal: Race and class in elite college admission and campus life*. Princeton, NJ: Princeton University Press.

Feagin, J. R., H. Vera, and N. Imani. 1996. *The agony of education: Black students at a white university*. New York: Routledge.

Fischer, M. J. 2008. Does campus diversity promote friendship diversity? A look at interracial friendships in college. *Social Science Quarterly* 89 (3): 631–655.

Fiske, S. T. 1998. Stereotyping, prejudice, and discrimination. In *The Handbook of Social Psychology*, 4th ed., ed. D. T. Gilbert and S. T. Fiske, 357–411. New York: McGraw-Hill.

Gaertner, S., and J. P. McLaughlin. 1983. Racial stereotypes: Associations and ascriptions of positive and negative characteristics. *Sociological Psychology Quarterly* 46 (1): 23–30.

Graham, L. O. 1999. *Our kind of people: Inside America's black upper class*. New York: Harper Perennial.

Granfield, R. 1991. Making it by faking it. *Journal of Contemporary Ethnography* 20 (3): 331–351.

Gurin, P. 2004. The compelling need for diversity in higher education: Expert report of Patricia Gurin. University of Michigan Admissions Lawsuits. Available at http://www.vpcomm.umich.edu/admissions/research/expert/gurintoc.html.

Gurin, P., with E. L. Dey, G. Gurin, and S. Hurtado. 2004. The educational value of diversity. In *Defending diversity: Affirmative action at the University of Michigan*, ed. P. Gurin, J. S. Lehman, and E. Lewis, 97–188. Ann Arbor: University of Michigan Press.

Gurin, P., E. L. Dey, S. Hurtado, and G. Gurin. 2002. Diversity and higher education: Theory and impact on educational outcomes. *Harvard Educational Review* 72 (3): 330–367.

Gurin, P., J. S. Lehman, E. Lewis, E. L. Dey, S. Hurtado, and G. Gurin. 2004. *Defending diversity: Affirmative action at the University of Michigan*. Ann Arbor: University of Michigan Press.

Gurin, P., and B. (Ratnesh) A. Nagda. 2006. Getting to the what, how, and why of diversity on campus. *Educational Researcher* 35 (1): 20–24.

Gurin, P., B. (Ratnesh) A. Nagda, and G. E. Lopez. 2004. The benefits of diversity in education for democratic citizenship. *Journal of Social Issues* 60 (1): 17–34.

Harper, S. R. 2006. Peer support for African American male college achievement: Beyond internalized racism and the burden of "acting white." *Journal of Men's Studies* 14 (3): 337–358.

Harper, S. R., and S. Hurtado. 2007. Nine themes in campus racial climates and implications for institutional transformation. In *Responding to the realities of race on campus: New directions for student services, No. 120*, ed. S. R. Harper and L. D. Patton, 7–24. San Francisco: Jossey-Bass.

Harper, S. R., and A. H. Nichols. 2008. Are they not all the same? Racial heterogeneity among black male undergraduates. *Journal of College Student Development* 49 (3): 199–214.

Harper, S. R., and L. D. Patton, eds. 2008. *Responding to the realities of race on campus: New directions for student services, No. 120*. San Francisco: Jossey-Bass.

Harper, S. R., and S. J. Quaye. 2007. Student organizations as venues for black identity expression and development among African American male student leaders. *Journal of College Student Development* 48 (2): 127–144.

Harvard Financial Aid Initiative. 2011. *Shoestring Strategies for Life @ Harvard: A Guide for Students on a Budget*. Cambridge, MA: Harvard College. Available at http://isites.harvard.edu/fs/docs/icb.topic556953.files/ShoestringStrategies.pdf.

Henderson-King, D., and A. Kaleta. 2000. Learning about social diversity: The undergraduate experience and intergroup tolerance. *Journal of Higher Education* 71 (2): 142–164.

Hogan, D. E., and M. Mallott. 2005. Changing racial prejudice through diversity education. *Journal of College Student Development* 46 (2): 115–125.

Horvat, E. M., and A. L. Antonio. 1999. "Hey, those shoes are out of uniform": African American girls in an elite high school and the importance of habitus. *Anthropology and Education Quarterly* 30 (3): 317–342.

Hoyt, S. K. 1999. Mentoring with class: Connections between social class and the developmental relationships in the academy. In *Mentoring dilemmas: Developmental relationships within multicultural organizations*, ed. A. J. Murrell, F. J. Crosby, and R. J. Ely, 189–210. Mahwah, NJ: Lawrence Erlbaum.

Hughes, M., and B. R. Hertel. 1990. The significance of color remains: A study of life chances, mate selection, and ethnic consciousness among black Americans. *Social Forces* 68 (4): 1105–1120.

Hunter, M. L. 2005. *Race, gender, and the politics of skin tone*. New York: Routledge.

Hurst, A. L. 2010. *The burden of academic success: Loyalists, renegades, and double agents*. Lanham, MD: Lexington Books.

Hurtado, S. 2005. The next generation of diversity and intergroup relations research. *Journal of Social Issues* 61 (3): 595–610.

———. 2007. Linking diversity with the educational and civic missions of higher education. *Review of Higher Education* 30 (2): 185–196.

Hurtado, S., L. Arellano, C. Wann, M. Cuellar, C. Alvarez, and L. Colin. 2009. The climate for diversity: Studying student perceptions and experiences in the first year of college. PowerPoint presentation given at the Association for Institutional Research, Atlanta, June 2. Available at http://www.heri.ucla.edu/dle/downloads/AIR09_Climate_for_Diversity.pdf.

Hurtado, S., K. A. Griffin, L. Arellano, and M. Cuellar. 2008. Assessing the value of climate assessments: Progress and future directions. *Journal of Diversity in Higher Education* 1 (4): 204–221.

Inkelas, K. K., K. E. Vogt, S. D. Longerbeam, J. Owen, and D. Johnson. 2006. Measuring outcomes of living-learning programs: Examining college environments and student learning and development. *Journal of General Education 55* (1): 40–76.

Keith, V. M., and C. Herring. 1991. Skin tone and stratification in the black community. *American Journal of Sociology* 97 (3): 760–778.

Kernahan, C., and T. Davis. 2010. What are the long-term effects of learning about racism? *Teaching of Psychology* 37 (1): 41–45.

Kezar, A., P. Eckel, M. Contreras-McGavin, and S. J. Quaye. 2008. Creating a web of support: An important leadership strategy for advancing campus diversity. *Higher Education: The International Journal of Higher Education and Educational Planning* 55 (1): 69–92.

Kirwan, W. E. 2004. Diversity in higher education: Why it matters. In *What makes racial diversity work in higher education*, ed. F. W. Hale, xxi–xxiv. Sterling, VA: Stylus.

Klonoff, E. A., and H. Landrine. 2000. Is skin color a marker for racial discrimination? Explaining the skin color–hypertension relationship. *Journal of Behavioral Medicine* 23 (4): 329–338.

Laird, T.F.N., M. E. Engberg, and S. Hurtado. 2005. Modeling accentuation effects: Enrolling in a diversity course and the importance of social action engagement. *Journal of Higher Education* 76 (4): 448–476.

Lareau, A., and E. B. Weininger. 2003. Cultural capital in educational research: A critical assessment. *Theory and Society* 32:567–606.

Lawler, S. 1999. "Getting out and getting away": Women's narratives of class mobility. *Feminist Review* 63 (1): 3–24.

Legault, L., J. N. Gutsell, and M. Inzlicht. 2011. Ironic effects of anti-prejudice messages: How motivational interventions can reduce (but also increase) prejudice. *Psychological Science* 22 (12): 1472–1477.

Lehmann, W. 2009. Becoming middle class: How working-class university students draw and transgress moral class boundaries. *Sociology* 43 (4): 631–647.

Levin, S., C. van Laar, and J. Sidanius. 2003. The effects of ingroup and outgroup friendships on ethnic attitudes in college: A longitudinal study. *Group Processes and Intergroup Relations* 6 (1): 76–92.

Locks, A. M., S. Hurtado, N. A. Bowman, and L. Oseguera. 2008. Extending notions of campus climate and diversity to students' transition to college. *Review of Higher Education* 31 (3): 257–285.

Longerbeam, S. D. 2010. Developing openness to diversity in living-learning program participants. *Journal of Diversity in Higher Education* 3 (4): 201–217.

Lubrano, A. 2004. *Limbo: Blue-collar roots, white-collar dreams.* Hoboken, NJ: Wiley.

Mallett, R. K., Z. R. Mello, D. E. Wagner, F. Worrell, R. N. Burrow, and J. R. Andretta. 2011. Do I belong? It depends on when you ask. *Cultural Diversity and Ethnic Minority Psychology* 17 (4): 432–436.

Marcoux, J-S. 2009. Escaping the gift economy. *Journal of Consumer Research* 36 (36): 671–685.

McCauley, C., M. Wright, and M. E. Harris. 2000. Diversity workshops on campus: A survey of current practice at U.S. colleges and universities. *College Student Journal* 34 (1): 100–114.

McConahay, J. B. 1986. Modern racism, ambivalence, and the Modern Racism Scale: Prejudice, discrimination, and racism. In *Prejudice, discrimination, and racism*, ed. J. F. Dovidio and S. L. Gaertner, 91–125. San Diego: Academic Press.

McLaughlin, A., B. T. Dill, S. Harley, and D. Rosenfelt. 2009. Instituting a legacy of change: Transforming the campus climate through intellectual leadership. In *Doing diversity in higher education: Faculty leaders share challenges and strategies*, ed. W. R. Brown-Glaude, 17–38. New Brunswick, NJ: Rutgers University Press.

Meacham, J., and C. Barrett. 2003. Commitment to diversity in institutional mission statements. *Diversity Digest* 7 (1–2): 6–7, 9. Available at http://www.diversity web.org/digest/vol7no1-2/meacham-barrett.cfm.

Milem, J. F., M. J. Chang, and A. L. Antonio. 2005. *Making diversity work on campus: A research-based perspective.* Washington, DC: Association of American Colleges and Universities. Available at http://www.aacu.org/inclusive_excellence/documents/Milem_et_al.pdf.

Misa, K., N. Denson, V. Sáenz, and M. J. Chang. 2006. The educational benefits of sustaining cross-racial interaction among undergraduates. *Journal of Higher Education* 77 (3): 430–455.

Multi-university intergroup dialogue research project guidebook. 2011. Available at http://sitemaker.umich.edu/migr/files/migr_guidebook.pdf.

Myers-Lipton, S. J. 1996. Effect of a comprehensive service-learning program on college students' level of modern racism. *Michigan Journal of Community Service Learning* 3:44–54.

Nagda, B. (Ratnesh) A. 2006. Breaking barriers, crossing borders, building bridges: Communication processes in intergroup dialogues. *Journal of Social Issues* 62 (3): 553–576.

Nagda, B. (Ratnesh) A., and P. Gurin. 2007. Intergroup dialogue: A critical-dialogic approach to learning about difference, inequality and social justice. *New Directions for Teaching and Learning* 111:35–45.

Nagda, B. (Ratnesh) A., P. Gurin, N. Sorensen, and X. Zúñiga. 2009. Evaluating intergroup dialogue: Engaging diversity for personal and social responsibility. *Diversity and Democracy* 12 (1): 4–6. Available at http://www.diversityweb.org/DiversityDemocracy/vol12no1/vol12no1.pdf.

Nagda, B. (Ratnesh) A., and X. Zúñiga. 2003. Fostering meaningful racial engagement through intergroup dialogues. *Group Processes and Intergroup Relations* 6 (1): 111–128.

Orfield, G., E. D. Frankenberg, and C. Lee. 2002/2003. The resurgence of school segregation. *Educational Leadership* 60, no. 4 (December/January): 16–20.

Ostrove, J. M. 2003. Belonging and wanting: Meanings of social class background for women's constructions of their college experiences. *Journal of Social Issues* 59 (4): 771–784.

Paluck, E. L., and D. P. Green. 2009. Prejudice reduction: What works? A review and assessment of research and practice. *Annual Review of Psychology* 60:339–367.

Pascarella, E. T., C. T. Pierson, G. C. Wolniak, and P. T. Terenzini. 2004. First-generation college students: Additional evidence on college experiences and outcomes. *Journal of Higher Education* 75 (3): 249–284.

Pendry, L. F., D. M. Driscoll, and S.C.T. Field. 2007. Diversity training: Putting theory into practice. *Journal of Occupational and Organizational Psychology* 80 (1): 27–50.

Perez, A. D., and C. Hirschman. 2009. The changing racial and ethnic composition of the U.S. population: Emerging American identities. *Population and Development Review* 35 (1): 1–51.

Pettigrew, T. F. 1998. Intergroup contact theory. *Annual Review of Psychology* 49:65–85.

Pettigrew, T. F, and L. R. Tropp. 2006. A meta-analytic test of intergroup contact theory. *Journal of Personality and Social Psychology* 90 (5): 751–783.

———. 2008. How does intergroup contact reduce prejudice? Meta-analytic tests of three mediators. *European Journal of Social Psychology* 38 (6): 922–934.

Pettigrew, T. F., L. R. Tropp, U. Wagner, and O. Christ. 2011. Recent advances in intergroup contact theory. *International Journal of Intercultural Relations* 35:271–280.

Phelps, R. E., D. B. Altschul, J. M. Wisenbaker, J. F. Day, D. Cooper, and C. G. Potter. 1998. Roommate satisfaction and ethnic identity in mixed-race and white university roommate dyads. *Journal of College Student Development* 39:194–203.

Piaget, J. 1975. *The equilibration of cognitive structures: The central problem of intellectual development.* Chicago: University of Chicago Press.

Pike, G. R., and G. D. Kuh. 2006. Relationships among structural diversity, informal peer interactions and perceptions of the campus environment. *Review of Higher Education* 29 (4): 425–450.

Reason, R. D., and N. H. Evans. 2007. The complicated realities of whiteness: From color blind to racially cognizant. In *Responding to the realities of race on campus: New directions for student services, No. 120,* ed. S. R. Harper and L. D. Patton, 67–75. San Francisco: Jossey-Bass.

Reay, D., G. Crozier, and J. Clayton. 2009. "Strangers in paradise"? Working-class students in elite universities. *Sociology* 43 (6): 1103–1121.

Reay, D., M. E. David, and S. J. Ball. 2005. *Degrees of choice: Social class, race, gender and higher education.* Stoke-on-Trent, UK: Trentham Books.

Rice, K. L., and J. R. Brown. 1998. Transforming educational curriculum and service learning. *Journal of Experiential Education* 21 (3): 140–146.

Rothman, S., S. M. Lipset, and N. Nevitte. 2003. Does enrollment diversity improve university education? *International Journal of Public Opinion Research* 15 (1): 8–26.

Rubin, M. 2012. Social class differences in social integration among students in higher education: A meta-analysis and recommendations for future research. *Journal of Diversity in Higher Education* 5 (1): 22–38.

Rudenstine, N. L. 2001. The proper consideration of race in higher education. *Journal of Blacks in Higher Education* 33:114–117.

———. 2004. Diversity and learning at Harvard: An historical view. In *What makes racial diversity work in higher education: Academic leaders present successful policies and strategies,* ed. F. W. Hale, 61–72. Sterling, VA: Stylus.

Rudman, L. A., R. D. Ashmore, and M. L. Gary. 2001. "Unlearning" automatic biases: The malleability of implicit prejudice and stereotypes. *Journal of Personality and Social Psychology* 81 (5): 856.

Ryan, J., and C. Sackrey, eds. 1984. *Strangers in paradise: Academics from the working class.* Boston: South End Press.

Saddler, T. N. 2010. Mentoring and African American undergraduates' perception of academic success. In *The evolving challenges of black college students,* ed. T. L. Strayhorn and M. C. Terrell, 179–200. Sterling, VA: Stylus.

Sáenz, V. B., H. N. Ngai, and S. Hurtado. 2007. Factors influencing positive interactions across race for African American, Asian American, Latino, and white college students. *Research in Higher Education* 48 (1): 1–38.

Schofield, J. W., L.R.M. Hausmann, F. Ye, and R. L. Woods. 2010. Intergroup friendships on campus: Predicting close and casual friendships between white and African American first-year college students. *Group Processes and Intergroup Relations* 13 (5): 585–602.

Sears, D. O., and P. J. Henry. 2003. The origins of symbolic racism. *Journal of Personality and Social Psychology* 85 (2): 259–275.

Shelton, J. N., and J. A. Richeson. 2006. Ethnic minorities' racial attitudes and contact experiences with white people. *Cultural Diversity and Ethnic Minority Psychology* 12 (1): 149–164.

Shelton, J. N., J. A. Richeson, and J. Salvatore. 2005. Expecting to be the target of prejudice: Implications for interethnic interactions. *Personality and Social Psychology Bulletin* 31 (9): 1189–1202.

Shook, N. J., and R. H. Fazio. 2008a. Interracial roommate relationships: An experimental field test of the contact hypothesis. *Psychological Science* 19 (7): 717–723.

———. 2008b. Roommate relationships: A comparison of interracial and same-race living situations. *Group Processes and Intergroup Relations* 11 (4): 425–437.

Sidanius, J., S. Levin, C. van Laar, and D. O. Sears. 2008. *The diversity challenge: Social identity and intergroup relations on the college campus.* New York: Russell Sage Foundation.

Sidanius, J., C. van Laar, S. Levin, and S. Sinclair. 2004. Ethnic enclaves and the dynamics of social identity on the college campus: The good, the bad, and the ugly. *Journal of Personality and Social Psychology* 87 (1): 96–110.

Skrentny, J. D. 2001. *Color lines: Affirmative action, immigration, and civil rights options for America.* Chicago: University of Chicago Press.

———. 2002. *The minority rights revolution.* Cambridge, MA: Belknap Press of Harvard University Press.

Smith, D. G. 2009. *Diversity's promise for higher education: Making it work.* Baltimore: Johns Hopkins University Press.

Smith, S. S., and M. R. Moore. 2000. Intraracial diversity and relations among African-Americans: Closeness among black students at a predominantly white university. *American Journal of Sociology* 106 (1): 1–39.

Smith, T. W. 2000. *Taking America's pulse II: NCCJ's 2000 survey of intergroup relations in the United States.* New York: National Conference for Community and Justice.

Solórzano, D., M. Ceja, and T. Yosso. 2000. Critical race theory, racial microaggressions, and campus racial climate: The experiences of African American college students. *Journal of Negro Education* 69 (1–2): 60–73.

Sorensen, N., B. (Ratnesh) A. Nagda, P. Gurin, and K. E. Maxwell. 2009. Taking a "hands on" approach to diversity in higher education: A critical-dialogic model for effective intergroup interaction. *Analyses of Social Issues and Public Policy* 9 (1): 3–35.

Stephan, W. G., and K. Finlay. 1999. The role of empathy in improving intergroup relations. *Journal of Social Issues* 55 (4): 729–743.

Stewart, A. J., and J. M. Ostrove. 1993. Social class, social change, and gender. *Psychology of Women Quarterly* 17 (4): 475–497.

Strayhorn, T. L., and M. C. Terrell. 2010. *The evolving challenges of black college students: New insights for policy, practice, and research.* Sterling, VA: Stylus.

Strayhorn, T. L., M. C. Terrell, J. S. Redmond, and C. N. Walton. 2010. "A home away from home": Black cultural centers as supportive environments for African American collegians at white institutions. In *The evolving challenges of black college students,* ed. T. L. Strayhorn and M. C. Terrell, 122–137. Sterling, VA: Stylus.

Stuber, J. 2011a. *Inside the college gates: How class and culture matter in higher education.* Lanham, MD: Lexington Books.

———. 2011b. Integrated, marginal, and resilient: race, class, and the diverse experiences of white first-generation college students. *International Journal of Qualitative Studies in Education* 24:117–136.

Sue, D. W. 2010. *Microaggressions in everyday life: Race, gender, and sexual orientation.* Hoboken, NJ: Wiley.

Sue, D. W., J. Bucceri, A. I. Lin, K. L. Nadal, and G. C. Torino. 2007. Racial microaggressions and the Asian American experience. *Cultural Diversity and Ethnic Minority Psychology* 13 (1): 72–81.

Sue, D. W., C. M. Capodilupo, and A.M.B. Holder. 2008. Racial microaggressions in the life experience of black Americans. *Professional Psychology: Research and Practice* 39 (3): 329–336.

Sue, D. W., C. M. Capodilupo, G. C. Torino, J. M. Bucceri, A.M.B. Holder, K. L. Nadal, and M. Esquilin. 2007. Racial microaggressions in everyday life: Implications for clinical practice. *American Psychologist* 62 (4): 271–286.

Tatum, B. D. 1997. *"Why are all the black kids sitting together in the cafeteria?" And other conversations about race.* New York: Basic Books.

Thomas, K. R. 2008. Macrononsense in multiculturalism. *American Psychologist* 63 (4): 274–275.

Tokarczyk, M. M., and E. A. Fay, eds. 1993. *Working class women in the academy: Laborers in the knowledge factory.* Amherst: University of Massachusetts Press.

Torres, V., M. F. Howard-Hamilton, and D. L. Cooper. 2003. *Identity development of diverse populations: Implications for teaching and administration in higher education. ASHE-ERIC Higher Education Report,* vol. 29, no. 6. San Francisco: Jossey-Bass.

Towles-Schwen, T., and R. H. Fazio. 2006. Automatically activated racial attitudes as predictors of the success of interracial roommate relationships. *Journal of Experimental Social Psychology* 42 (5): 698–705.

Trail, T. E., J. N. Shelton, and T. V. West. 2009. Interracial roommate relationships: Negotiating daily interactions. *Personality and Social Psychology Bulletin* 35 (6): 671.

Tropp, L. R. 2006. Stigma and intergroup contact among members of minority and majority status groups. In *Stigma and group inequality: Social psychological perspectives,* ed. S. Levin and C. V. Laar, 171–191. Mahwah, NJ: Lawrence Erlbaum.

———. 2007. Perceived discrimination and interracial contact: Predicting interracial closeness among black and white Americans. *Social Psychology Quarterly* 70 (1): 70.

Tropp, L. R., and R. A. Bianchi. 2006. Valuing diversity and interest in intergroup contact. *Journal of Social Issues* 62 (3): 533–551.

Tropp, L. R., and T. F. Pettigrew. 2005. Relationships between intergroup contact and prejudice among minority and majority status groups. *Psychological Science* 16 (12): 951.

Turner, M. R. 2004. The office of African-American affairs: A celebration of success. In *What makes racial diversity work in higher education: Academic leaders present successful policies and strategies*, ed. F. W. Hale Jr., 113–122. Sterling, VA: Stylus.

Umbach, P. D., and G. D. Kuh. 2006. Student experiences with diversity at liberal arts colleges: Another claim for distinctiveness. *Journal of Higher Education* 77 (1): 169–192.

University of Michigan. n.d. *Michigan diversity report: Michigan student study: An assessment of students and alumni's experiences and outcomes with diversity.* Ann Arbor: University of Michigan. Available at http://www.oami.umich.edu/images/MSS%20DIVERSITY%20REPORT.pdf (accessed December 14, 2011).

U.S. Census Bureau. 2012. Table 229 and Table 230. In *Statistical abstract of the United States: 2012.* Washington, DC: U.S. Census Bureau. Available at http://www.census.gov/compendia/statab/2012/tables/12s0229.pdf.

van Laar, C. V., S. Levin, S. Sinclair, and J. Sidanius. 2005. The effect of university roommate contact on ethnic attitudes and behavior. *Journal of Experimental Social Psychology* 41 (4): 329–345.

Vars, F. E., and W. G. Bowen. 1998. Scholastic aptitude test scores, race, and academic performance in selective colleges and universities. In *The black-white test score gap*, ed. C. Jencks and M. Phillips, 457–479. Washington, DC: Brookings Institution Press.

Wade-Golden, K., and J. Matlock. 2007. Ten core ingredients for fostering campus diversity success. *Diversity Factor* 15 (1): 41–48.

Walpole, M. 2003. Socioeconomic status and college: How SES affects college experiences and outcomes. *Review of Higher Education* 27 (1): 45–73.

Walton, G. M., and G. L. Cohen. 2007. A question of belonging: Race, social fit, and achievement. *Journal of Personality and Social Psychology* 92 (1): 82–96.

———. 2011. A brief social-belonging intervention improves academic and health outcomes of minority students. *Science* 331 (6023): 1447–1451.

Waters, M. C. 1999. *Black identities: West Indian immigrant dreams and American realities.* Cambridge, MA: Harvard University Press.

Watson, L. W., M. C. Terrell, D. J. Wright, F. A. Bonner II, M. J. Cuyjet, J. A. Gold, D. E. Rudy, and D. R. Person. 2002. *How minority students experience college: Implications for planning and policy.* Sterling, VA: Stylus.

Wentworth, P. A., and B. E. Peterson. 2001. Crossing the line: Case studies of identity development in first-generation college women. *Journal of Adult Development* 8 (1): 9–21.

Winkle-Wagner, R. 2009. *The unchosen me: Race, gender, and identity among black women in college.* Baltimore: Johns Hopkins University Press.

Zúñiga, X., E. A. Williams, and J. B. Berger. 2005. Action-oriented democratic outcomes: The impact of student involvement with campus diversity. *Journal of College Student Development* 46 (6): 660–678.

Zweigenhaft, R. L., and G. W. Domhoff. 1991. *Blacks in the white establishment? A study of race and class in America.* New Haven, CT: Yale University Press.

———. 2006. *Diversity in the power elite: How it happened, why it matters.* Lanham, MD: Rowman and Littlefield.

———. 2011. *The new CEOs: Women, African American, Latino, and Asian American leaders of Fortune 500 companies.* Lanham, MD: Rowman and Littlefield.

Index

Elizabeth Aries is Professor of Psychology at Amherst College. She is the author of *Men and Women in Interaction: Reconsidering the Differences*; *Adolescent Behavior: Readings and Interpretations*; and *Race and Class Matters at an Elite College* (Temple).

Richard Berman is an independent scholar and a singer/songwriter.